Dr B.R. Ambedkar's Philosophy in Contemporary India

Dr B.R. Ambedkar's Philosophy in Contemporary India

Emanual Nahar

KALPAZ

First Published, 2017

Published by

Kalpaz Publications
C-30, Satyawati Nagar,
Delhi – 110052
E-mail: kalpaz@hotmail.com
Ph.: 9212142040

Printed at: G. Print Process, Delhi

Cataloging in Publication Data—DK

Courtesy: D.K. Agencies (P) Ltd. <docinfo@dkagencies.com>

Nahar, Emanual, author.

Dr. B.R. Ambedkar's philosophy in contemporary India / Emanual Nahar.

pages cm

ISBN 9789351282952

1. Ambedkar, B. R. (Bhimrao Ramji), 1891-1956—Political and social views. 2. Dalits—India—Social conditions. 3. Women—India—Social conditions. 4. Social justice—India. I. Title.

HT720.N34 2017 DDC 305.56880954 23

Contents

List of Contributors

1. **Professor Emanual Nahar,** Professor in Political Science – USOL and Director- CSSEIP and Dr B.R. Ambedkar Centre Panjab University, Chandigarh.
2. **Dr Nisha Bhargava,** Pricipal MCM, DAV College Sector-32, Chandigarh.
3. **Dr Navjot Kaur,** Associate Professor, Department of Political Science, Panjab University, Chandigarh.
4. **Dr Ranjay Vardhan,** Senior Assistant Professor in Sociology, Post Graduate Government College for Girls, Sector-42, Chandigarh.
5. **Dr Neeru Sharma,** Associate Professor, Department of Political Science, B.D. Arya College, Jalandhar, Punjab.
6. **Dr Gobind Chandra Sethi,** Assistant Professor, Department of Political Science, Post Graduate Government College, Sector-46, Chandigarh.
7. **Mrs Jatinder Walia and Mrs Reena Kushwaha,** Assistant Professor, Department of Political Science, Post Government Graduate College of Girls, Sector-11, Chandigarh.
8. **Dr Amandeep,** Assistant Professor, Department of Evening Studies, Panjab University, Chandigarh.
9. **Rohini Arora,** Assistant Professor, SGGS College, Sector-26, Chandigarh.
10. **Dr Mona Arora,** Assistant Professor, Department of Sociology, SD College, Sector-32, Chandigarh.
11. **Jasbir Kaur, Assistant Professor,** Department of Political Science, Khalsa College for Women, Civil Lines, Ludhiana, Punjab.
12. **Devinder Kaur, Assistant Professor,** Department of Political Science, Guru Gobind Singh Khalsa College, Kamalpura, Distt-Ludhiana.

13. **Dr Nirmal Singh,** Assistant Professor, University Institute of Legal Studies, Panjab University, Chandigarh.
14. **Dr Kanchan Chandan,** Research Associate, Centre for the Study of Social Exclusion and Inclusive Policy, Panjab University, Chandigarh.
15. **Mrs Manjinder Kaur,** Research Assistant, Centre for the Study of Social Exclusion and Inclusive Policy, Panjab University, Chandigarh.
16. **Dr Sucheta Singh,** Research Assistant, Centre for the Study of Social Exclusion and Inclusive Policy, Panjab University, Chandigarh.
17. **Archana Thakur,** Assistant Professor, Department of Political Science, Khalsa College, Ghardiwala, Hoshiarpur, Punjab.
18. **Parambir Brar,** Research Scholar, Centre for the Study of Social Exclusion and Inclusive Policy, Panjab University, Chandigarh.
19. **Tarminder Kaur,** Assistant Professor, Department of Sociology, SD College, Sector-32, Chandigarh.
20. **Parveen Kumari,** Research Scholar, Department of Political Science, Jammu University, Jammu.
21. **Navneet Kaur,** Assistant Professor in Sociology, Post Graduate Government College for Girls, Sector-42, Chandigarh.
22. **Shayama Bangar,** Research Scholar, Department of Political Science, Panjab University, Chandigarh.

Foreword

Bharat Ratna, Baba Saheb Dr B.R. Ambedkar, the Principal Designer of Constitution of India, is well-known not only as the Architect of Indian Constitution and a Legislator-par-excellence but also as a great academician and a dynamic reformer. Baba Saheb was endowed with an intellectual vigour that is rarely seen in men. For that reason, it is always a paying proposition to study Ambedkar to enrich our understanding and sharpen our analysis of the various problems facing our society. There is a persistent need to re-examine Baba Saheb's thoughts in the context of changing socio-political, economic and educational scenario of contemporary world.

Baba Saheb wanted the emancipation of underprivileged and down-trodden masses so he carried on a struggle against the domineering Hindu society at political, social, cultural and intellectual levels in his pursuit to build a brave new society where all castes may enjoy equal status and dignity. He was not fighting against any particular caste but against casteism as such which divides people and weakens the social fabric. He opined that a society that is segregated into various castes, religions, and gender biases should be liberated from its shackles.

He always vied for the equality of social status for women whom he had always observed to be bound by the man dominance. He considered women as a vital component in the socio-economic development in every society of the world. He measured the progress of a community by the degree of progress which women have achieved. This shows the intensity of his inclination towards women empowerment.

Baba Saheb held views which looked radical at that time but they proved relevant with the passage of time and hold good even today. But his ideology often met with disapproval and crticism because he condemned the derogatory caste structure of Indian society. He encountered numerous hardships as he belonged to a lower caste. He had to bear embarrassments throughout his childhood and he grew up facing humiliation in the hands of his mentors and counterparts. But despite having options to lead a comfortable life, he chose to lead a modest way of living and to work for the cause of oppressed and depressed classes and find lasting solutions to the long vexed social problems of our country. The societal adversities and hardships back home could never lower the resolve of Baba Saheb.

But still there has always been an attempt to belittle his significance by confining him almost entirely to the question of Dalit upliftment. His contribution is no less significant in other spheres like economy, polity, secularism and foreign relations which need to be realised by the non-dalit society.

The Constitution of India is the best example to support this averment. The pioneering efforts of Baba Saheb, while drafting the constitution were never backed by the thought of any caste or community specific. He uniquely contributed in providing to each and every individual of India, the best constitution in the world irrespective of his caste, colour or creed. But sadly the personality that belonged to every individual of this country is kept hooked to the Dalits alone.

So the book **"Dr B.R. Ambedkar's Philosophy in Contemporary India: Issues and Challenges"** which is a by product of a successful ICSSR sponsored National Seminar organised by CSSEIP, Punjab University, Chandigarh is an assembled work from papers presented by learned and distinguished experts, academicians and research scholars during the National Seminar that attempts to recapitulate and place on record the views of visionary Baba Saheb on social justice, caste-based discrimination and dalit identity.

I personally feel that more we admire and appreciate Baba Saheb and his vision, more enlightened we become for our times. So this book gives an in-depth historical as well as contemporary and analytical account of conflicting concerns. The study also analyses various development policies regarding the marginalised sections and their implementation. I am glad that the book has been edited by

Professor Emanual Nahar, Director Dr Ambedkar Centre and CSSEIP, Punjab University, Chandigarh, and hope it should serve as an important source of information for the researchers, academicians, Social Welfare Department and social workers working for the downtrodden sections of the society.

Dr Charanjit Singh Atwal

Speaker, Punjab Legislative Assembly

Introduction

The word Dalit—literally translating to "oppressed" or "broken"—is generally used to refer to people who were once known as "untouchables", those belonging to castes outside the four-fold Hindu Varna system. The number of Scheduled Castes (SCs) in India increased by 35 million during the decade ranging from 2001 to 2011. Dalits have been oppressed, culturally subjugated, and politically marginalised. The principles of untouchability and "purity and pollution" dictate what Dalits are and are not allowed to do; where they are and are not allowed to live, go, or sit; who they can and cannot give water to, eat with, or marry; extending into the minutia of all aspects of daily life. Moreover, discrimination for Dalits does not end if they convert from Hinduism to another religion. In India, Islam, Sikhism, and Christianity (among other religions) maintain some form of caste despite the fact that this contradicts their religious precepts. As a result, dominant castes maintain leadership positions while Dalit members of these religions are often marginalised and flagrantly discriminated against. For example, Dalit Christians are provided separate burial areas from non-Dalit Christians.

Dr Babasaheb Ambedkar is a constant source of inspiration to the people of India especially the vast suffering masses, because his ideas, principles and actions continue to have relevance as the contradictions in social and economic life persist even today. *Bharat Ratna*, Dr Ambedkar was a man of versatile genius, great economist, constitutionalist, social reformist, political thinker, a champion and a *Messiah* of downtrodden and above all a great humanist. He took utmost care to draft the liberal Constitution, making the citizens of this nation to enjoy the fundamental rights without any discrimination on the basis of caste, colour and creed, place of birth, religion or sex. All through his life he strived to establish the basic principles - Liberty, Equality and Fraternity in all walks of life. He, being a revolutionary thinker and spokesman of the depressed people of India, who are socio-culturally discriminated, exploited, deprived and disadvantaged, has fought against all the socio-cultural, economic and political forces throughout his life. He stressed on the empowerment of the oppressed as one of the means of their emancipation from exploitation and injustice, which operate in various social forms of violence against the oppressed. Dr Ambedkar held pragmatic and uncompromising views on the amelioration of the sufferings of the *Dalit* category. He came out vociferously and eloquently in support of adequate representation and constitutional safeguards for the depressed classes. Dr Ambedkar felt that the untouchables should come forward in union and play a leading role in the eradication of caste demolition of the Brahminical system. He felt a strong need for the social reconstruction of the Indian Society.

With a view of creating casteless and classless social order, Dr Ambedkar endeavoured to set basic everlasting human values such as equality, liberty, fraternity and social justice. These fundamental ideas and values of his life, have become the fountain of inspiration of self-respect, self-confidence, rationality and practical humanism. He wanted to build a new India, a strong united India free from the burden of history of hatred and exploitation.

Political Parties and Dr B.R. Ambedkar

An interesting free-for-all in B.R. Ambedkar's name is going on among political parties in India. For political parties in India, Dr Bhimrao Ambedkar, it seems, has become more of an agenda to further their electoral interests. With almost all parties trying to encash dalit votes by usurping Ambedkar legacy, one of the foremost thinkers that the country has produced is being reduced to just a dalit icon. Leading from the front is BSP chief Mayawati whose 'social engineering' model of politics has been largely dependent on dalit votes which she lost in 2014. The otherwise inaccessible former Chief Minister of Uttar Pradesh used the 'Ambedkar Jayanti' to hit out at the Bharatiya Janata Party (BJP) and the Congress for trying to Ambedkar and grab dalit votes.

The Congress has left no stone unturned in celebrating Ambedkar since the 1990s, forgetting that it was the Congress that was instrumental in cancelling a holiday on Ambedkar Jayanti long ago — to instead declare holiday on Tilak Jayanti. At that time it seemed like massaging Maharashtrian pride was more important to the party than bothering about the feelings of many who revered Ambedkar as a messiah of the dalits. For, by the 1970s, that is what Ambedkar had been reduced to. That particular episode set in motion a series of events that eventually resulted in the emergence of the All India Backward (SC, ST, OBC) and Minority Communities Employees Federation (BAMCEF) and the Bahujan Samaj Party (BSP).

Since April 14 – which marked the 125th birth anniversary of Bhimrao Ambedkar – both the BJP and the Congress have been vying to appropriate Ambedkar's legacy, at least in part, to gain political mileage. The BJP particularly has its eye on polls in Bihar later this year.

Prime Minister Narendra Modi is going to head the committee that will oversee various activities and events to celebrate Ambedkar over the next year.

And a resurgent Rahul Gandhi is headed to Ambedkar's birthplace, Mhow, to finally kick off the Congress' celebrations. The RSS too has planned a series of events to commemorate Ambedkar. Their mouthpiece *Organiser* had published a special 200-page edition on Ambedkar for his birth anniversary on April 14. The RSS is keenly arguing that the Dalit icon actually supported 'ghar wapsi'.

In the state of Punjab, the dalit community has largest population. Akali Dal, Bharatiya Janta Party and Congress party has left no stone unturned to organise dalits in own favours. From some years, dalit votes are shifting from Congress and opted for alternatives whenever they could find them. In Punjab, BSP has failed to fulfil the political aspiration of dalits and dalit leadership got scattered in different parties. After winning the Lok Sabha election in 2014, the BJP changed its electoral strategy. In assembly elections in Haryana and Maharashtra, the BJP did not enter into alliance with its traditional allies. This may have implications for its SAD-BJP alliance in Punjab. This may pose a challenge to the survival of regional parties, as the BJP has regionalised its parties.

Why Ambedkar, Why Now?

There's the cynical explanation: that the desperate scramble for Ambedkar's legacy is merely an extension of 'vote bank' politics. This would especially hold true after the BSP rout in the general elections, following which the national parties are keen to capitalise on the Dalit vote in the Hindi Belt.

However, apart from the pragmatic considerations of electoral politics, there is much to be said for Ambedkar as a man whose legacy fits in perfectly into post-liberalisation India. Also the BJP, during its national executive in Bengaluru, decided to celebrate Ambedkar's birth anniversary in a big way. Since then, with an eye on Uttar Pradesh Assembly elections in 2017, the BJP's state unit is going all-out to woo dalit voters. The party has already organised 1,000 special camps in dalit localities across the state as part of its nationwide membership drive.

And how could the ruling Samajwadi Party (SP) leave behind the in competition. UP CM Akhilesh Yadav made a master political stroke by declaring December 6-Ambedkar's death anniversary- a 'public holiday'.

At the heart of this competition, as witnessed in the wake of Ambedkar's 125th birth anniversary on Tuesday, is the perceived loosening of Bahujan Samaj Party's (BSP) grip on dalits which were, till very recently, considered a strong vote bank of the party. The shift of dalit votes towards BJP in 2014 served as a warning call for BSP as well as the Congress while giving fresh hopes of making inroads among dalits to the BJP.

The weakening of BSP in UP has motivated other parties to try to win over dalit votes. The new-found love for Ambedkar among political parties stems from dalit vote bank's interest in going for alternatives other than BSP. But by relating Ambedkar to one section of society (dalits), political parties have ended up dishonouring a national icon, feel experts.

It's quite unfortunate that rather than treating Ambedkar as an icon of national prominence, the political parties have reduced him to a dalit icon. Relating him to a particular section of society would be doing injustice to his stature.

BJP and the Congress Party laid claim to Ambedkar even though he regarded Hinduism as inhuman and the Congress leader Mahatma Gandhi as a charlatan who pretended to support Dalits while strongly defending India's brutal caste system.

Dalits are at the very bottom of India's caste system and are born into degrading work like dry latrine cleaners and scavengers. They are forbidden from marrying higher caste partners, drinking from the same wells, sharing food and in some places even casting their shadow or leaving footprints because they are regarded as 'polluting'. The battle for Ambedkar's legacy reflects his enduring popularity among India's Dalit population and fierce competition for their votes.

Dr B.R. Ambedkar was a towering figure of astonishing vision, which spoke against social and economic inequalities and worked all his life for the upliftment of the depressed classes. Ambedkar, a pioneer of social justice and architect of the Indian constitution not only safeguarded the interests of the weaker sections of the Indian society but also tried to bridge the gap between the legal theory and social practice. He was concerned about the development and welfare of the depressed and weaker sections of the society. He fought for their betterment and opened a path of progress for the depressed sections through constitutional reforms. He fought for their emancipation and made them aware of their rights with a view to end exploitation. Ambedkar's quest for social justice can be visualised in the philosophy, policy and ideals of the constitution of India. Ambedkar was of the opinion that Social Justice can be dispensed in a free social order in which an Individual is end in itself. He fought relentlessly to establish a society based on democratic ideas of liberty, equality and fraternity. He was in favour of that establishment of socio-economic and political equality not just as a slogan but also as concrete policy. Ambedkar's contributed a legal framework for the upliftment of the downtrodden sections of the Indian society by incorporating relevant provisions in the Indian constitution. The creation of an egalitarian social order still remains an unfulfilled wishful thinking.

There is a great need to acquire and enrich the teachers, scholars, students as well as the concerned people of India with Dr Ambedkar's vision of nation and society by getting them involved in research studies, field work based on extension service programmes and activities to refresh and motivate them to contribute towards making India a strong nation, free from all kinds of discrimination. In this backdrop, Centre for Study of Social Exclusion and Inclusive Policy, Punjab University, Chandigarh organised a National Level Two-day Seminar. The Seminar was held under the sponsorship of ICSSR, Punjab University, Chandigarh. The main objective of the Seminar was to envisage deliberations on the relevance of Dr Ambedkar's ideas, thoughts and perspectives in the contemporary socio-economic and political scenario prevailing in India. Eminent scholars were involved in the deliberations that critically reflected on this subject and opened up different views and perspectives. Following were the main objectives of the Seminar:-

(i) To understand and analyse the concept of caste discrimination, identity and social philosophy of Dr Ambedkar.

(ii) To understand and examine Dr Ambedkar's views on social justice.

(iii) To deliberate upon theoretical framework of Dr Ambedkar on Indian Brahminical caste system, and his contribution to understand caste system and its operational mechanism.

(iv) Dr Ambedkar's philosophy as an inspirational source for post-independence Dalit movements and Assertions.

(v) Relevance of Dr Ambedkar's philosophy in the era of globalisation.

The National Seminar was of two days i.e. 27-28 March, 2015. Many eminent scholars from various universities and colleges participated in the deliberations during the Seminar. Various issues related to Dr Ambedkar's ideas, thoughts and perspectives in the contemporary socio-economic and political scenario prevailing in India was discussed during the technical sessions of the National Seminar. Dr Emanual Nahar, Director, Dr Ambedkar Centre and Centre for the Study of Social Exclusion and Inclusive Policy welcome all the distinguished guests and introduce the theme of the National Seminar while inaugural address was given by Professor M.M. Puri, former Vice Chancellor of Punjab University, Chandigarh. Dr Ajit Singh Chahal from Meerpur University was key note speaker while Presidential Remarks was given by Professor Jagroop Shekhon, Department of Political Science, Guru Nanak Dev University, Amritsar. Nearly 30 papers were presented in the two-day National Seminar.

Professor Emanual Nahar discussed Dr B.R. Ambedkar's views on democracy, social and economic justice, gender equality, national unity and religious belief provide important inputs in quest for finding solutions to some of the demanding questions of present times. The relevance of Ambedkar's thought will remain – democratic system is working, institutions are getting strength, caste system is getting negated though slowly, dalits are increasingly getting their say and rightly so, social integration is coming around. All these positive traits in Indian system and establishment have come about due to sound edifice given by Dr Ambedkar. The need of the hour is to highlight and safeguard those facets in Ambedkar's personality and thinking that help in ensuring a social change. The radical part of Ambedkar's legacy which will strengthen the forces fighting for radical social transformation should be safeguarded and emulated. Ambedkar's life and work cannot be ignored by anybody in our country who is concerned about changing the society.

Dr Nisha Bhargava's paper makes an attempt to review the political and economic philosophy of Dr Ambedkar. The first section reviews his political philosophy and in the second, his views on Indian economy are discussed. The final section explores the relevance of his philosophy in the globalised era. The study tends to conclude that by espousing globalisation, we are moving away from Ambedkar's socialist philosophy. Consequently, our current policies are in stark contrast with Ambedkar's vision and mission. Considering the growing uncertainties and negative outcomes of globalisation, we need to reconsider our liberal policies. We must keep in mind Dr Ambedkar's prescriptions for removing the ills of our economy and polity if we desire to have inclusive growth.

Dr Navjot Kaur discusses that Ambedkar devoted most of his intellectual, social and political efforts for securing social justice to the discriminated, deprived and downtrodden sections of society in India. One such effort was to enter the profession of journalism in 1920s as the Chief Spokesman of the voiceless, penniless and helpless millions of untouchables and exploited masses, starting different papers such as; 'Mook Nayak', 'Bahishkrit Bharat', 'Samata' and 'Janata'. He threw light on the history of social discrimination and led socio-cultural movement and utilised his papers as powerful means of struggle for social revolution; providing a forum to the cause of the oppressed and the downtrodden. In this background, it would be worthwhile to revisit B.R. Ambedkar's philosophy and canon of journalism and his contribution as a journalist to bring about a social justice in Indian society. An attempt would also be made to understand as to what Ambedkar considered to be the role of newspapers to establish an egalitarian society.

Dr RanjayVardhan tries to analyses in his paper that Dr Ambedkar wanted the untouchables or 'dalits' to follow some principles in life so that they could attain a respectable status by their own efforts as a community. He recommended "Pancha-sutras" for them. Ambedkar made an appeal to his community to change its style of life to suit to the needs of time. He wanted them to dress well and have self-respect for themselves. The paper makes an attempt to study social, cultural and political efforts of Dr Ambedkar in ameliorating the conditions of Dalits. The paper concludes that chief aim of Dr Ambedkar was to bring about a revolution in the way of life of the dalits and in their aspirations for themselves and for their children. Dr Ambedkar in his efforts to raise the status of dalits considered the caste system one of the great obstacles. He expressed his great disappointment with the caste as well as varna system. He supported the Anti-Untouchability League which launched a campaign all over the country to secure for the depressed classes enjoyment of their civil rights such as taking water from the village wells, admission of the children in village schools etc. Ambedkar had the honour of giving to the people of India their Constitution.

Dr Neeru Sharma discusses the issue of social justice found its place in the very Preamble of the Indian Constitution. It expressed solemn resolve to secure to all Indian citizens 'Justice, Social economic and political; equality of status and opportunities and to promote among them all fraternity assuring the dignity of the individual and unity and integrity of the nation'. Thus, it is evident that the main intention of the constitution-makers was to provide justice, equality and dignity. Dr B.R. Ambedkar being the Chairman of the Draft Committee took various initiatives to check discrimination with depressed classes. Provisions for reservation were included in Various articles of the Indian Constitution. But after the 70 years of independence, Dalits are facing discrimination and are victims of inequitable social system. Seventy-third amendment provided reservation for SC/STs in Panchayati Raj Institutions. Even here Dalits met the same fate. Present paper makes an humble attempt to study discrimination with Dalits in Panchayati Raj Institutions. Paper sums up that if government is really interested in empowering underprivileged it must revive the practice of capacity building programme for Dalits. The intention of this study is to expose the fact that untouchability still prevails in Indian Society.

Discusses in her paper that B.R. Ambedkar has a unique place among modern Indian thinkers. For his whole life he fought for the rights of dalits. He roused the dalit consciousness to fight for the eradication of dalit discrimination. But inequality and discrimination still continue in Indian society. Her paper makes an humble attempt in this direction. It analyses gross deprivation and inequality persisting in South Asia as well as in India. It sums up that B.R. Ambedkar needs to be reinvented in era of privatisation and growing role of corporate sector where dalits are marginalised.

Dr Gobinda Chandra Sethi's paper indicates that dalits were deprived from their rights and living in harsh condition. Now-a-days, it is to remind not only age-old oppression by depriving from basic amenities but also the dominance of super-structure over the sub-structure. An upper stratum of the society was the suppressor but the lower was suppressed. It was the order of the then society expose the fact about upper caste supremacy over the sub-castes in different forms or pattern in the prevailing society perennially. Dalit comprises SCs, STs and all the manual workers subservient to Brahminical order. This further symbolises a struggle for recognition of self-identity, expression of historical reality of oppression due to caste-based untouchability and occupations and a determination for creation of egalitarian society. Indian society has mechanisms that integrate by allowing them to hold together in order to restore the state of harmony or stability. Dalit community is excluded from enjoyment of social, economical, educational and political opportunities. It has long history of struggle to fight against caste discrimination. Social Inclusion is the removal of institutional barriers and the enhancement of incentives to increase the access of diverse individuals and groups to development opportunities. Constitutional provisions have enabled Dalits to have their greater access to services, resources and development opportunity.

Mrs Jatinder Walia and Mrs Reena Kushwaha's paper investigates the contribution of B.R. Ambedkar in the context of social justice and also measures at what level it achieve success. Dr Babasaheb Rao Ambedkar is the man of millennium for social justice since he was the first person in history to successfully lead a trade of securing social justice to vast section of humanity. He believed that root cause of social injustice in India lies in the caste system. He himself being member of low caste was victim of ill-treatment. He argued that a true democracy in India could prevail only when no kind of discrimination would exist in Indian societies. So, he struggled throughout his life for the downtrodden. When he became a member of the drafting committee, he mentioned special provisions in fundamental rights, directive principles and provision to set up constitutional machinery for scheduled castes, scheduled tribes and women. These are considered as some of his great efforts. Today, his ceaseless efforts have brought changes in Indian societies. Educated people are accepting inter-caste marriages and give respect to people of all strata. But still now there is need of awareness because it happens only in metro cities.

Dr Amandeep analyses the writings and political activities of Dr Babasaheb Ambedkar who made significant contributions to the anti-caste movement. Ambedkar's thoughts are the sole inspiration for Dalit Literature. Ambedkar stood for the social liberation, economic emancipation and political advancement of the downtrodden. Dalit writers found Self-respect through Ambedkar ideas and agitations. It further analyses how Ambedkar has remained a source of inspiration of Dalit writers. The three cornerstones of Ambedkar aesthetics are – empiricism, constitutionalism and conversion, one succeeding the other in a dynamic continuum. It needs be stressed here that Dalit aesthetics during Ambedkar's time itself undergoes shifts as it strives to seek authentic ways to empowerment.

Rohini Arora in her paper highlights the women empowerment is multi-dimensional concept. Dr B.R. Ambedkar had said that education is the key to achieve success. This statement focuses on education as the prime dimension of empowerment for women. This key concept acts as the baseline for women empowerment in India in which Ambedkar had given emphasis on education of women which is the foundation of economic empowerment. Education enhances employment opportunities for women and their ability to make decisions. Her paper focuses on Ambedkar's views on education as tool for women empowerment and role of ICT in implementing his views in today's digital era.

Dr Mona Arora's analyses that Dr Ambedkar was a scholar as much as a man of action. Ambedkar tried hard to show the mechanisms of the caste system and clarified the origin of untouchability in order to support his fight for equality. For him, if the lower castes were not in a position to overthrow their oppressors, it was because of two reasons: they had partially internalised hierarchy; and because of the very characteristics of caste-based inequality.

Mrs Jasbir Kaur elaborates in her paper that Ambedkar was not only the father of Indian Constitution; he was a great freedom fighter, political leader, philosopher, thinker, economist, editor, social reformer, revivalist of Buddhism and was first Indian to break down the barriers in the way of advancement of women in India. He argued for extensive economic and social rights for women. He stated that women should be given all round development more importantly social education, their well being and socio-cultural rights. He emphasised that each and every section of Indian women be given their due share and it is a must to maintain and protect dignity and modesty of women. He translated many of his ideas and visions into specific policies and institutions during his stint as the architect of Indian constitution and as the law minister of India.

Devinder Kaur highlights in her paper about Dr Ambedkar's concept of social justice means a mode of life to give every man his right place in society. Its precepts may be: to live honourably, to give respect to all, to injure no one, and to give every man his due without any artificial discrimination in mind and unnatural classification in society. Ambedkar admits that it is a problem not merely of distributing the material abundance among the people but basically a mode of life based on mutual respect and regard, a feeling of fellowship as equal members of a society. Hence the measure of social justice is not material progress, but the abundance and proliferation of human values among the people. Now-a-days it is a wider and broader concept. We can include linguistic and religious minorities, schedule castes and schedule tribes, deprived and untouchables, mentally challenged, physically disabled and women etc. under the umbrella of social aspect of justice.

Due to globalisation the social problems have also became worldwide or global. Privatisation and urbanisation have changed the role of welfare state to maintain and protect the social justice. This paper investigates the enlarged dimensions of social justice with the Ambedkar's idea of social justice in Indian society.

Dr Nirmal Singh's paper he discusses that the encounter of democracy with caste is a historical process accommodating two sets of opposed values. There is a common understanding that caste is antagonistic to democracy. Indeed, the hierarchical universe of the caste system is theoretically at odds with the equalitarian requirements of substantive democracy. The political culture of Indian society is leading to more and more social contradictions. On the one hand we aspire to become egalitarian society and, on the other, the caste culture negates this very aspiration. And what is more problematic we cannot become egalitarian without the help of this very caste culture, at least in economic sense. The present paper is an attempt to understand Ambedkar's views on caste system and Indian democracy. His paper has two-fold objectives, first, to understand and analyse caste system in India, and second, to explore Ambedkar's vision of social democracy.

Manjinder Kaur discusses in her paper that Dr B.R. Ambedkar championed the cause of women as well as the miserable plight of Scheduled Castes and Scheduled Tribes throughout his career. His contribution was great in the field of women's empowerment who advocated for the liberation of women and gender equality in India. If there any persons worked for women's liberation in India, they were none other than Dr Babasaheb Ambedkar, EV. Ramasamy Periyar and Jyotirao Phule. Without Dr Babasaheb Ambedkar, at least whatever so changes the position of women today in India would be only question mark. There were many leaders fought for the women's rights in India. Most of them were failed in their action. But Dr Babasaheb Ambedkar was the only person who changed the effort via Law.

Dr Sucheta Singh's paper highlights that Dr B.R. Ambedkar to be a genius and was known as a greater thinker, philosopher, jurist-par excellence, prolific writer, social activist and critic and strode like a colossus in the Indian socio-political scene unto his death, his thoughts never received adequate attention in the generality of Indian society just because he was born as an untouchables. He provides a powerful source of inspiration to formulate a feminist political agenda which simultaneously addresses the issues of class, caste and gender. Ambedkar had deep faith in the fundamental rights-in equal rights of man and women, in the dignity of the individual and in the social and economic justice. In India, basically women are oppressed and are not treated on par with men. Moreover dalit women are oppressed among oppressed and slaves of slaves. Her present paper tries to throw lights on Ambedkar's view on the problems of women and its relevancy in present scenario with special reference to Dalit women.

Archana Thakur discusses Dr Ambedkar's thought that Hinduism in practice would be an obstacle to healthy social developments and political democracy in India. The idea of converting to another religion in order to escape from the caste system logically ensued from Ambedkars analysis of Hinduism, whose originality and strength laid in its demonstration that in this civilisation social hierarchy was consubstantial to religion. To leave it was thus the only means to attain equality. So, he thought of Buddhism which he rightly considers was very modern in its to way of thinking and would be an answer to social disparities created by Hinduism. In this article my hypothese is Why did Ambedkar choose Buddhism to liberate his Depressed Classes, not other religion? Was his failure in politics leading him to Buddhism? Lastly, after a thorough analysis, she concluded that he converted to Buddhism because of his failure and frustration with politics in finding a way to uplift the life of the untouchable people justice.

Parambir Brar highlights in her paper that Bhim Rao Ambedkar had experienced various discriminations in his early life by virtue of being born in an untouchable family. He wanted to get rid off from such ill-treatments which make him suffer intellectually as well as socially. For this, he sorted to convert into another religion which will act as substitute to Hinduism for the simple reason that the Hindu religion does not recognise the principles of equality on the basis of social status and also, it fosters inequality by insisting upon grading people on the basis of Chaturvarna system. So, he started looking towards Sikhism because this religion would not alienate the converts from Hindu culture as Sikhism is an offshoot of Hinduism only but due to some differences with Sikh leaders of contemporary period and prevalence of untouchability among Sikhs, this conversion could not take place and as a result, Ambedkar, along with his followers sought for Buddhism instead of Sikhism as an alternative way towards salvation.

Tarminder Kaur intended to understand Caste system from the view point of Dr B.R. Ambedkar and his vision of Caste ridden Indian society. He comprehensively analysed the factors responsible for operational success of Caste system and its continuity from centuries. This paper highlight the theoretical contribution of Dr B.R. Ambedkar to approach Indian society from a different perspective with special reference to depressed and downtrodden lowest rung of Indian Caste system i.e. Scheduled Caste and Untouchables. The role of Dr B.R. Ambedkar as a social reformer and a National Political Leader is also discussed.

Parveen Kumari attempts to highlight the relevance of Dr B. R. Ambedkar's ideas on the inclusion and empowerment of women in general and Dalit women in particular who carry the double burden of gender and caste oppression in the larger framework of society. Dr B.R. Ambedkar mobilised a large number of Dalit women to join the various phases of his movements – be it the historic Mahad Satyagraha of 1927, or the Nasik Satyagraha of 1930 or his conversion to Buddhism in 1956. Dalit women have benefitted in several ways from his initiatives. Some Dalit women took up the pen to articulate their experiences of victimisation. The paper attempts a study of Baby Kamble's narrative *The Prisons We Broke* to analyse why Dalit women have great reverence for their 'Babasaheb' and why he is still considered a Messiah by Dalits. It was Ambedkar's awakening regarding the rights of Dalits which ultimately moved them from periphery to centre.

Navneet Kaur discusses in her paper that Dr B.R. Ambedkar emerged during a period when the caste-based discrimination was at its peak. Jyotiba Phule as well as Chatrapati Shahu ji Maharaj already attempted so many ways to provide the education as well as Employment to the Untouchables respectively whereas Gandhi was attempting the efforts to 'Change the Hearts' of the upper castes. During this period, Dr Ambedkar emerged as a Scholar, Philosopher, Social-Activist as well as a Reformer who sincerely raised-up the Caste-based issues in the British Councils, 3-Round Table Conferences as well as during the Constituent Assembly Debates. This paper is, therefore, an attempt to examine analytically the efforts of Dr Ambedkar for removing the Untouchability from the Hindu Society and their influence in present democratic India.

Shayama Bangar highlights in her paper that India has produced many social and political thinker and philosopher in the course of her long and chequered history. Among the galaxy of thinkers and philosophers of India, Bharat Ratna Dr Babasaheb Ambedkar occupies undoubtedly the most important place. He "has carved out for himself a unique position in society, whatever label he wears in future, Dr Ambedkar is not the man to allow himself to be forgotten. Dr Bhim Rao Ambedkar, popularly known as Babasaheb Ambedkar, was one of the architects of the Indian Constitution of the Independent India. Dr Ambedkar a determined fighter and a deep scholar has made significant efforts to lead the society on the path of Liberty, Equality and Fraternity. While his views on various social, economic and political aspects have been analysed, his approaches to Indian foreign policy especially most conflicting issues of Indian foreign policy (China and Kashmir issue) have remained a rain shadow area. This paper highlights Dr Ambedkar's thought on China and Kashmir issue which are the most conflicting issues of the Indian foreign policy.

1

Dr B.R. Ambedkar's Philosophy in Contemporary India: Threats and Relevance

— *Emanual Nahar*

Abstract

Dr B.R. Ambedkar's views on democracy, social and economic justice, gender equality, national unity and religious belief provide important inputs in quest for finding solutions to some of the demanding questions of present times. The relevance of Ambedkar's thought will remain – democratic system is working, institutions are getting strength, caste system is getting negated though slowly, dalits are increasingly getting their say and rightly so, social integration is coming around. All these positive traits in Indian system and establishment have come about due to sound edifice given by Dr Ambedkar. The need of the hour is to highlight and safeguard those facets in Ambedkar's personality and thinking that help in ensuring a social change. The radical part of Ambedkar's legacy which will strengthen the forces fighting for radical social transformation should be safeguarded and emulated. Ambedkar's life and work cannot be ignored by anybody in our country who is concerned about changing the society.

Introduction

Dr B.R. Ambedkar was an astute political leader, constitutionalist, jurist, economist, thinker and a transformational social reformer whose philosophy has an abiding relevance today. Dr Ambedkar played a seminal role in the drafting the constitution. The life and work of Dr Ambedkar is a testament of his tireless fight against the abhorrent practice of untouchability and the unjust caste system on behalf of the oppressed and the poor. His emphasis on dignity, unity, freedom and rights for all citizens, and particularly the less fortunate segments of our people is adequately reflected in the Constitution.

As democratic India prepares to celebrate the 125th year of his birth, Babasaheb Ambedkar stands taller than he ever did before—his role in the struggle for a modern, democratic, and socially just India greatly enhanced at the expense of various other outstanding national figures who were contemporaries and opponents during the great battles of the freedom movement era. This is essentially because the deep-seated and central problems spotlighted by his life, struggles, studies, and experimentation in ideas remain alive and kicking while the searching and often profound questions he raised about Indian society remain basically unanswered.

I. Dr Ambedkar – A Champion Reformer and Social Democrat

It was B.R. Ambedkar that identified the cause of the retardation of the Indian creativity, which is also the source of the retardation of the mindsets of people of other South Asian countries. He saw that purely by way of mental exercises this bondage cannot be broken. What needed to be broken were the social linkages which had tied up the minds of the people over centuries. To this, he gave and for the understanding of this processes he devoted his time. And his way of understanding was not by reading into the text of the past but into the lives of the ordinary folk of India spread in that vast country.

Dr Ambedkar was well-versed on history and the political theories, which have been produced in the process of struggles for democracy. He was also deeply aware of the history of minority problems in the world. He understood that if a minority problem is not properly resolved entire civilisations can be destroyed in conflicts which would not only destroy the minorities but entirety of society.

He had a number of interesting ideas to say about complicated and difficult national issues—Kashmir, language, nationhood, citizenship, ethnicity, and so on. His analysis lit up the field for a proper democratic understanding of co-operative federalism and Centre-State relations in India. On international questions and foreign policy, his approach was that of a conservative dissenting from non-alignment and from the Nehruvian, not to mention the Left's world view.

The social and class basis of the following he commanded; the radical nature of his social questioning; his passion for social justice; his openness to modern, scientific, and rational ideas; his unyielding secularism and forward-looking views on a number of questions, especially on the condition and future of women, and on what it took to make a civil society; his great intellectual gifts, tireless curiosity, and wide-ranging interests; his ability to concentrate on attainable, practical goals; and his constructive sense of realism— marked him out as a unique kind of leader.

It was he who forced India to confront the reality of discrimination by facing up to the reality of caste oppression. And he did so bluntly, in a manner which youngsters today would call "in your face". Not for him the mealy-mouthed platitudes of the well-meaning: he was prepared to rage against the injustice of social discrimination, and to do so in every forum available to him. It was an attitude that Indian society was not prepared for, but at a time when Indians were fighting for their freedom from foreign rule, it was both appropriate and necessary that Indians should fight equally against domestic oppression.

Dr Ambedkar rejected what he saw as the patronising indulgence of the Gandhian approach to untouchability. The Mahatma called them "Harijans" – 'Children of God'. Dr Ambedkar rejected the word - after all, he argued, aren't we all children of God? He used, instead, the Marathi and Hindi words for the 'excluded' (Bahishkrit), the 'oppressed' (Dalit) and the 'silent' (Muka) to define the outcastes. So even while fighting British rule, Dr Ambedkar was a tireless and courageous advocate of the Dalit cause, an enemy of superstition, and an iconoclast who had contempt for traditions that he felt deserved no sanctity.

As a nationalist, he was sensitive to the charge that he was dividing Indians at a time when they needed to be united against the British. His critics forget that Gandhiji himself acknowledged Dr Ambedkar's "sterling patriotism", brilliantly displayed in the first Round Table Conference. When Dr Ambedkar demanded separate electorates for downtrodden people, Mahatma Gandhi undertook a fast unto death until an unconvinced. Dr Ambedkar, fearing mass reprisals if the Mahatma died, caved in. Gandhiji, who abhorred untouchability, believed that the answer lay in the social awakening of caste Hindus rather than in building walls of separation.

Dr Ambedkar, who lived with the daily reality of caste discrimination, was not convinced that the entrenched practices of traditional Hinduism could ever disappear. In the end, he found a Constitutional solution to remedy the injustices, he fought against all his life. As a political leader, Dr Ambedkar was better at articulating powerful ideas than in creating the structures to see them through. None of the three parties he founded ever acquired the following or the permanence that his ideas deserved. But the Constitution of which he was the principal author remains the best instrument for pursuing his ideas. The leader and spokesman of a community left his greatest gift to all communities - a legacy that belongs to all of us, and one of which we are yet to prove ourselves wholly worthy. Let us hope that this 125th anniversary year is not spent entirely in platitudes, but in an honest recognition of the life and the message of one of the greatest son of India.

This paper is an attempt to explore the threats to Dr Ambedkar's Philosophy and approach. The study also evaluates and highlights relevance of Dr Ambedkar in present Indian socio-political scenario.

II. Relevance of Dr Ambedkar's Philosophy in Contemporary India

As the government and political parties trip over each other to commemorate the 125th birth anniversary of Dr Babasaheb B.R. Ambedkar today, it would be a pity if the life of this extraordinary Indian were reduced to one issue - his championship of the Dalit cause - just as much as it would be wrong to gloss over his path-breaking role in that monumental endeavour.

Dr Ambedkar is such an icon today that we fail to fully appreciate the remarkable scale of what he accomplished. To be born into what was called an 'untouchable' family in 1891, and that too as the 14th and last child of a poor Mahar subedar in an Army cantonment, would normally have guaranteed a life of neglect, poverty and discrimination. Not only Dr Ambedkar rise above the circumstances of his birth, but he achieved a level of success that would have been spectacular for a child of privilege.

Dr Ambedkar emphasised the anti-social, anti-progress character of an unjust social order as well as its vital connection, through networks of force and ideology, with political power. The caste system, in his analysis, militated against fraternity, "sanghatan and co-operation for a good cause", public charity and broad-based virtue and morality.

Dr Ambedkar's ideal would be a society based on liberty, equality, and fraternity. He specified that his ideal society would be mobile; there would be "social endosmosis. There would be fraternity, which was only another name for democracy, and democracy was primarily a mode of associated living, of conjoining communicated experience and breeding an attitude of respect and reverence towards fellow human beings.

Two of his political admonitions are of particular contemporary relevance. Do not lay liberties at the feet of a great man; in politics, bhakti or hero-worship is a sure road to degradation. Make political democracy a social democracy; resolve the contradictions, else they will undermine democracy itself.

Ideologically, Ambedkar may have stood to the right of centre, but at times he moved sharply the other way, to the radical side. This happened especially when his ideas, campaigns, and political organisational work were backed by powerful mass movements, for example during the 1938 workers' struggle in Mumbai against the Anti-strike Bill. He was the builder of the Independent Labour Party, which did not take off at the all-India level but yielded some useful political, ideological, and organisational lessons to the opposition around the country.

The current national situation is framed by the political and social ascendancy of the Hindu Right and the ideological and political offensive by majority communalism and social reaction. Hindutva is even attempting, against the grain of history, to appropriate Ambedkar's legacy. In this situation, his uncompromising analysis of the caste system, of chaturvarnya and sanatana dharma, of notions of pollution, of unalterable or rigid social hierarchy, and of the implications of the hegemony of the *shastras* must be read, re-read, and made part of a national debate. His major theoretical exposition of such questions is contained in a 1936 presidential address which stirred up a hornet's nest, the radical Annihilation of Caste to which the writer Arundhati Roy, in a long introductory essay, has provided fresh meaning and context. This intellectual contribution to the building of a new India must be ranked on a par with Babasaheb's signal and justly celebrated contribution to the making of a Republican Constitution.

Dr B.R. Ambedkar's solid contribution to constitutional and institution-building aside, he had a great deal to say about democracy as a real way of life and about citizens' rights, about authoritarianism, and also about a healthy democratic political system. He detested hereditary, dynastic rule and a one-party system. "To have popular government run by a single party is to let democracy become a mere form for despotism to play its parts from behind it," is a typical Ambedkar formulation. He warned: "Despotism does not cease to be despotism because it is elective. The real guarantee against despotism is to confront it with the possibility of its dethronement, of its being laid low, of its being superseded by a rival party." Ambedkar clearly had little use for political stability premised on a single-party rule, or on a social philosophy of "letting sleeping dogs lie".

Dr B.R. Ambedkar's views on democracy, social and economic justice, gender equality, national unity and religious belief provide important inputs in quest for finding solutions to some of the demanding questions of present times. The relevance of Ambedkar will remain – democratic system is working, institutions are getting strength, caste system is getting negated though slowly, dalits are increasingly getting their say and rightly so, social integration is coming around. All these positive traits in Indian system and establishment have come about due to sound edifice given by Dr Ambedkar.

The 2G scam and some wrong doing by the system are being pin pointed and checked by the CAG and other watchdog agencies. Dr Ambedkar speaking in the Constituent Assembly highly placed the office of the CAG. The judiciary is active proactive. The executive is afraid of the parliament. The system of checks and balance is working. India has started asserting itself, as visualised by Dr Ambedkar long before the relations with China and Pakistan went sore after our independence. Dr Ambedkar's thinking on our China policy was to assert on the issue of Tibet and sit and negotiate with Pakistan on the basis of ground realities on the border. These important aspects of our foreign policy have to be given a fresh look. It is satisfying to note that the elections are being held regularly though not yet fully free from faults.

III. Threat to Ambedkarism

There are so many organisations and Non Government Organisations in the name of Babasaheb Ambedkar in India and abroad also. The NGO's are more interested in collecting money from the government exchequer rather than spreading the real message of Dr Ambedkar. The Neo-intelligentsia from amongst Dalits especially Bureaucrats, Doctors, Engineers etc. are least concerned and bothered about the significance of Ambedkarism and his philosophy. They relate Ambedkar with reservation only. They are busy enjoying their pseudo status and want to enjoy all benefits on the name of Dr Ambedkar in the society. Added to it is the fact that they are not at all telling their children about Ambedkar and other social reformers of Dalit society. Ironically most of them even themselves do not know about Ambedkar beyond reservation. In some cases they have even started hiding their caste and identity also and marrying their children in upper caste Hindus.

The Neo-pseudo rich culture in Dalits who have earned a lot after getting benefits of reservation is also a big threat to the survival of Ambedkarite thoughts. This class within caste in fact could have worked for spread of Ambedkarite thoughts but they are busy enjoying pseudo rich culture and are transferring same to their children. They are not creating an interest among their children to struggle in life, they make things easy for their children. In fact, they are not aware of the future implications of this fast emerging phenomenon of neo-pseudo rich culture. They shirk from discussing plight of their caste and their forefathers in front of their children. They hesitate to show their own identity and caste in public places.

Limited Space for Dr Ambedkar's Philosophy

Some of the communal organisations, political parties and caste groups in India are providing limited space for Dr Ambedkar's Philosophy and reducing the value of his ideas. Even some of the fanatic groups are mixing their philosophy with Hindutva and left Marxist ideology. These groups are playing politics to capture the vote bank. By creating such type of division, these groups wants to show only that Dr Ambedkar is a leader of Scheduled Castes and wanted to give the status of sub-national leader in India.

History of India also certifies that Dr Ambedkar was a mass leader because in 1942 and 1945, he organised big rallies of women and dalits in the Mumbai Province for the protection and upliftment of weaker sections of the society. On the other side, history also certifies that many fanatics communal Hindu leaders did not want to see him as a national leader of India and gave him little space in the national politics.

Diminishing Use of Reservations

India's Constitution, adopted in 1950, inaugurated the world's oldest and farthest-reaching affirmative action programme, guaranteeing scheduled castes and tribes - the most disadvantaged groups in Hinduism's hierarchy - not only equality of opportunity but guaranteed outcomes, with reserved places in educational institutions, government jobs and even seats in parliament and the State Assemblies. These "reservations" or quotas were granted to groups on the basis of their (presumably immutable) caste identities. The logic of reservations in India was simple: they were justified as a means of making up for millennia of discrimination based on birth. It was a small way of compensating the millions of unfortunates who suffered daily the inequities and humiliations of untouchability. Even BJP emerged as a Dalit Party in Uttar Pradesh and came in power by adopting Dr Ambedkar's philosophy. With the refusal of big industrial houses even to entertain the proposal of reservation in jobs for people belonging to Scheduled Castes/Tribes in private companies, the question whether government at the Centre will be able to fulfill its promise of providing job reservations to the SC/STs in the private sector or has once again started begging for an answer.

Reservations became more political in 1989, when the VP Singh-led government of the day decided to extend their benefits to Other Backward Classes (OBCs), based on the recommendations of the Mandal Commission. The OBCs hailed from the lower and intermediate castes who were deemed backward because they lacked "upper caste" status.

Neo-Liberal Policies and Dalits

Dalit intellectuals are extremely agitated at the destructive nature of neo-liberal policies. They are noticing the failure and diminishing use of reservations, which were termed as a 'boon' given by Ambedkar, realising that they cannot save reservations without fighting neo-liberal policies. They are also agitated at the attempts by the Hindutva forces to derail the debate on caste-based oppression and inequality from political agenda by pushing forward their revanchist nationalism, revivalist patriotism and moribund feudal culture. These dalit intellectuals cannot break the existing disappointment in the dalit movement and move forward unless these forces identify specific ideas of Ambedkar which can help them fight against the forces that are trying to impose their hegemony by promoting neo-liberal policies, communalism and cultural reaction.

Reservation as a solution to empowering people in a caste-ridden Indian society averred that reservation is losing its efficacy in an era where more jobs are being created in private rather than government sector. As caste system is deep-rooted in society and creates socio-economic imbalances, it is important to have reservations till such time that his disparity is removed from society in totality.

Actually, the purpose of reservations is to uplift the Dalits and change their status and promote equality. But it is in fact that 61 per cent of Dalits are agricultural labour, 56 per cent Dalits have been reported living below the poverty line and about 47 per cent are working in informal sector. In the public sector, 14 per cent jobs are reserved for scheduled castes but only 10 per cent were filled because there is no proper policy of implementation of reservation. Job prospects in government sector is responsible and escaping from their accountability.

Politicisation of Dr Ambedkar

There's the cynical explantation: that the desperate scramble for Ambedkar's legacy is merely an extension of 'vote bank' politics. This would especially hold true after the BSP rout in the general elections, following which the national parties are keen to capitalise on the Dalit vote in the Hindi Belt. However, apart from the pragmatic considerations of electoral politics, there is much to be said for

Ambedkar as a man whose legacy fits in perfectly into post-liberalisation India.

Dr Ambedkar received the Bharat Ratna in 1990 - at a time when India was on the cusp of economic liberalisation and dealing with anti-Mandal protests. Ambedkar suddenly appeared to be the perfect founding father of the nation – ripe to be celebrated at last. His egalitarian credentials too, are beyond reproach - right through his life he was one of the most ardent spokespersons for the rights of Dalits, women and labourers. But most importantly for India's major Centre and Centre-Right parties, Ambedkar was an economic liberal. It is this mix – the egalitarian and the capitalist – that makes Ambedkar a prime candidate for every major national party to appropriate, in today's India.

Every Political Party is talking about Dr Babasaheb Ambedkar's life and work today. One of the reasons for this spurt in interest might be the 125th birth anniversary of Ambedkar. However, the interest shown by political parties on Ambedkar today has got other strong political reasons. Ambedkar's life work was to a large extent in the pre-independence period. He passed away on December 6, 1956. It was not even a decade since achieving independence at that time. And it was not even five years after the promulgation of constitution, in whose drafting he had played a major part. Though there were attempts by the ruling parties in the last seven decades of independent India to appropriate the legacy of Ambedkar to suit their interests, never were these efforts so intense as we are witnessing them today.

Merchants of Dalit Voters through Dr Ambedkar

Dalit organisations, Dalit political parties and other political parties are doing permanent claims on Dr Ambedkar and have opportunist alliance with dalit organisations. BSP is claiming itself as the only political party protecting interests of Dalits in India.

The Congress party is trying to re-embrace Ambedkar with a view to win back the lost support of dalits and other weaker sections. Dalits and other weaker sections who remained for a long time as the solid vote bank for the Congress, started moving away from it in many states after the introduction and pursuance of neo-liberal policies which severely harmed their interests. Now, realising the importance of wearing a pro-poor mask and to regain its lost vote base, it is straining to restore the eminence of Ambedkar in its strategy of wooing the weaker sections.

Fanatic groups are also showing keen interest in Ambedkar as they consider his philosophy and personality a huge hindrance for the realisation of its Hindutva project. To overcome this hindrance, it is trying to appropriate Ambedkar by sanitising and distorting his ideas and transform him into a supporter of Parivar's revanchist ideology. To realise this, Sangh Parivar is pursuing a two pronged strategy – attack the dalits and browbeat them into submission; and appropriate Ambedkar's personality by distorting his ideas.

After the assumption of power by BJP at the Centre, physical attack against dalits and other weaker sections have increased manifold. Recently, in the state of Gujarat, Dalit community's people were beaten very miserably. The manner in which the organisers of Ambedkar-Periyar Study Circle in IIT Madras were harassed, the way the Central Government played a role in the events that led to the suicide of Rohith Vemula of University of Hyderabad, clearly expose their intentions to establish an 'upper-caste culture' in the name of 'Indian culture'. One cannot forget the book written by Arun Shourie sometime back demeaning the personality of Ambedkar.

Sangh Parivar clearly knows that it cannot erase the ideas of Ambedkar by simply attacking him. That is why it is pursuing the second part of its strategy – of appropriating Ambedkar, by distorting his teachings to suit the needs of their Hindutva project. They are campaigning that Ambedkar is a social reformer who had tried to reform and better Hinduism and a great nationalist who rejected Islam and Christianity, by converting to Buddhism, which is a part of Indian culture. They are trying to place Ambedkar in the pantheon of the leaders and ideologues of Sangh Parivar.

However, these attempts by the Sangh Parivar and the BJP lack honesty. The ideas expounded by Ambedkar throughout his life are completely against the ideas of Hindutva forces. He expended his entire life to annihilate the caste system and expose those teachings and ideas of Hinduism that uphold the caste system. Ambedkar had firmly believed that as long as Hinduism exists, brahmanical caste system and untouchability will exist and so, dalits can be liberated only if they are free from its stranglehold. It is for this reason that only after intense thinking he left Hinduism and joined Buddhism along with his followers. Therefore the efforts by the Sangh Parivar forces to depict Ambedkar as a reformer of Hindu religion are not going to convince anybody especially the oppressed sections.

An entirely different type of process is occurring among those organisations and intellectuals, who claim that they are the real inheritors of Ambedkar's legacy. The failure of slogans like, 'political power' to dalits and other weaker sections in achieving substantial progress in the fight against caste system and liberation of dalits, has placed some of them in a dilemma. Faced with this situation, a section of organisations and individuals are losing their hope on the prospects of social change and are happily allowing themselves to be co-opted by the ruling classes. These co-opted sections are trying to create the impression that the advance of few individuals among dalits will lead to the advancement of all. But these illusions are fast disappearing in the face of realities faced by dalits. In effect, capitalist system deliberately promotes some individuals from the weaker sections into the upper rungs of the society in order to ensure the stability of its social system. The slogan, 'share in power' is a practical expression of this desire of the capitalist system to promote a few individuals from the weaker sections into the ranks of the ruling class.

Communists are also showing greater interest now, than earlier, in the legacy of Ambedkar. Unlike the BJP and the Congress, Communists want to preserve and carry forward the radical part of Ambedkar's legacy in the interest of dalits and other weaker sections. Naturally, this elicited some well-meaning and some mischievous criticisms. Many of the detractors are questioning the sincerity of communists in working for the annihilation of caste system.

Communist Agenda Regarding Dr Ambedkar

Communists never forgot or ignored the objective of annihilation of caste system. It is not an accident that Bhagat Singh had written an essay against caste system in 1928 and also on socialism when he was in prison. This only goes to prove that whoever thinks about establishing a socialist system in our country, cannot ignore the necessity of annihilation of caste system. It will not be an exaggeration to state that apart from Phule and Ambedkar, there is no organisation other than the Communist Party, which was in the forefront in the fight against caste system and its oppressive forms. The political lives of most of the communists started with the fight against caste system. Elimination of caste discrimination was an important component in all the rural peasant struggles led by them. The weakness of communists is not in identifying or fighting caste discrimination. It lies in the failure to understand the dialectical relationship between the struggles for annihilation of caste and abolition of classes and in the uni-dimensional thinking that abolition of classes will automatically lead to the elimination of caste system. This weakness is not confined to the question of caste alone. This applies to the understanding of women's issue and cultural issues too. Communists realised this long back and hence do not have any inhibition in carrying forward the radical ideas of Ambedkar in fighting caste oppression.

Although Ambedkar's basic ideology and communist ideology are completely opposite poles, Communists have never failed to acknowledge the glorious efforts of Ambedkar in fighting caste system and for the welfare of dalits and other weaker sections. Communists intend to move forward by taking all the good in Ambedkar's legacy, identifying and developing those ideas that are useful for social change and leaving out those ideas and actions that do not suit the present times.

Policies and Programmes against Dr Ambedkar's Approach

Caste in contemporary times has become a political tool for the ruling class to severe its social oppression over Dalits and also for economically exploiting the working classes. The present government, while carrying forward its Hindutva agenda, it is simultaneously assisting the multinational corporates. While implementing pro-corporate moves like Land Acquisition Bill, Insurance Bill, Labour Laws, corporate favour budget, 100 per cent FDI in PSUs etc and paving way for to give more benefits to the corporate sector, it is communally polarising the common people by the ban on ***cow slaughtering,*** **ghar vapsi** programmes and promoting Vedas etc.. In the name of '***Swadeshi***' they are selling mother India and dividing her children in the name of communalism. As part of this, now they are revisionising Ambedkar and projecting him as an icon for their vote politics. Ambedkar proposed to annihilate the caste by destroying Hinduism. He says, "You must destroy the Religion of the Shrutis and the Smritis. Nothing else will avail". "Hinduism is a veritable chamber of horrors and it must die for caste to vanish". But in the contemporary days, when caste is supporting the economic exploitation, it can only be annihilated by taking forward struggle against caste simultaneously with the struggle against recolonisation.

The ruling classes in our country are trying to convert Ambedkar into an innocuous symbol to suit their class rule. His statue has become an important part in this scheme. All Ambedkar's statues, without any variation, are sculpted with a copy of the Constitution in his hand, as if to show that he had done nothing substantial in his life, except for drafting the Constitution. There is no doubt about Ambedkar's role in the drafting of our Constitution and it isn't an exaggeration to praise him as the architect of our Constitution. Apart from Ambedkar's huge role in ensuring reservations for the weaker sections, we can clearly see his stamp in drafting a liberal and democratic Constitution. In spite of all these, we should not forget that the basic character of our Constitution is safeguarding private property. All those aspects concerning common people are relegated to directive principles, instead of making them fundamental rights. Anybody can understand what kind of Constitution would have emerged if Ambedkar was given complete freedom in its drafting from the memorandum he had submitted to the Constituent Assembly.

Invoking Nationalism

According to Dr B.R. Ambedkar nationalism cannot be generated by slogans only, it it possible by providing adequate representation by providing adequate methods and by spreading of education among downtrodden people if the society and also by maintaining dignity of the Dalits. Dr Ambekar rightly said that anti-national feelings can only come due to economic conflicts and social injustice. Today, some of the fanatic groups in India are spreading terror and fear in society but these things are not helpful to create nationalism. It is only social feeling and oneness brings nationalism in the minds of the people not the slogans like – 'Laal Salam' or 'Bharat Mata ki Jai'. Whatever the colour – red, blue or saffron are only symbolic but not helpful for nationalism. Only the sense of belonging or social feeling can create nationalism more stronger.

Present Political Democracy is not a Social Democracy

His faith in democracy, which he shared with Jawaharlal Nehru, is also one of his proud legacies to our country. Whereas some saw Ambedkar, with his three-piece suit and formal English, as a westernised exponent of occidental constitutional systems, he was inspired far more by the democratic practices of ancient India, in particular the Buddhist sanghas.

Ambedkar saw in the institutions of Indian democracy that he was helping to create, the best guarantee for the future development and welfare of his own people, the oppressed and marginalised of India. He fought hard to introduce into the Constitution fundamental protections and guarantees of civil liberties for individual citizens.

Ambedkar also convinced the Constituent Assembly that it was not enough to abolish untouchability: what was needed to undo millennia of discrimination and exploitation was a system of affirmative action to uplift the oppressed, including reservations of jobs in the civil services, schools and universities. This gave India the world's oldest and farthest-reaching affirmative action programme, which guarantees not only equality of opportunity but of outcome, with seats reserved for Dalits in government jobs, universities and even in Parliament.

Through his role Dr Ambedkar ushered in momentous change into Indian society and politics, but to him it had not come fast enough. He saw the entrenched practices of Hindu society as something he had to reject. "I am born a Hindu," Dr Ambedkar declared in 1936, "but I swear I will not die a Hindu." Twenty years later he died a Buddhist, months after converting with hundreds of thousands of his followers at a public ceremony.

The present democracy is not a social democracy. It has destroyed democratic values and public spirit. Recently, attrocities on dalits in Gujarat and Rohit Vermulla's case that caste-based hierarchy, Brahmanical caste-based society is still existing. Violence against Dalits is increasing day by day. Caste consciousness has become a serious threat to India's unity and integrity. Even Dalit Samaj has become de-facto. In the present democracy, state is escaping from social responsibility and leaving education and health in the hands of market forces and corporate sector. It will increase inequalities and challenge the social justice concept of Dr Ambedkar.

Political Democracy – One man and One Vote was not enough, principles of liberty, equality and fraternity could not be divorced from each other. Even to save political democracy, it was necessary to ensure social justice and equality in our social justice and equality in our social and economic life at the earliest possible. Dr Ambedkar in his final address in the constituent assembly argued that we must make our political democracy a social democracy as well. Political democracy cannot last unless it lies at the base of social democracy. It means social democracy was the ultimate goal of his life because social democracy provides socio-economic and political justice and also creates social harmony and destroys caste system.

Conclusion

The need of the hour is to highlight and safeguard those facets in Ambedkar's approach and thinking that help in ensuring a social change. The radical part of Ambedkar's legacy which will strengthen the forces fighting for radical social transformation should be safeguarded and emulated. Ambedkar's life and work cannot be ignored by anybody in our country who is concerned about changing the society.

Ambedkar's political thought is still very relevant to not only to the politics of India but also to politics in South Asia in general. South Asian countries are today facing deep crises, unable to develop political and social institutions to guarantee stability to their societies primarily because of centuries of oppressive and social political systems that were their heritage due to the caste system. The caste system essentially was a system of domination by a small group, called Brahmins, who developed most sophisticated forms of cunning into the social control systems of their time in a way that even for centuries they could maintain their dominance. The damage that was done in the process of repression that accompanied the creation and the maintenance of the caste system have become the obstacles to the development of the intelligence the creativity and the capacity of all the people to deal with contemporary problems. Their past holds them in their bondage. The bonds are so deeply engrained into the very nervous systems that generation after generation people are reproduced with mentalities that prevent them from realising the capacity for freedom and capacity for deeper social communion in each other in their social context.

Although, some faultiness emerged in the Indian society, in spite of these fault lines, there are problems within the society. The constitution is on track and India on rails. Institutions like Commissions, CAG, Public institutions are getting strength. His Philosophy is providing the Gap between practical and theory and also combining materialism and spiritualism. The whole credit goes to Dr B.R. Ambedkar. There is no way fault of our constitution provisions and drawbacks are only in implementation process. And it depends upon our executive, political class and the state. The constitution of India and its provisions are guiding us in difficult time and uniting spirit of our nation. In the conclusion, we can say there is need to change the mindset.

References

1. Ambedkar B.R. (1989), Dr Babasaheb Ambedkar Writings and Speeches Vol. V, Government of Maharashtra Publication, Mumbai.
2. Ambedkar, B. R. (1990), "Who were Sudras?" Writing and Speeches – (Vol. 7), Ed.Department, Government Maharashtra, India.
3. Bandyopadhyay, S. (2000), "Transfer of Power and the Crisis of Dalit Politics in India, 1945-47", Modern Indian Studies, 34(4), 2000, p. 913.
4. Barnwal, Bijay K. (2014), Dr B.R. Ambedkar's Quest for Gender Equality Its Relevance in Contemporary Feminist Discourse, Online International Interdisciplinary Research Journal, {Bi-Monthly}, Volume-IV, Issue-II, March-April.
5. Bharati, A.K. (2001), Dr Ambedkar's Vision for Dalit Upliftment: Extract from a Souvenir. National Conference on Dalit Organisations, New Delhi. Centre for Alternative Dalit Media (CADAM), Delhi.
6. Busi, S. N. (1997), Mahatma Gandhi and Ambedkar Crusader against caste and Untouchability, Palak Prakashan, Jalandhar, India.
7. Dr B. H. Damji and A. P. Jamma (2012), "Dr B. R. Ambedkar's thought on agriculture and its relevance to current agriculture in India" Review of Research.
8. G. Austin, (1999), "Working a Democratic Constitution: The Indian Experience", Oxford University Press, pp. 19-20.
9. Jafferlot, C. (2005), Dr Ambedkar and Untouchability: Analysing and Fighting Caste, Oxford University Press, New Delhi.
10. Jatava, D.R. (2001), Political Philosophy of Dr Ambedkar, National Publishing House, Jaipur and New Delhi.

11. Kashyap, Subash. (ed.), Perspectives on the Constitution. Delhi: Shipra Publication, 1993.
12. Keer Dhananjay (1963), Life and Mission of Dr Ambedkar. Budhbhoomi Prakashan Nagpur, p. ix.
13. Mathew, Thomas. (1991), Ambedkar: Reform or Revolution. New Delhi: Segment Books.
14. Michael, S.M. (2007), Dalits in Modern India : Vision and Values. Sage Publication.
15. Navayan, Karthik (2012), Dr Ambedkar Contribution in Law and Justice for the Upliftment of the Disadvantaged. National Seminar on Ambedkar's Contribution for the Upliftment of the Disadvantaged. 2nd and 3rd September, 2010, Seminar Hall, MGNIRSA.
16. Ronki Ram (2010), Dr Ambedkar, Neo-Liberal Market-Economy and Social Democracy in India, 5 Human Rights Global Focus, 12-38.
17. S.M. (1998), "Ambedkar and Indian nationalism", The Economic and Political Weekly, 7 March 1998, p. 518.
18. Shashi, S.S., (ed.), Ambedkar and Social Justice-Volume II, Director Publications Division, Ministry of Information and Broadcasting, Government of India, Patiala House, New Delhi,1992.
19. Urmilesh (2013), Illogical statement on Dalit Philosophy. Dainik Jagran, Daily Hindi News Paper, Bhagalpur, City edition, Year 1, Issue 212, 02 February 2013, p.12.
20. Zelliot, E. (2005), From Untouchable to Dalits: Essays on Ambedkar Movements, Manohar, New Delhi.

2

Dr Ambedkar's Economic and Political Thought: Relevance in Globalised Era

— ***Nisha Bhargava***

Abstract

Dr B. R. Ambedkar played a crucial role in the social reform movement in India.His life mission was annihilation of caste and he worked for it throughout his life. When he was given the responsibility of drafting the Constitution of free India, he introduced many safeguards to protect the interests of untouchables and minorities. Besides evincing keen interest in Indian polity, he also expressed his views on various aspects of economy such as agriculture, finance, planning and so on. He opined that socialism had the solution to various problems of Indian Economy. Unfortunately, his dream of a socialistic pattern of society has already been sacrificed in the era of globalisation. Moreover, his dream of a casteless society is also likely to remain a delusion due to the persisting caste consciousness in Indian society. Besides our social dilemmas, we have longstanding economic issues which could not be resolved under the mixed economy regime and we hope to sort them out through globalisation and liberalisation. The present study makes an attempt to review the political and economic philosophy of Dr Ambedkar. The first section reviews his political philosophy and in the second, his views on Indian economy are discussed. The final section explores the relevance of his philosophy in the globalised era. The study tends to conclude that by espousing globalisation, we are moving away from Ambedkar's socialist philosophy. Consequently, our current policies are in stark contrast with Ambedkar's vision and mission. Considering the growing uncertainties and negative outcomes of globalisation, we need to reconsider our liberal policies. We must keep in mind Dr Ambedkar's prescriptions for removing the ills of our economy and polity if we desire to have inclusive growth.

[**Keywords:** *Untouchables, Democracy, Socialism, Poverty, Globalisation*].

Introduction

The institution of caste has been an integral part of Indian society since ages. Various social reformers such as Raja Ram Mohan Roy, Gandhiji, Jyotiba Phule, Narayan Guru and Ambedkar have tried to abolish caste system. But the efforts to create a casteless society have largely been unsuccessful. Dr B.R. Ambedkar played a crucial role in the social reform movement in India. He was an institution personified. He was a statesman, philosopher, economist and a prolific writer. He studied abroad and practiced law for some years. He had suffered as a child as he belonged to the Mahar caste (treated as untouchables). Therefore, he worked for improving the condition of minorities and untouchables in India. Ambedkar believed that to eliminate untouchability, the entire caste system had to come to an end. He said, "As long as caste system is there, untouchability will not go. All these Hindu reformers are complaining only of untouchability but have no programme to abolish caste.[1] When India gained independence in 1947, he became the first law minister of Independent India. Soon thereafter, he was appointed the Chairman of Drafting Committee of the Constitution of India.

Dr Ambedkar's Political Philosophy

Ambedkar realised that caste was deeply entrenched in Hindu social framework. Therefore, he visualised the establishment of a casteless and classless society. He said, "My ideal would be a society based on liberty, equality and fraternity. An ideal society should be mobile, should be full of channels for conveying a change taking place in one part to other parts. In an ideal society there should be many interests consciously communicated and shared. There should be varied and free points of contact with other modes of association. In other words, there must be social endosmosis. This is fraternity, which is only another name for democracy. Democracy is not merely a form of government. It is primarily a mode of associated living, of conjoint communicated experience. It is essentially an attitude of respect and reverence towards one's fellow men".[2] Thus, democracy to him was an instrument for bringing social equality among men.

Ambedkar was deeply concerned about the drawbacks of caste system. He opined, "caste is an enclosed class,".[3] He believed that caste system which had Brahmins at the apex and Shudras at the bottom, had done irreversible damage to Indian society. He observed, "The effect of caste on the ethics of the Hindus is simply deplorable. Caste has killed public spirit. Caste has destroyed the sense of public charity. Caste has made public opinion impossible. A Hindu's public is his caste. His responsibility is to his caste. His loyalty is restricted only to his caste. Virtue has become caste-ridden, and morality has become caste-bound."[4]

Throughout his life, Ambedkar strived to make untouchables aware of their rights. Zelliot states, "Ambedkar planned his programmes to bring the untouchables from the state of dehumanisation and slavery into one of equality through the use of modern methods based on education and the exercise of legal and political rights. Ambedkar sought to awaken in the untouchables an awareness of their debased condition and common interests that would promote the unity needed for development of effective organisations and mass action".[5]

It may be mentioned that Ambedkar was not satisfied with his own efforts and capabilities (within the 'nationalist frame), to provide the untouchables their due share in the society and at a time he even considered inviting the intervention of the United Nations. He says, "I had prepared a report on the condition of the Scheduled Castes for submission to the United Nations. But I did not submit it. I felt that it would be better to wait until the Constituent Assembly and the future Parliament was given a chance to deal with the matter. The provisions made in the Constitution for safeguarding the position of the Scheduled Castes were not to my satisfaction. However, I accepted them for what they were worth hoping that the government will show some determination to make them effective.[6] As such it may be inferred that he did not really have full faith in parliamentary democracy. He was of the opinion that untouchables did not enjoy the same *values* as the so called superior castes. Therefore, he argued that the minorities needed to be given a higher share of representation in political, social and economic spheres than their actual percentage in the population so that they are empowered to stand up to the tyranny of the majority. To protect the interests of untouchables and downtrodden, he made adequate provisions in the constitution of India and he will always be remembered as the great architect of the constitution. He was also a guardian of social justice and a supporter of socialism and planning.

The Economic Views of Ambedkar

Dr Ambedkar expressed his views on various aspects of economy such as agriculture, finance, planning and so on. He focussed primarily on economic, social and political aspects of various problems. He pointed out that government should plan its economic activities in such a way that there is ample scope for productivity enhancement and for the growth of private entrepreneurship. He was a hard-core socialist. However, he did not support communism as communism supports revolution and violent means. He believed that societal transformation should be brought in a peaceful and democratic manner. Neither did he believe in disappearance of state. He opined that state was fundamental for existence of humans. His economic thoughts remain relevant even today.

(i) Economic Dimensions of Society and Polity

Though he took up social and political issues, the economic dimensions of these issues were his primary concern. He realised the fact that wealth brought power and Shudras had suffered basically because they were poor and underprivileged. Therefore, along with social and political power he wanted to economically strengthen them. Ambedkar was a staunch supporter of socialism and he rejected the policy of laissez faire. Therefore, he favoured public ownership of means of production. Besides, he recommended that government should play an active role in formulating policies for removal of poverty and inequalities.

(ii) His Views on Financial Sector

His insights on financial sector primarily focus on origin and evolution of provincial finance in India. He wrote on provincial decentralisation of imperial finance. His seminal work on public finance, *National Dividend of India: A Historical and Analytical Study* sheds light on his views on public finance. Here, he elaborates on the financial relations between British and the state governments during the period 1833 to 1921 when there was centralisation of public finance.

Dr Ambedkar was of the opinion that financial constraints were due to weak fiscal policy. Besides, the taxable capacity of people was low. Ambedkar suggested a strong fiscal policy where expenditure should be made on productive ventures. He also advocated the nationalisation of insurance sector in India.

(iii) Agrarian Reforms

Agriculture was one of the primary concerns of Ambedkar. He was aware of the fact that sub-division and fragmentation of land holdings in India had an adverse impact on agricultural productivity. The basic problem of Indian agriculture according to him was that it was unable to generate investible surplus. This led to underutilisation of resources and the problem of disguised unemployment. This further increased cost of production and reduced agricultural productivity.The weaknesses of agricultural sector which was the backbone of Indian Economy were a major hurdle in the country's economic growth. He suggested consolidation of land holdings to increase productivity. He further suggested that government should acquire surplus land from individuals and should provide standard sized holdings to farmers for cultivation.

(iv) Industrialisation

Dr Ambedkar suggested that basic industries should be established by the government as the private sector did not have required capital to invest in large scale ventures. He was not against private enterprise however; he disliked the concentration of economic power in private hands. He realised the fact that industrialisation and agricultural development could lead to mutual development of each other due to linkage effects.

(v) The Currency Issue

Dr Ambedkar disfavoured the gold exchange standard as it lacked stability and caused inflation. He also opposed linking of rupee with gold. He suggested that India should create a managed inconvertible currency and discard the gold exchange standard and the gold reserve standard. Ambedkar opined that gold exchange standard saves gold and increases its supply. Consequently, its value is depreciated and it becomes unsuitable as a standard of value. He strongly criticised Keynes for advocating gold exchanged standard and favoured a modified gold standard.[7]

(vi) On Equal Distribution

Dr Ambedkar stressed on the need for nationalisation of the major sectors of economy. It was essential for optimising production and for ensuring that gains of development are shared equally by all. He believed that socialism was necessary for India's development and if private capital was given priority over socialism, it would lead to growing social and economic disparities. The creation of a robust public sector and nationalisation of insurance sector in India were the key step in that direction. Ambedkar suggested that state should acquire all land and distribute it among the poor. He wanted a progressive transition of society, without glaring social and economic inequalities which were characteristic of capitalist system of production.[8] He believed that the relations between labour and capital can be harmonised by promoting labour welfare and eliminating exploitation.

(vii) Labour Welfare and Social Security

Ambedkar was a proponent of trade unionism and he supported worker's participation in industrial management. He laid special emphasis on the need to introduce employment exchanges and social security measures such as earned leave for regular employees and other welfare measures for their well-being. He opined that industrial peace will prevail only if there is social and distributive justice. He suggested same welfare measures (such as provident fund, workers' compensation, health insurance and pension) for industrial as well as agricultural labour.

(viii) Caste System and its Economic Aspects

Dr Ambedkar realised that caste-based division of Indian society was a major hindrance in the way of economic development. It created a compartmentalised society where people having some particular skills could not find work in other professions. Due to this reason, there were instances when jobs were available and men were not and sometimes men were there and they could not find jobs suitable for their skills. There was thus complete lack of inter-caste professional mobility. This not only led to unemployment of a large number of people but was also one of the root causes of the problem of poverty of masses. This also caused underutilisation of resources and a high level of inefficiency in resource allocation.[9] What was most frustrating was that people were compelled to remain in a particular occupation due to their caste and they had no other option. Thus, the system of untouchability had wrecked the economy of the country. A major proportion of population (i.e. the untouchables) had no basic rights such as right to education, right to property and so on. In a nutshell we can say that Ambedkar wanted state to play a major role in the development of our country.

Relevance of Ambedkar's Philosophy in the Era of Globalisation

The Indian economy entered a new era with the New Economic Policy of 1991 which marked the onset of Liberalisation, Privatisation and Globalisation in the country. The policy generated a firm belief among masses that globalisation would do wonders to Indian Economy by streamlining economic growth and by bringing an end to the long-standing economic, political and social issues. In particular, it was expected that the problems of poverty, caste system, inequality, exploitation, financial instability etc. will have ready solutions. However, more than two decades after, not only the prevailing problems continue to haunt us but new issues have also cropped up. There have been various positive outcomes of globalisation such as communications revolution, increase in foreign trade, employment generation, expansion of medical, health and educational services and so on. There has been a sure march towards free trade as the economy is being opened up and controls are being reduced. In a nutshell, Indian Economy has observed a robust growth during the last two decades. However, there is an eerie similarity between the globalisation of today and the colonialism of the nineteenth century.

Under the present scenario, Dr Ambedkar's views are as relevant as these were during his times.Today, uncertainties are growing and growth lacks inclusivity as one-third of India's population still lives below poverty line. Moreover, caste consciousness, instead of disappearing has been strengthening due to continuation of the reservation policy of government. On one hand there are gaping economic inequalities and on the other, we are moving away from mixed economy and socialism in the name of privatisation.

Banking and insurance sectors have been privatised. There is however, a lack of financial inclusion. The agriculture sector which once observed green revolution is facing stagnation and the condition of farmers is deplorable. Industrial growth has decelerated however, monopoly capital and concentration of economic power is growing. Financial volatility is on the higher side as there are wide fluctuations in the value of our currency. Though there has been an expansion of social services, these have become prohibitively expensive and inaccessible to the poor. Though more employment opportunities have been created in service sector, there is a growing tendency towards adhocism and increasing working hours. All these are the consequences of privatisation and globalisation. Though globalisation is now firmly entrenched in our economic and social framework, we can still avoid some of its negative fallouts. For this, the government has to regulate the key economic sectors and indicators. Besides, the government should formulate its monetary and fiscal policies in such a manner that our basic social and economic objectives (as envisaged by Ambedkar) are not overlooked and we are able to have inclusive growth. The new government is making commendable efforts in that direction. Recently, Prime Minister Narendra Modi has launched an ambitious programme under the name *Make in India*. The programme envisages transforming India by making it a manufacturing hub while eliminating unnecessary regulations, making bureaucratic processes efficient and making government more transparent, responsive and accountable.[10] Through this programme, our government expects MNCs to come to India for manufacturing products instead of just marketing products built elsewhere. The primary purpose of the programme is to challenge China's dominance in the world of manufacturing. The programme is likely to generate employment for taking advantage of our demographic dividend.[11] Besides, the *Make in India Initiative*, a number of programmes have been started to make growth more meaningful and inclusive.

Conclusion

Though Ambedkar is known more for his political philosophy, his views on economy are equally thought provoking. He believed that socialism had the solution to various problems of Indian Economy and Polity. He wanted equal distribution of wealth and he wanted equal social status for all citizens. He wanted to eliminate caste system and he worked for it throughout his life. It won't be an exaggeration to say that he was one of the greatest Indian statesmen if greatness is measured in terms of the impression made on the society and contribution made for its furtherance and reform. He made sustained efforts in this direction all his life through his writings and activities. When he was given the responsibility of drafting the Constitution of free India, he introduced sufficient safeguards to protect the interests of untouchables and minorities. Evidently, the condition of untouchables is much better today than it was a century earlier. Nevertheless, there is one lacuna. Initially the reservation policy was to continue till such time as and when the situation of Dalits improved. However, the continuation of reservation policy has reinforced and strengthened the caste consciousness among masses. The dream of a socialistic pattern of society has already been sacrificed in the name of liberalisation and privatisation. Under present scenario, the dream of a casteless society is also likely to remain a delusion and the persisting caste consciousness poses a serious threat to the unity and integrity of the country. Besides our social dilemmas, we have longstanding economic issues which could not be resolved under the mixed economy regime and we hope to sort them out through globalisation and liberalisation. However, we must keep in mind Dr Ambedkar's prescriptions for removing the ills of our economy and polity. Only then we can have inclusive growth.

References

1. Ambedkar, B.R. 1987, *Go for Conversion*. Dalit Sahitya Academy, Bengaluru, p. 14.
2. Ambedkar, B.R. 1979, *Writings and Speeches*, Vol. 1. Education Department, Government of Maharashtra, Mumbai.
3. Ambedkar B.R., 1916, *Castes in India-Their Mechanism, Genesis and Development*, paper presented at New York.
4. Ambedkar, B.R. 2000, *Annihilation of Caste*. Blumoon Books (first published May 1936).
5. Ambedkar, B.R. 1951, In his Resignation Letter on 10 October. Available at http://www.india-seminar.com/2009/601/601_s_anand.htm.Last accessed on 12 March 2015.
6. Dr Krishan Gopal, Dr Jagdish Lal, Sarabjeet S Sharma, "*Thoughts and Ideas of Gandhi, Nehru, Tagore and Ambedkar*", Jawahar publishers and distributors, New Delhi-16,1994, p. 223.

7. Kuber, W. N. 1991, *Ambedkar: A Critical Study*, People's Publishing House, New Delhi, p. 280.
8. Lal, S. and K. S. Saxena. (Ed). 1998, *Ambedkar and nation building*. Rawat Publications: New Delhi, pp. 94-95.
9. Mahapatra, R. 2014. Making Sense of 'Make in India,' *Down to Earth*, 16-31 October, p. 58.
10. The Financial Express. 2014, Narendra Modi's clarion call to investors – Let's Make in India, soon the world will come to us. *News item*, September 25.
11. Zelliot, Eleanor. 1979, Learning the Use of Political Means: The Mahars of Maharashtra, in *Caste in India*, (Ed. Rajni Kothari), Orient Longman Publishers, Delhi.

3

B.R. Ambedkar's Quest for Social Justice through Journalism

— *Navjot Kaur*

Abstract

Ambedkar devoted most of his intellectual, social and political efforts for securing social justice to the discriminated, deprived and downtrodden sections of society in India. One such effort was to enter the profession of journalism in 1920s as the Chief Spokesman of the voiceless, penniless and helpless millions of untouchables and exploited masses, starting different papers such as; 'Mook Nayak', 'Bahishkrit Bharat', 'Samata' and 'Janata'. He threw light on the history of social discrimination and led socio-cultural movement and utilised his papers as powerful means of struggle for social revolution; providing a forum to the cause of the oppressed and the downtrodden. In this background, it would be worthwhile to revisit B.R. Ambedkar's philosophy and canon of journalism and his contribution as a journalist to bring about a social justice in Indian society. An attempt would also be made to understand as to what Ambedkar considered to be the role of newspapers to establish an egalitarian society.

*[**Keywords:** Ambedkar, social revolution, oppressed, social justice].*

Introduction

Press, called as the fourth estate in the political terminology, the other three being government, opposition and judiciary, is a vital pillar of a free democratic society. Democracy ensures freedom and guarantees expression of views to create and influence public policy. By giving citizens an opportunity to have their say, democracy binds them with a sort of vital tissue to government. There are, thus, not only outgoing currents of commands and ordinances issued from the central seat of authority, but also incoming currents in the form of suggestions, desires and grievances of people.

Democracy is best qualified constantly to adjust the supply of control to social needs and favours a wholesale social equilibrium. It deepens the sense of social obligation. An extraordinarily powerful communication is periodical literature and the most potent of such literature is the daily press. Walter Lippmann, the political scientist attached great deal of importance to the daily press in educating the people and forming opinion, which Ambedkar called as the 'Bible of democracy'.

Freedom of press is a pre-requisite for the growth and development of a healthy public opinion, as it needs an alert and informed participation not only in purely political processes but also in efforts of the community to adjust its socio-economic life to increasingly complex circumstances. Democratic society, therefore, needs a clear and truthful account of events, of their background, and their causes; a forum for discussion and informed criticism; and a means whereby individuals and groups can express a point of view or advocate a cause.[1] Ambedkar vehemently criticised the Indian Press Act of 1910, which had put severe restrictions on the press. He was against the suppression of the right of public meeting, the right to personal freedom and the right to freedom of discussion.

The first Press Commission, which was established in 1952 under Justice Rajadhyaksha, explains freedom of the press as, "Freedom to hold opinions, to receive and to impart information through the printed word without any interference from any public authority".[2] Thus, a free and impartial press is indispensable for the successful functioning of a democratic government. It acts as a jealous guardian of the rights and liberties of citizens and is a forum for the discussion of public policies, enabling the government to feel the pulse of the people. Ambedkar accorded a pride of place to freedom of speech and expression as one of the main objectives of the Constitution, as envisaged in its preamble, and that is to secure liberty of thought and expression to all citizens. In order to give effect to this objective, 'freedom of speech and expression' has been guaranteed as a fundamental right under Article 19(1)(a) to all citizens, subject only to the restrictions, which may be imposed by the state under clause (2) of that article.[3]

Ambedkar entered the profession of journalism in 1920s as the Chief Spokesman of the voiceless, penniless and helpless millions of untouchables and exploited masses, starting different papers such as; 'Mook Nayak', 'Bahishkrit Bharat', 'Samata' and 'Janata.' He threw light on the history of social discrimination and led socio-cultural movement and utilised his papers as powerful means of struggle for social revolution; providing a forum to the cause of the oppressed and the downtrodden. As G.B. Molt, one of the great American journalists says that,

"...the press is a full fledged institution in our modern world and the various media utilised by the press are generally called by, and now professionally united, under the common name of journalism."[4]

But Ambedkar felt that, "Journalism in India was once a profession. It has now become a trade."[5] In his opinion, journalism has a moral function, i.e., to give the news uncoloured, without any motive, which, to his dismay, is not regarded by "journalism in India its first and foremost duty."[6] He found the press in India under the complete monopoly of the ruling classes, the biggest enemy of the oppressed classes. The Indian press does not adequately focus on the untold miseries of the weak and the oppressed.

The following observations made by A.D. Gorwala aptly reveal the hopeless condition of the Indian press.

"Thus, press in India certainly has the capacity to educate. For reasons that no doubt appear valid to large sections of it, it has chosen not to exercise that capacity to any large extent. Left free, seeing the present deplorable condition of all standards in this land, it may mend its way and begin to fulfill its proper functions. Deprived of freedom, regulated and confined by government instructions and order, it will cease to be anything but a propaganda organisation."[7]

Ambedkar felt that Indian press lacked social commitment hence he focused his writings more than adequately on revealing the untold miseries of the untouchables and the most oppressed classes in his papers. He gave them a great scope to make use of his papers as their mouthpiece. He took to journalism as champion of the cause of the weak and the oppressed. He was an exceptional journalist of his times; while most of the journalists did their best to champion the cause of the haves, he put forth his best efforts to champion the cause of the have nots. He, therefore, denounced the writings of the Congress journals "as the writing done by drum boys to glorify their heroes."[8] He observed that for a journalist in India, to accept a hero worship has become its principal duty under it, the news gives place to sensation, reasoned opinion to unreasoning passion, in place of appeal to the minds of responsible people, to appeal to the emotions of the irresponsible.

To articulate the problem of Dalits, Ambedkar started a paper under the title 'MookNayak', meaning leader of the dumb, with some financial help from the Maharaja of Kolhapur through Dottaba Pawar. The unwelcome reception that 'MookNayak' received, is very succinctly put in by Keer:

"How violent and unfavourable were the times can be seen from the fact that the 'Kesari' refused even to announce its publication although solicited to do so as a paid advertisement! And this happened when Tilak was yet alive![9]

In the first issue of the 'MookNayak', Ambedkar unambiguously announced the aim of the paper to awaken depressed to their disabilities.[10] 'MookNayak' tried to create greater awareness among the weaker sections of the society about their status, problems and prospects. However, the paper could not survive for long due to economic constraints and lack of social support.

After a gap of seven years, on April 3, 1927, the fortnightly vernacular 'Bahishkrit Bharat' was launched, as he realised that a paper is the most important channel of communication between the leader and the masses. He said in this connection thus:

"A leader without a paper is like a bird without wings."[11]

Obviously, to run a press was not an economically viable venture and then the rude revelation that there were no buyers if the paper is dedicated to a social cause; indeed the financial constraints always remained in the forefront, making it difficult for him to carry it on. And another important factor responsible for this was the community, whose cause he was representing, did not buy it, as they could not read or write, due to illiteracy and ignorance amongst them. That apart, he was not prepared to compromise with his professional values. He did not become an agent of the capitalists. He never had any inclination towards commercialisation of his paper.

His editorial after editorial in a crisp and fearless style, impressed upon the government to punish the wrong doers and trespassers who opposed the welfare of the downtrodden people. G.S. Lokhande also observed: "the name of the weekly was changed into Bahishkrit Bharat' or 'Ex-communicated India" in the year 1927, signifying that most of the untouchables were kept segregated from the various villages. Therefore, he exhorted the untouchables to rise in revolt against the shastras, which sanctified the oppressive social customs, and simultaneously making the caste Hindus aware of their responsibility for the welfare and uplift of the downtrodden."[12]

On the eve of his departure for England to attend Round Table Conference in 1930, he was given a grand send-off by the untouchables in Mumbai, presenting him with a purse as a token of their abiding gratitude for his selfless services to their cause. He gratefully thanked the organisers especially "Shankar Rao S. Pasha, who had spent large sums on his movement and declared that a fortnightly paper named 'The Janata', (the people) would soon be published in place of Bahishkrit Bharat – the Excluded India."[13] However, later, 'Samata', was considered more appropriate signifying the message of equality and ceaselessly pleading for the removal of all the existing social barriers.

Again, in 1931, his companions Deorao Naik and Kadrekar started a new fortnightly paper called the 'Janata' – the people - with a vowed mission to educate the people in citizenship rights and responsibilities. It also sought to make the people aware of their patriotic duty to protect the independence and integrity of the country.

Ambedkar's efforts received due appreciation. The Times of India, Mumbai (April, 21) observed:

> "Without political and economic power, the Harijans will find it hard to attain social equality, and Dr Ambedkar has done well in realising this fact."[14]

The Mumbai Chronicle wrote:

> "Ambedkar brooded day in and day out over the unending inhumanity to his community and it was no wonder, therefore, that his devotion to the Harijans was unequalled, if not exceeded...."[15]

The Press indeed recognised and appreciated the services and scholarship of Ambedkar.

In 1956, the weekly 'Janata' was baptized and re-named, as 'Prabhuddha Bharat', which means "Enlightened and Self-disciplined India", emphasising the responsibilities of the people as free citizens. Rights involve responsibilities. In fact, they are two sides of the same coin. Human rights, though essentially individualistic in form and content, have profound social significance and, therefore, a moral dimension. Civilised social life, which alone can provide the basis for individual creativity and excellence is impossible in the absence of a code of ethics to regulate and sustain it."[16]

Thus, the Press has to be committed objectively to the ethical conduct. His basic message, of course, was that the control of minds by some powerful individuals through press and other means of communication were bad. Such a control retarded the movement; he held rationally that journalism should not be allowed to become the handmaid of the corrupt and dominant sections of the society, for maintaining their status quo and promoting their vested interests.

Conclusion

Ambedkar felt that Indian press lacked social commitment hence he focused his writings more than adequately on revealing the untold miseries of the untouchables and the most oppressed classes in his papers. He gave them a great scope to make use of his papers as their mouthpiece. He took to journalism as champion of the cause of the weak and the oppressed. He was an exceptional journalist of his times; while most of the journalists did their best to champion the cause of the haves, he put forth his best efforts to champion the cause of the oppressed.

Ambedkar was in every sense people-oriented, committed to value-based journalism, writing regularly and vigorously for enlightenment and advancement of dalits, women, peasants, workers and all other oppressed people. Instead of making money out of this profession or to glorify hero worship, his papers contained volumes of information on religion, culture, caste-system, economy, polity, secularism, socialism, democracy, equality, liberty, justice, fraternity, education, modernisation, development and so on and so forth. Thus, his papers aimed at bringing about transformation in the lifestyles of millions of neglected men and women, as he did not find even a single newspaper, which was committed to abolition of untouchability and emancipation of the depressed classes.

References

1. Keer, Dhananjay (1991), *Dr Ambedkar Life and Mission*. Popular Prakashan: Mumbai, p. 358.
2. *Ibid,* p. 345.
3. *Ibid,* p. 345.
4. *Ibid,* p. 41.
5. *Ibid,* p. 41.
6. *Ibid,* p. 80.
7. Lokhande, G.S. 1982, (2nd ed) *Bhimrao Ramji Ambedkar—A Study in Social Democracy*, Intelectual Publication: New Delhi, p. 230.
8. G.S. Lokhande, op. cit., p. 231.
9. Mann, Gian Singh, *Journalism-Concept and Controversy*. Gagan Publications: Ludhiana, 1988, p. 16.
10. Quoted by Sarkar, R.C.S. (1984), *The Press in India.* S. Chand and Co. Ltd.: New Delhi, p. 32.
11. R.C.S. Sarkar, op. cit., p. 36.
12. Report of Ambedkar, B.R. (1979), *Dr Babasaheb Ambedkar: Writings and Speeches*, Vol.1 (compiled by Vasant Moon), Education Department, Government of Maharashtra, Mumbai, p. 277.
13. *Ibid,* p. 227.
14. The First Royal Commission on Press, pp. 100-01, Quoted in Patil, V.T.: Studies in Ambedkar (New Delhi, Devika Publications) 1995, p. 290.
15. The first Press Commission report, Part-I, p. 358, Quoted in Patil, V.T.: *Studies in Ambedkar*, Devika Publications, New Delhi, 1995, p. 289.
16. The Weekly 'Janata' was renamed as 'Prabhuddha Bharat'.

4

Ambedkar and Dalits: A Sociological Perspective

— *Ranjay Vardhan*

Abstract

Dr Bhim Rao Ambedkar was a great modern social thinker, a born fighter, a famous advocate and a humanist. He was an institution in himself in promoting the welfare of the dalits and in elevating their status. With the advent of Ambedkar in political arena during 1920s, the issue of social reform got a new direction. He was of the opinion that until and unless the downtrodden themselves come forward to fight their battle, no one could alleviate their position. Through his social-movement he wanted to instil in the minds of the dalits the ideas of self-dignity, self-confidence and self-respect. The paper makes an attempt to study subaltern approach of Ambedkar and social, cultural and political efforts in ameliorating the conditions of Dalits. The paper concludes that chief aim of Ambedkar was to bring about a revolution in the way of life of the dalits and in their aspirations for themselves and for their children. He supported the Anti-Untouchability League which launched a campaign all over the country to secure for the depressed classes enjoyment of their civil rights such as taking water from the village wells, admission of the children in village schools etc. Ambedkar had the honour of giving to the people of India their Constitution.

*[**Keywords:** dalits, revolution, depressed classes, constitution].*

Introduction

Dr Bhim Rao Ambedkar took a leading role in promoting the welfare of the dalits and in elevating their status. He took many steps to reform the ways of the dalits. He fought against many of the injustices done to the untouchables by establishing a political party and a couple of organisations for the untouchables. He had made a detailed study of the problem of untouchability, its origin, development etc. He had made it clear that his main aim in life was to remove the practice of untouchability and to take the so-called "untouchable community" towards socio-economic equality and justice. Through his social-movement, he wanted to instil in the minds of the dalits the ideas of self-dignity, self-confidence and self-respect. Ambedkar wanted the untouchables or 'dalits' to follow some principles in life so that they could attain a respectable status by their own efforts as a community. He recommended "Pancha-sutras" for them. Ambedkar made an appeal to his community to change its style of life to suit to the needs of time. He was able to bring changes and social mobility in the caste system which was then a closed system of stratification. The paper makes an attempt to study subaltern approach of Ambedkar and social, cultural and political efforts in ameliorating the conditions of Dalits. Ambedkar took an anti-dogmatic stance and never accepted anything in the name of authority. He gave a vision that even the ideologies are bound by tenet of impermanence and nobody should claim their validity beyond their times. His thought and action was for ending all kinds of exploitation and bring revolutionary changes in the caste system.

Subaltern Perspective by Dr B.R. Ambedkar

The word 'subaltern' as given in the Oxford Dictionary stands for the general attitude of subordination, which is expressed in terms of caste, class, age, gender, office or any other ways. It includes the characteristics of defiance and submission. Thus, in literal sense; it conveys 'view from below'; i.e., a view or understanding from the bottom of society or the flow of knowledge from below. Ambedkar was of the opinion that until and unless the downtrodden themselves came forward to fight their battle, no one else could alleviate their grievances. No one else could know better than about their own state of affairs. He impressed upon the people to understand own affairs themselves. According to him, self-awakening could provide them necessary strength to fight against evils in society. In the subaltern approach Ambedkar said that dalit themselves have to come forward to take up the herculean task of their emancipation and empowerment.

It was an approach that looked at the problem of dalits from the below. Another aspect of this approach for the emancipation of Dalits and their empowerment was his distinct formulation of Indian Nationalism in opposition to the dominant discourse of Hindu Nationalism. His alternative form of nationalism popularly known as 'Dalit-Bahujan Samaj' constructed a new discourse of Indian nationalism. It aimed at establishing a casteless and classless society where no one could be discriminated on the basis of birth and occupation. Before we proceed further, let us understand who is a Dalit.

Who is a Dalit?

Dalits, a modern term for untouchables in India, are underprivileged people in all social, economic, cultural and political fronts of our society which led to their misery, discrimination, exploitation and oppression by the caste dominated social stratification of India. The Constitution of India classifies Dalits as Scheduled Castes (SCs). The term Dalit was used prominently in 1973, 17 years after the death of Dr Ambedkar. The Dalit Panthers used the term "dalit" in its manifesto. The Dalit Panthers had used the term in much broader sense where they included in it the Scheduled Castes, Tribes, Other Backward Castes or Classes, Minorities, Women and Economically Poor of other Castes and Communities and to some of his vigorous strives made for generating a considerable amount of socio-political consciousness among them (Nandu Ram, 1995). The untouchables or dalits have lived in India since centuries together. According to the thesis of Ambedkar the untouchables and untouchability originated in India after second Century A.D. especially after Manu- the Hindu Lawgiver- wrote his Smriti. But the notion of untouchability was attached to them much later sometimes in fourth Century A.D. when the Dharamshastras proscribed the inter-caste relations and prescribed more stringent rules and practices to crystallise the caste system and regulate the inter-caste relations. During this period, the untouchables got engaged in several types of defiled occupations like disposing of the dead, leather works, scavenging, etc. since then they have been serving the people of other castes as menial workers, labourers, servants, watch and ward men, etc. and living in separate houses.

Untouchables have always remained indispensable in rural or urban India and playing vital role in the social setup. However, the caste system has subjugated the lower castes and exploited them for two millennia and it represented institutionalisation of the most heinous inequality by the Hindu religion as ordained by its Gods, became the prime target of Ambedkar life. He attacked it from the standpoint of its victims- the untouchables. He waged many battles; initially targeting the citadels of Brahminism- the custodian of the Hindu religious code, and later he politicised the battle, realising the ineffectiveness of the former. He worked continuously for the achievement of this objective. His struggle extended well beyond the class struggle and encompassed all other forms of exploitation. Due to his caste, Ambedkar faced a bitter taste of discriminatory treatment. He and his brother had to carry gunny bags inside the classroom as they were not allowed to sit on chairs. They were not allowed to drink water or mix with children. Teachers would not check their answer books as they feared pollution. He internalised the multiple deprivations of the dalits as a whole and it sowed the seeds of discontentment with the Hindu social system.

Ambedkar and Dalit Movement

Social reformers like Narayan Guru (1854-1928), Jyotiba Phule (1827-1890) and Ramaswamy Naicker (1879-1973) launched massive struggles for dignity of dalits throughout India. However, Ambedkar represent one of the towering names who not only represented them as their leader but also gave them their significant position both politically and constitutionally. He joined Baroda State Service after returning from studies in US and UK as part of his scholarship agreement. He worked as Secretary in the Defence Office of Maharaja of Baroda State but he faced insults while at work due to his low caste origin. At times, even peons hurled files on him and water was not served during official functions. At officer club, he was made to sit in the corner and he found difficulties in getting rented accommodation. He was evacuated from a rented house and he had to spend day in public garden from where he left for Mumbai. Such incidents guided and ignited Ambedkar to work for protection of dalit rights and upliftment of dalits. In 1924, he started legal practice in Mumbai and founded Bahishkrit Hitkarni Sabha (Depressed Class Institute) for dalit upliftment. He roused dalit consciousness to fight for the eradication of dalit discrimination; to claim equality of treatment, status and opportunity;

to enjoy equally all rights and to respect dignity of the persons. He became a crusader for the rights of dalits in India.

The Dalit movement, in the familiar sense of organised resistance of the ex-untouchables to caste oppression, may not be traced beyond colonial times. However, in a wider sense of the struggle of lower castes against the hegemony of Brahminical ideology, it has to coexist with the history of caste itself. The broad framework of caste remaining the same, the Dalit movement could also be seen in a historical continuum with its previous phases. In another sense, it could be taken as the articulation phase of the numerous faceless struggles against the iniquitous socio-economic formation ordained by the caste system that has occupied vast spaces of Indian history. By any reckoning it seems to have done well in identifying its friends and foes, putting in place its strategies and tactics and more importantly, carving out a space for itself in every sphere. It kept pace with the changes taking place in socio-political sphere during the colonial times and thus displayed significant learning during this phase. However, it could not do so thereafter when it had to consolidate its gains particularly in the context of substantial changes that befell during the post-independence times.

Ambedkar recounted the experience of the depressed classes and the immense sacrifices made by them to secure minimum human rights under the aegis of Hinduism. Ambedkar fought for the rights of workers and peasants and adopted various means to safeguard dalit rights. He launched a movement against dalit discrimination by creating public opinion through his writings in periodicals like Mook Nayak, Vashishrit Bharat and Equality Janta. He also launched various movements. One of the memorable struggles of dalits was the Vaikkom Satyagraha in Travancore which asserted the right of dalits to worship in Hindu temples without hindrance. Another temple entry movement took place at Kalaram Temple, Nasik in Maharashtra State.

Before this movement, dalits were denied entry into the temples. Mahad March was another significant movement to take water from public watering places. He organised the dalit rally to assert their legal right to take water from Chowdar tank of Mahad which was made public tank in 1869. In 1923, the Mumbai Legislative Council passed a resolution that the dalits be allowed to use all public watering places.

Mahad Municipality also passed a resolution on 5 January, 1927 that it had no objection in allowing dalits to use the tank. He convened a conference on 18-20 March 1927 and exhorted the dalits to go to Chowdar tank and exercise their right to take water from it. There was a resistance from upper caste Hindus but the dalits exercised their right to drink water from Chowdar tank. The demand for safeguards and protection of Scheduled Castes (earlier called Depressed Class) has a long history dating to Montague-Chelmsford Reform of 1919 during the British Raj period. Ambedkar had been closely involved in the struggle to give Scheduled Caste people solid statutory safeguard. In 1924, Dr Ambedkar started legal practice in Mumbai and founded Bahishkrit Hitkarni Sabha (Depressed Class Institute) to ameliorate the condition of Dalits. He roused Dalit consciousness, started the movement for eradication of Dalit discrimination and granting of equality of treatment. His effort was that Dalits should enjoy all rights, equality of status and opportunity and respect for the dignity of Dalits.

Ambedkar in 1930s

The 1930s marked changeover of Ambedkar to party politics. In the late 1920s and especially in the 1930s when he had formed his Independent Labour Party, he took up the cause of tenants (from both the dalit Mahars and the caste Hindu Kunbis) in the Konkan region of Maharashtra. He was a delegate at the Round Table Conference in London, where he asked for separate electorate for the Dalits. The British Government partly agreed with his arguments in the arbitration (Communal Award) which was announced on August 14, 1932. Mahatma Gandhi feared that such a step would threaten Hindu unity and went on a fast in Yervada jail at Poona. This move forced Ambedkar to leave his demand for separate electorates and to sign "Poona Pact" on September 14, 1932. Ambedkar was unhappy with this development. In 1936, he created his first political party, the Independent Labour Party (ILP), in anticipation of forthcoming 1937 elections which were to be held within the framework of Govt. of India Act, 1935. This Act more powers to provincial governments and assemblies. His party fielded candidates in Mumbai Presidency and Central Provinces where it had some success. Ambedkar was elected along with nine others.

With the support of radicals then in the Congress Socialist Party, the Independent Labour Party organised a huge march of 20,000 peasants to Mumbai in 1938, the largest pre-independence peasant mobilisation in the region. In the same year, Ambedkar joined with the Communists to organise a strike of Mumbai textile workers in protest against a bill about to be introduced by the British Government to curve labour strikes. Ambedkar took the lead in condemning the bill in the assembly and argued that the right to strike was simply another name for the right to freedom of assembly.

The contribution of Ambedkar in context of Punjab cannot be ignored, due to his efforts eight seats got reserved for scheduled caste people in the Punjab State Legislative Assembly under Government of India Act, 1935. The other most important contribution was that he was successful in getting repealing of Land Alienation Act 1901 that barred them from ownership of land under the Article 372(2) of the constitution to which Scheduled Caste are greater indebted to him. In India, scheduled caste social mobility largely took place after independence largely due to processes of urbanisation, modernisation, sanskritisation, spread of education, development of transport and means of communication, etc. Socialist model of development with emphasis on growth with distributive justice, individual freedom, equality, fraternity and opportunities for development created avenues for social mobility particularly scheduled caste social mobility.

Changes in the world scenario due to Second World War accelerated the change in Indian politics and governance. Without consulting Congress, British had involved India which resulted in resignation of its representatives from eight provincial governments it controlled. Britishers in order to involve Indians in the war, co-opted leaders of small political parties such as the Muslim League, the Hindu Mahasabha and the ILP in support for the war. This gave an opportunity to Ambedkar to join the Defence Advisory Committee in 1941 and later he was appointed as Ministry of Labour in 1942. In the same year he established Scheduled Castes Federation (SCF) and to broaden his political base concentrated on untouchables. In elections to provincial assemblies of March 1946 he himself and his party were defeated by Congress, but he continued his work.

Ambedkar and Drafting of Indian Constitution

On August 15, 1947 Jawaharlal Nehru appointed him as Minister of Law later on August 29; he was made head of the committee charged with the drafting of the Constitution (the Drafting Committee). Constitution outlined a favourable framework for social reform specifically abolition of untouchability, prohibition of all discriminations and reservations for SCs and STs. Ambedkar saw to it that the welfare of the Scheduled Caste people were guaranteed in Constitution of India in the form of reservation in legislative, employment and educational fields. In addition to these, Ambedkar in January, 1950 launched a campaign for revision of Hindu Code Bill which regulated matrimonial relations, inheritance, adoption, etc. for reforming Hindu society. However, a proposal was not approved by Congress and he resigned from the government in September 1951. He joined socialists but the alliance was defeated in elections in 1951-52. He subsequently lost faith in Hinduism and converted to Buddhism. He chose Dusshhera to convert to Buddhism in a big ceremony in which thousands of untouchables also converted to Buddhism. His last work was dedicated to Buddhism which was titled "The Buddha and his Dhamma" which was published after his death in 1957.

Three Principles of Dalit Movement: "Education, Agitation and Organisation"

Dr Ambedkar suggested three principles to govern the "dalit movement". These principles are: "education, agitation and organisation". (i) Education is essential for helping the dalits to take out their mask of ignorance; (ii) Agitation becomes inevitable to fight against all the exploiters and cheats; (iii) Organisation is necessary to thrash out individual differences, to realise community interests and to fight for a common cause collectively. After the All-India Depressed Class Conference in Nagpur in 1942 Ambedkar declared, "My final word of advice is to educate, agitate, organise and have faith in yourself. It is a battle for the reclamation of human personality".

Dr Ambedkar tried to show that whatever might be the origin of caste system, it has been the most unjust social order in actual necessity. He made Hindus aware of the great tension-generating social problems which must be tackled; otherwise it could harm not only Hindu society but also the social and political fabric of society. He believed that the economic and political issues should be resolved only after achieving the goal of social justice. If priority is given to the issue of political emancipation, it would mean transfer of power from foreign rule to upper caste Hindus who will not do justice with Scheduled Castes. The injustices against SCs will continue. He considered casteism as an expression of mental slavery of the Hindus and real change could come only if we do away with the evil of casteism. He believed that emancipation of untouchables automatically involved emancipation of the Hindu society as a whole. He called for arousal of self-respect of untouchables. His efforts brought tremendous success and the reservations have altered the very edifice of caste system. Sociologically, the basic structure of society has changed. The four varnas can be seen working together, dining together, travelling together, intermix freely and even celebrate festivals and functions together. SCs have become officers, landlords, businessmen, teachers, doctors, engineers, etc. and are getting best education. In some parts of Punjab, there are few instances where upper caste men can be seeing working in the fields of SCs. Politically too they are becoming powerful and they can be seen occupying the seats of power.

Conclusion

Ambedkar was a great champion of the dalit cause because he succeeded in turning the depressed class movement into a revolutionary movement throughout India. Ambedkar was of the opinion that until and unless the downtrodden themselves came forward to fight their battle, no one else could alleviate their grievances. His subaltern approach gave a new direction to dalit movement. Today India has witnessed the oppressed classes walking on the streets of cities and villages with confidence and poise; of course many despicable acts of discrimination and violence against the dalits still occur. Yet, the juggernaut of equality is rolling on remorselessly and forcefully. He searched for solutions, explored strategies and in doing so; set the Dalits on the path of ardour emancipation. The paper concludes that chief aim of Dr Ambedkar was to bring about a revolution in the way of life of the dalits and in their aspirations for themselves and for their children. Dr Ambedkar in his efforts to raise the status of dalits considered the caste system one of the great obstacles. He expressed his great disappointment with the caste as well as Varna system. He supported the Anti-Untouchability League which launched a campaign all over the country to secure for the depressed classes enjoyment of their civil rights such as taking water from the village wells, admission of the children in village schools etc. Ambedkar had the honour of giving to the people of India their Constitution. His efforts have yielded results and there has been an upsurge in the status of Dalits.

References

Aggarwal, S., 1991, Dr B.R. Ambedkar: The man and his Message: A Commemorative Volume, Prentice Hall of India, New Delhi.

Chalam, K.S., The Relevance of Ambedkarism in India, Rawat Publications, Jaipur and New Delhi, 1993.

Chalam, K.S., Modernisation and Dalit Education: Ambedkar's vision, Rawat Publications New Delhi, 2008.

Chatterjee, Partha, 1994, Caste and Subaltern Consciousness, Oxford University Press, New Delhi.

Hutton, J.H., 1946, Caste in India; Its nature, functions and origins, Cambridge University Press, London.

Jadhav, N., 1993, Dr Ambedkar's Economic Thought and Philosophy, Popular Prakashan, Mumbai.

Jaffrelot Christopher, 2005, Dr Ambedkar and Untouchability Analysing and Fighting Caste, Permanent Black, Delhi.

Jatava, B.R., Ambedkar in Modern World, ABD Publishers, Jaipur, 2008.

Jatava, D.R., Sociological Thoughts of B.R. Ambedkar, ABD Publishers, India, 2001.

Kapoor, S.K., 2013, Dr B.R. Ambedkar and Caste Mobilisation, Swastik Publications, New Delhi.

Krishan, Asha, Ambedkar and Gandhi, Emancipators of Untouchables in Modern, International Journal of Multidisciplinary Educational Research ISSN: 2277-7881 volume 1, issue 2, June 2012, Himalaya Publishing House, Delhi, 1997.

Massey, James, B.R. Ambedkar, A Study in Just Society, Centre for Dalit/ Subaltern studies, Manohar, 2003.

Naik, C.D., Thoughts and Philosophy of Dr B.R. Ambedkar. Sarup and Sons, New Delhi, 2003.

Narayan, J.S., Rao, Somasekhar, A., and Audiseshaiah, K., B.R. Ambedkar, His relevance Today, Gyan Publishing House, New Delhi, 1994.

Omvedt, Gail (1994), Dalit and Democratic Revolution: Dr Ambedkar and the Dalit Movements in Colonial India, Sage, New Delhi.

Prasad, Suraj Nandan, 2010, Life and Works of Ambedkar, ABD Publishers, Jaipur.

Reddy, L.V., Narayana, M.L., and Rao, Digumarti Bhaskara, Education for Dalits, Discovery Publishing House, New Delhi, 2004.

Sharma, S.P., Ambedkar and Socio-political Revival in India, Vista International Publishing House, Delhi, 2009.

Shukla, J.J., B.R. Ambedkar, Gandhi and Tagore, (Comparative study on Education), Karnavati Publication, Ahmedabad, 1998.

Shyam Lal and Saxena, K.S., 1998, Ambedkar and Nation Building (edited), Rawat Publications, Jaipur.

5

Ambedkar's Concept of Social Justice and Discrimination in Panchayati Raj Institutions

— *Dr Neeru Sharma*

Abstract

The issue of social justice found its place in the very Preamble of the Indian Constitution. It expressed solemn resolve to secure to all Indian citizens 'Justice, Social, economic and political; equality of status and opportunities and to promote among them all fraternity assuring the dignity of the individual and unity and integrity of the nation'. Thus, it is evident that the main intention of the constitution-makers was to provide justice, equality and dignity. Dr B.R. Ambedkar being the Chairman of the Draft Committee took various initiatives to check discrimination with depressed classes. Provisions for reservation were included in various articles of the Indian Constitution. But after the 70 years of independence, Dalits are facing discrimination and are victims of inequitable social system. 73rd amendment provided reservation for SC/ STs in Panchayati Raj Institutions. Even here Dalits met the same fate. Present paper makes an humble attempt to study discrimination with Dalits in Panchayati Raj Institutions. Paper sums up that if government is really interested in empowering under-privileged it must revive the practice of capacity building programme for Dalits. The intention of this study is to expose the fact that untouchability still prevails in Indian Society.

Introduction

The present paper is a humble attempt to present what social justice was meant according to Dr B.R. Ambedkar and how reservation given to Dalits in PRIs have created positive or negative results. The ideals of social justice denote brotherly relations of a citizen with other citizens of the society. It tries to justify that caste discrimination has not ended, although the state claims it has abolished the caste system. During the 'World Conference Against Racism' in Durban in 2001, the Indian Government repeatedly claimed it had abolished the caste system and provided enough mechanisms to do away with caste but the reality is that in changed circumstances, caste discrimination takes different forms.[1] The question remains to be answered will those in power take note of this unsavory situation and rectify it early. This paper is a scholastic enquiry on the discrimination with Dalits in PRIs in the milieu of the post 73rd Constitutional Amendment Act in the Indian Constitution.

B.R. Ambedkar on Social Justice

The fundamental meaning of this concept of 'Social justice' is to bring a just society. The main objective of this concept is to uplift the women, Scheduled Castes and Scheduled Tribes in the Society and pull them to the mainstream of the society. So far as Dr B.R. Ambedkar's vision of social justice is concerned he is real earnest, sacrificed his whole life for amelioration of the women and Dalits. He strongly fought against the prevalent caste system and gender discrimination in the society and ventured to secure social justice to these sections of the society. In one of his debate in the Constituent Assembly he expressed his views that, all of us desire that this unfortunate class could be entitled to the same privileges as members of the other communities without any hindrance from anybody.[2] He made clear that if any community or person will violate this provision it will impose duty on the state to stop such violation through the law, because the constitution contains ample provisions.[3]

To Ambedkar, social justice is the philosophy of good life. It is not only a prime democratic value, but also a prime social ethic and an instrument of social transformation. Social justice is the crowning glory of Ambedkar's ideology. In a diverse, plural and divisive Indian society, the relevance of his concept of social justice can hardly be denied.

Social justice is the hinge of Ambedkar's ideology; it is the hypen that joins, the buckle that fastens the plural society in a harmonious way. In that sense, his social justice is the true principle of social life, meant to eliminate the plight of the depressed, to uproot the outworn doctrines of Hindu scriptures, and to move the society forward through consensus and consideration to the goals of liberty, equality and fraternity. Overall, social justice is a useful concept that forms the heart and soul of the Indian Constitution as it is meant to wipe every tear from every eye. It is socio-economic revolution aiming to transform the Indian society and at the same time without disrupting the unity and harmony of the organic way of life. Its relevance, therefore, can hardly be refuted in the Indian context.

According to Dr B.R. Ambedkar, social justice means a complete change in the fundamental notions of life. It means a complete revolution in our look and in attitude towards men and things. It means a new and vibrant life for all. But such a new life cannot enter a body that is dead. His reference was to Hindu society which was an antique and out-dated society. He, therefore, argued: 'But a new life cannot enter a body that is dead. New life can enter only in a new body. The old body must die before a new body can come into existence and a new life can enter into it. To put it simply, the old must cease to be operative before the new can begin to enliven and to pulsate. This is what I meant when I said you must discard the authority of the Shastras and destroy the religion of the Shastras.[4]

Ambedkar was a true and sincere democrat. For him, political democracy without social and economic democracy was a double deception. He warned that as long as there are inequalities on the social and economic front there can be no political democracy, except in name of form. Unlike most of the Indian leaders, he never indulged in unnecessary glorification of the Indian civilisation. He frankly pointed out to the several weaknesses that the Indian society suffered from. He honestly admitted that "Democracy was top dressing on the Indian soil which is essentially undemocratic". He believed that constitutional morality is not national sentiment and it has to be cultivated.[5]

73rd Amendment and Reservation

Dr B.R. Ambedkar provided reservation provisions for upliftment of Dalits and 73rd amendment is without any doubt enhancement of his this effort. Reservation being the modus by which Dalits could get into power sharing is seen as a means of disgrace by the upper caste segment. In Panchayati Raj Institutions there are two major means of discrimination. One is that Dalits are kept away from Panchayat proceeding, developmental work, schemes etc., and another is that wherever Dalits are in power by virtue of reservation they are targeted and their posts are declared null and void after a certain period of time.[6]

Twenty-four years have passed since the Act on new Panchayati Raj Institutions (PRI) was put in place by the 73rd Amendment (1992). There were high hopes of empowering rural India's neglected sections of society- women and Dalits- through reservation of seats in elections to panchayat bodies. The reform was seen, understandably, as a major step in the direction of Dalit liberation.

In ancient India, the panchayat system was based on the age-old caste system, social status and family. Although the local self-government concept was introduced in 1882, it took more than 100 years for the local self-government institutions to become a part of the Indian Constitution. While tremendous possibilities have been opened up in the areas of development, social justice, people's participation and grass-roots democracy, but at many places Dalits are being discriminated. Reservation of seats and offices of the chairpersons for Scheduled Castes (SCs) and Scheduled Tribes (STs) in proportion to their population has the potential to radically change the socio-political structure of this country. Although historically excluded groups and communities are now included in these decision-making bodies (more than 660,000 elected members, i.e. 22.5 per cent, in the rural and urban local bodies are from SCs and STs), there has been a sharp increase in caste-based violence in the panchayats in the last 24 years. Panchayat-related caste violence continues unabated and has become a part of the social reality today. Unfortunately, while upper caste groups are committing atrocities against the lower castes, the latter do not have a supportive redressal mechanism. Since the police is not under the authority of panchayats, Dalits are being subjected to violence with the connivance of the state administration and the local police. Yet after more than two decades of its functioning, many feel that nothing much has come out of this exercise. The reasons are not far to seek. From Day One, hard-core caste Hindu opponents of Dalits seemed bent on making the system non-functional inasmuch as it benefited Dalits. The 1992 constitutional amendment introduced systematic reservation of political positions for Dalits (besides women) in institutions of governance at the grass-roots level.

Discrimination with Dalits

The panchayat elections are a nightmarish experience for Dalits. Several elections in reserved panchayats could not be held because not a single nomination paper was filed in the face of threats from upper caste people. In many panchayats, Dalit candidates are living in terror because filing their nomination papers is seen as an act of defiance. Dalit voters are often prevented from voting in many panchayats.[7]

There have been instances where high caste groups have challenged the reservation for SCs and STs in a court of law, and when this attempt failed, they announced a boycott of elections. There are also numerous cases of Dalits being used as proxies, and being coaxed to carry out the dictates of the dominant castes. A recent study by Evidence, a Madurai-based organisation working on Dalit issues, has documented a series of discriminations against panchayat presidents spread over 10 districts in Tamil Nadu. The study finds that 94 per cent of the 171 Dalit panchayat presidents studied have not been given any training; seven panchayat presidents were not allowed to sit on chairs; all the 171 panchayat chiefs have complained of discrimination by caste Hindus; and 32 of them have given in writing charges of discrimination. The study also shows that the majority of panchayat presidents are ignorant about the need to fight untouchability.[8]

When Dalits seek empowerment through participation in the political process either at the panchayati raj level or through representation in Parliament/State Assemblies, they face the powerful onslaught of dominant castes, often abetted by political parties. There seems to be a growing trend to dislodge the elected heads of gram sabhas and panchayats, who belong to Dalit communities.

S. Palraj, elected president of the Nakkalamuthanpatti village panchayat in Tirunelveli district in Tamil Nadu, said that Dalit panchayat president's fears cannot be dismissed as unfounded as his predecessor, Jakkaiyan, was murdered on November 22, 2006, for choosing to ignore the diktats of persons belonging to the dominant caste in running the local administration. Palraj was allegedly threatened that he would meet the same fate if he tried to function independently. Recalling the circumstances that forced him to the village, Palraj said: I have not been allowed to occupy my seat in the Panchayat office. Upper Caste members asked me not to enter the office premises. They wanted me to collect a certain amount of daily expenses and leave the job of running the Panchayat to them. They compelled me to sign the office records maintained by them."[9] Thirty-five reserved panchayat presidents in Sivaganga district have gone on record admitting caste discrimination in their areas. Evidence, a human rights organisation claimed that untouchability practices prevailed in a majority of the 85 reserved panchayats in Sivaganga district, which was evident from various forms of discrimination such as two-tumbler system at teashops.

In Usilangulam, the panchayat president, A. Kundumani, said the burial ground for Dalits was occupied by a caste Hindu who was now cultivating crops there. "We are burying the dead one over the other on a small promboke land. Being the president, I clean the overhead water tank at regular intervals as the person in-charge refuses to take my instructions. The Kayalarkoil union officials do not even allow me to enter the office for any discussion. Similar atrocities are prevailing in other reserved panchayats."[10]

Arasanoor panchayat president T. Devaraj said caste Hindus tried to dominate him in official proceedings. Though all the 700 Dalit families in the panchayat were living under acute poverty conditions, their names were not included in the Below Poverty Line (BPL) list. "The caste Hindus do not allow Dalits to enjoy the benefits of schemes meant for BPL category. Even my name was not included till recently. Not a single rupee was allotted for development works in this panchayat since I became the president. An engineering college in the locality refuses to pay property tax and professional tax," he said even after becoming the panchayat president, Mr. Devaraj alleged that he was forced to beat the `dandora' to convey good or bad news to the villagers.[11]

Caste bias is so visible in these villages that one need not make enquiries. When police or revenue officials come for inspections, the Dalits prefer not to complain fearing retaliatory action. "In the patriarchal system, there are lots of struggles for women to win the election. And within the system, Dalit women have to struggle more than other women. It is very difficult for them to win the election because nobody believes that they have the ability to carry out panchayat works. Everyone plays politics with them and against them just because they- dominant castes and men – never want Dalit women to control the panchayat administration.... Men never accept women's leadership and there is a need for specific attention to this by making proper use of the reservation policy as Babasaheb's blessing to us. Dalit women have to reap the benefits of this opportunity by actively engaging themselves in creating models of leadership."[12] According to Dalit women elected representatives in Ahmedabad district in Gujarat, "Consensus candidates who get selected are usually illiterate, poor people who are influenced by dominant castes on whom they depend for employment. Whoever becomes President through consensus always has to act as a pawn of the village." Similarly, Dalit women elected representatives in Cuddalore district in Tamil Nadu stated, "It is completely wrong to be elected unopposed or unanimously. This way of election is an instrument to strengthen the power of the dominant castes. Not only this, it is against democratic rights, freedom and equality. This is another kind of violence that dominant castes use against us."[13]

"Being the majority, the dominant castes could not accept the idea of being under a 'low' caste Dalit leader. So, for namesake they made me, a Dalit, the President. The dominant caste Vice President and other dominant caste members took away from me all powers and responsibilities. I did not even convene a meeting. I went to the panchayat office only when I was asked to go... I functioned like this because I have no education and belong to a low caste. Though I was given training, I was in such a situation that I could not do anything at all. We cannot speak against the dominant caste men. Even the [government] officials do not care for us. When they come to the village or panchayat office, they do not force us to come and attend the meetings. They simply speak with the Vice President, deal official business with him and then leave the place. How can Dalits function well in such a situation?" said Thilagam, village panchayat President, of Coimbatore district in Tamil Nadu. Once elected dominant caste male control over panchayat resources and ingrained discriminatory attitudes continued to govern to a large extent on Dalit women panchayat representatives. Observations of the CERD Committee on the Indian Government's Report in 2007 that: "Dalit candidates, especially women, are frequently forcibly prevented from standing for election or, if elected, forced to resign from village councils or other elected bodies or not to exercise their mandate."[14]

A 2006 nation-wide indent a study designed by leading Indian sociologists, titled, "Untouchability in Rural India" suggests that Panchayat members of the scheduled castes remain discriminated against in most of their interactions with others, among dozens of other instances of daily discrimination, members of SCs remain barred from entry into places of worship in more than 50 per cent of villages surveyed, they are denied access to water facilities in more than 45 per cent of the villages.[15]

Various studies by different scholars in India revealed mix of factors why SC Sarpanches are unable to significantly improve the lot of SC villagers. First, to the degree that untouchability persists, SC Sarpanches are often not provided with the authority and respect that is traditionally accorded to the Sarpanch. Second, the Sarpanch's ability to aid SC villages is limited by the local political context. Electorally speaking, successful SC Sarpanches depend on a multi-caste coalition, and do not have a free hand in making decisions favourable to their own group.[16]

Dalit women are excluded from decision making. They are not in position to exercise their power. Wherever Dalit women have contested, they have faced stiff opposition and even been brutally attacked. The 73rd amendment provides for mandatory reservation for Dalit women to be elected to the local governing bodies. They are elected but not able to exercise their power. There are instances where Dalit women have been elected into local governance and through the reservation policy nominated as the president of the local governing unit called Panchayat. But when these women have endeavoured to exercise their role, it has met with resistance even to the extent of physical violence. A Dalit women president is not allowed to sit on a chair if the other caste members do not allow this. She is forced to be a mere figure head, while the functioning of the Panchayats is taken over by other upper caste members.[17]

The Dalit Panchayat president, P. Krishnaveni of Thalaiyuthu Panchayat in Tirunelveli, who was brutally attacked by a gang had been facing discrimination right from the day of her announcement to contest elections. She was not allowed to sit in the chair that was allotted for the elected president. Since May 2007, she had filed 12 complaints with the police and district administration about the discrimination. The fact finding team had found that Ms. Krishaveni had to seek the help of District Collector to execute her duties as vice-president had been the writing all attempts made by her to work independently. Sometimes to conduct meetings she had to seek police protection to conduct meeting. The fact finding team came to know that Dalit presidents belonging to 125 Panchayats in the district were subject to one form of discrimination or the other.[18]

Alleging discrimination by upper caste members against Dalit Sarpanches in various Gram Panchayat of Gujarat, Ahmedabad-based Dalit Adhikar Manch demanded amendments to the Panchayats acts to protect the right of Dalit Sarpanches in the State. At a press conference, the group presented around six Dalit who allegedly faced discrimination at the hands of upper caste members of their Gram Panchayats during their tenure as Sarpanches. Addressing the press conference Sanjay Parmar said that his village had local population of around 4200 and he was elected as Sarpanch on a reserved seat.[19]

'After I was elected as Sarpanch, other upper –caste members of the Panchayats started harassing me. They did not allow me to pass annual budget of the Panchayats without giving any substantial reason. The thing is that due to statutory provisions they cannot stop Dalits becoming Sarpanch, but they make sure that only those Dalits who become their rubber stamps stay.[20]

Conclusion

So present study sums up that instances of discrimination against Dalits have been reported more intensely and frequently in states like Rajasthan, Uttar Pradesh, Madhya Pradesh, Bihar, West Bengal, Andhra Pradesh, Tamil Nadu, and Karnataka, in which the Dalit population is concentrated. When the PRIs in their amended form were launched, governments at the Centre and in the States declared that the empowerment of Dalits by providing them reserved seats in PRIs would lead to the abolition of the practice of untouchability in the years to come. But the reality is that much more has to be done to achieve this, say, by delegating more authority and giving more funds to these institutions so as to create confidence among panchayat leaders. The government must revive the practice of conducting capacity-building classes for Dalit panchayat chiefs if it is really interested in further empowering elected panchayat functionaries and facilitating the underprivileged to fulfill their commitments to the people. What is needed today is to equip Dalits with what they need to ensure the achievement of the twin objectives of economic development and social justice.

The mass media, communication technology and spatial mobility have broken the isolation of villages. Incidents even in remote village panchayats are grabbing the national limelight. The new panchayat system, with all its current weaknesses, has helped to weave the village into the broader social fabric. In states and regions which have witnessed strong social movements, Dalit panchayat members have begun to assert their constitutional rights and the dominant castes have begun to accept these changes, though grudgingly. It holds out hope for the future.

Ambedkar's eventual belief in social democracy and social justice was visible when at the end of the Constituent Assembly he said, on 26th of January (1950), we are going to enter into a life of contradictions. In politics we will have equality; in social and economic life we will have inequality. How long shall we live this life of contradictions? We must remove this contradiction or else those who suffer inequality will blow up the structure of political democracy."[21]

The life of Dr B.R. Ambedkar is a saga of great struggles and achievements. Mahatma Gandhi aptly described him as 'a man who has carved out for himself a unique position in a society. On his 125th birth anniversary year Prime Minister Narendra Modi described B.R. Ambedkar as a 'Yug Pursh' (Man of the era) who lives in the hearts and minds of crores of Indians.

Remembering Dr B.R. Ambedkar on 14th April and (His birthday) and 6th December (His last breathe) can be meaningful if a objective reappraisal of his legacy is undertaken and a conscious effort is made to rededicate ourselves to the ideas for which he waged a heroic and valiant struggle all his life. This will be a true tribute to Baba Saheb.

References

1. The Hindu 24 June 2005, p. 15, Delhi.
2. Constituent Assembly Debates, Vol. VII, p. 661.
3. *Ibid.* p. 662.
4. B.R. Ambedkar, Untouchables -The Children of India's Ghetto," in Dr Babasaheb Ambedkar, Writing and Speeches, Vol. 5, Mumbai: Government of Maharashtra, 1989, pp. 10-12.
5. Dalmia, Vasudha and Sadna Rashmi, eds, The Politics of Caste Identity Cambridge University Press, p. 93.
6. Goldy, M. George, "Dalits, Panchayat Raj and Power Equations", 9 May 2007 at www.countercurrents.org , retirved on 15 March 2015.
7. George Mathew, "Panchayats: Hope for Dalit Rights," 1 May 2013 livemint.com
8. S. Viswanathan, "Constitutionally Empower Act," The Hindu, 18 June 2012 at http:www.thehindu.com
9. S. Dorairay, "Disempowered Dalits," Frontline, 9 September 2016 at http:/ /www.frontline
10. The Hindu, 22 June 2011, Madurai at www.thehindu.com, Accessed on 19 August 2016.)
11. *Ibid.*
12. Jayshree Mangubhai, et.at, "Dalit Women's Right to Political Participation in Rural Panchayati Raj," IDEAS, Madurai, p. 3.
13. *Ibid.* p. 4.
14. UN Document, CERD Committee on India, Report 1997, p. 19.
15. Simon Chauchard, "Dalit Sarpanches Matter! Political Reservations and the Evolution of Untouchability in Rural India at https://casi.sas.upenn.edu, Accessed on 20 August 2016.
16. *Ibid.*
17. Unheard voices – Dalit Women, Periodic Report on India, 70 Session of committee on the Elimination of Racial Discrimination, Geneva, January 2007, pp. 5-6.
18. The Hindu, op.cit.
19. The Indian Express, 28 May 2016.
20. *Ibid.*
21. Hindustan Times, 15 April 2015, p. 8, Jalandhar.

6

Constitutional Prerogatives in Mainstreaming of Dalit in India

— Gobinda Chandra Sethi

Abstract

The sense of feeling the word, "Dalit" is derived from the Hebrew language means community suppressed. It indicated that dalits were deprived from their rights and living in harsh condition. Now-a-days, it is to remind not only age-old oppression by depriving from basic amenities but also the dominance of super-structure over the sub-structure. An upper stratum of the society was the suppressor but the lower was suppressed. It was the order of the then society expose the fact about upper caste supremacy over the sub-castes in different forms or pattern in the prevailing society perennially. The victims of such oppression, deprivation but also to the hardship of their condition of life. Dalit comprises SCs, STs and all the manual workers subservient to Brahminical order. This further symbolises a struggle for recognition of self-identity, expression of historical reality of oppression due to caste-based untouchability and occupations and a determination for creation of egalitarian society. Indian society has mechanisms that integrate by allowing them to hold together in order to restore the state of harmony or stability. Dalit community is excluded from enjoyment of social, economical,educational and political opportunities. It has long history of struggle to fight against caste discrimination. Social Inclusion is the removal of institutional barriers and the enhancement of incentives to increase the access of diverse individuals and groups to development opportunities. Constitutional provisions have enabled Dalits to have their greater access to services, resources and development opportunity. Reservation policy of the government is an affirmative step in mainstreaming Dalits. Integrated intervention for empowerment, inclusion and people's mobilisation and continued advocacy for distinct recognition of Dalit issues demanding for special Dalit development programmes has been crucial to influence policies and ameliorate economic, social and cultural rights of Dalits. Government's openness and co-operation has encouraged the move, accelerated the process and heightened the progress. Articles 15, 16 and 17 of the constitution is an eye opener to bridge the gap of mainstream and marginalised section of India. Dalit's lobby and regular sharing of the situation of Dalits has gained support and solidarity from international donor community including UN agencies. This process was started from later 1990s and got momentum from mid of the last decade. It is still continued. The gap between the upper and lower strata still exists, despite of the constitutional provisions and the efforts of the government by making some remarkable measures. It has sparked multiple challenges engulf us to think a step ahead.

[**Key words:** *Dalit, Deprivation, Strata, Self-Identity, Constitutional Provisions]*.

Introduction

Dalit means all those people of different castes and sub-castes among the depressed classes who were traditionally subjected to invidious discriminations on grounds of untouchability, and categorised as the untouchables, downtrodden, exterior classes, depressed classes or Scheduled Castes. The organisational or institutional efforts made by Dalit leaders for the liberation of the downtrodden masses could be termed as Dalit movement. It is a movement of protest against untouchability, casteism and superstitions. It aims at the uplift of the Dalits to the level of non-Dalits. "Negatively speaking, it stands for rejection of the old traditional Hindu social order based on untouchability, socio-economic inequality, casteism, unscientific and irrational religious beliefs and customary servitude. Positively speaking, it stands for acceptance of a new social order based on equality, liberty, and social justice, scientific and rational religious or moral principles and social, economic, cultural and political development of the Dalit." It is the movement to regain self-respect and equal human status in the society.

Dalit Identity

It is the result of the consciousness of Dalits of their own identity as human beings, equally equipped with physical and mental capacities as other human beings, and equally entitled to enjoy all the human rights "without any infringement, abridgement or limitations." Double folded issues are directed towards Untouchability and its Eradication. Untouchability, as indicated above, has always been considered as social evil. Since long efforts had been made to eradicate it. Religious and social, reformers like Buddha, Ramanuja, Ramanand, Chaitanya, Kabir, Nanak, Tukaram and others, made great efforts to eradicate it as far as possible. The Brahmo Samaj and the Arya Samaj, and other social organisations by propaganda, education, and practical measures, did much to secure the social, religious and cultural equality to them.

Vision of Dr Ambedkar

Among the depressed classes also rose intellectuals, distinguished of whom was Dr Ambedkar, who struggled to secure for them the social recognition and human rights. The All India Depressed Association and the All India Depressed Classes Federation, the principal organisations of these classes, initiated a movement to improve their conditions. They aimed at improving their miserable economic conditions, and to spread education among them. They worked to secure for them the rights to draw water from public wells, admission to the schools, and to the use of roads; and enter the public temples. The Mahad Satyagraha for the right of water led by Dr Ambedkar was one of the outstanding movements of the untouchables to win equal social rights.

Constitutional Prerogatives

India has attempted many different strategies in mainstreaming Dalits by using the Constitutional Prerogatives or Safeguards. Some of the provisions are relating to uplift the downtrodden enumerated in the constitution, the supreme law of the land. Some of the provisions with its dimensions are discussed below:

Directive Principles of State Policy

Article 46 is a comprehensive article comprising both the developmental and regulatory aspects. It reads as follows: "The State shall promote with special care the educational and economic interests of the weaker sections, of the people, and in particular, of the Scheduled Castes and the Scheduled Tribes, and shall protect them from social injustice and all forms of exploitation."

Social Dimension

Article 17: "Untouchability" is abolished and its practice in any form is forbidden. The enforcement of any disability arising out of "Untouchability" shall be an offence punishable in accordance with law. To give effect to this Article, Parliament made an enactment, Untouchability (Offences) Act, 1955. To make the provisions of this Act more stringent, the Act was amended in 1976 and was also renamed as the Protection of Civil Rights Act, 1955. As provided under the Act, Government of India also notified the Rules, viz., the PCR Rules, 1977, to carry out the provisions of this Act. As cases of atrocities on SCs/STs were not covered under the provisions of PCR Act, 1955, Parliament passed another important Act in 1989 for taking measures to prevent the atrocities. This act known as the Scheduled Castes and the Scheduled Tribes (Prevention of Atrocities) Act, 1989, became effective from 30.1.1990. For carrying out the provisions of this Act the Govt. of India have notified the SCs and the STs (Prevention of Atrocities) Rules, 1995 on 31.3.1995. These acts helps dalits a healthy social protects from social life.

Dimension of Human Trafficking, Article 23

Article 23: Prohibits traffic in human beings and beggar and other similar forms of forced labour and provides that any contravention of this provision shall be an offence punishable in accordance with law. It does not specifically mention SCs and STs but since the majority of bonded labour belongs to SCs/STs this Article has a special significance for SCs and STs. In pursuance of this article, Parliament has enacted the Bonded Labour System (Abolition) Act, 1976. For effective implementation of this Act, the Ministry of Labour is running a Centrally Sponsored Scheme for identification, liberation and rehabilitation of bonded labour. Article 24 provides that no child below the age of 14 years shall be employed to work in any factory or mine or engaged in any other hazardous employment. There are Central and State laws to prevent child labour. This article too is significant for SCs and STs as a substantial portion, if not the majority, of child labour engaged in hazardous employment belong to SCs and STs.

Religious Dimension, Article 25(2)

Article 25(2) (b) provides that Hindu religious institutions of a public character shall be thrown open to all classes and sections of Hindus. This provision is relevant as some sects of Hindus used to claim that only members of the concerned sects had a right to enter their temples. This was only a subterfuge to prevent entry of SC persons in such temples. For the purpose of this provision the term Hindu includes Sikh, Jaina and Buddhist.

Educational and Cultural Dimension

Article 15(4) empowers the State to make any special provision for the advancement of any socially and educationally backward classes of citizens or for SC and ST. This provision has enabled the State to reserve seats for SCs and STs in educational institutions including technical, engineering and medical colleges and in Scientific and Specialised Courses. In this as well as in Article 16(4) the term 'backward classes' is used as a generic term and comprises various categories of backward classes, viz., Scheduled Castes, Scheduled Tribes, Other Backward Classes, Denotified Communities (Vimukta Jatiyan) and Nomadic/Seminomadic communities.

Political Dimension

Article 330 provides for reservation of seats for SCs/STs in the Lok Sabha. Article 332 provides for reservation of seats for SCs/STs in the State Vidhan Sabhas (Legislative Assemblies).

Article 334 originally laid down that the provision relating to the reservation of seats for SCs/STs in the Lok Sabha and the State Vidhan Sabhas (and the representation of the Anglo-Indian community in the Lok Sabha and the State Vidhan Sabhas by nomination) would cease to have effect on the expiration of a period of ten years from the commencement of the Constitution. This article has since been amended four times, extending the said period by ten years on each occasion. This provision was to expire in January 2000 but not ceased off. The reason behind indicates that the government realise the need of its continuation.

Dimension of Reservation and Service

Article 16(4) empowers the State to make "any provision for the reservation in appointments or posts in favour of any backward class of citizens which, in the opinion of the State, is not adequately represented in the services under the State". Article 16 (4A). Nothing in this Article shall prevent the State from making any provision for reservation in matters of promotion to any class or classes of posts in the services under the State in favour of the Scheduled Castes and the Scheduled Tribes which, in the opinion of the State, are not adequately represented in the services under the State". Article 335. "The claims of the members of the Scheduled Castes and the Scheduled Tribes shall be taken into consideration, consistently with the maintenance of efficiency of administration, in the making of appointments to services and posts in connection with the affairs of the Union or of a State". Article 320(4) provides that nothing in clause (3) shall require a Public Service Commission to be consulted as respects the manner in which any provision under Article 16(4) and 16(4). A may be made or the manner in which effect may be given to the provisions of Article 335.

Statutes and Legislations

There are a number of laws, both Central and State, which provide for safeguards to SCs/STs. Some of these emanate from the various Constitutional provisions. An illustrative list of such laws is given below:

The Protection of Civil Rights Act, 1955.

The Scheduled Castes and the Scheduled Tribes (Prevention of Atrocities) Act, 1989.

The Bonded Labour System (Abolition) Act, 1976.

The Child Labour (Prohibition and Regulation) Act, 1986.

Acts and regulations in force in different States to prevent alienation of land belonging to SCs/STs. In some States such provision exists in the Land Revenue Code.

Acts in different States for restoration of alienated land to SCs/STs.

The Position of Dalits in India Today

According to the 2001 census, scheduled castes comprise 16.2 per cent of the total population of India, that is, they number over 17 crore. Scheduled tribes comprise 8.2 per cent of the population, that is, they number over 8 crore. Both together constitute 24.4 per cent of the Indian population, that is, they together number over 25 crore. The six states that have the highest percentage of scheduled caste population are Punjab (28.9), Himachal Pradesh (24.7), West Bengal (23.0), Uttar Pradesh (21.1), Haryana (19.3) and Tamil Nadu (19.0). The twelve states that have the largest number of scheduled castes are Uttar Pradesh (351.5 lakhs), West Bengal (184.5 lakhs), Bihar (130.5 lakhs), Andhra Pradesh (123.4 lakhs), Tamil Nadu (118.6 lakhs), Maharashtra (98.8 lakhs), Rajasthan (96.9 lakhs), Madhya Pradesh (91.6 lakhs), Karnataka (85.6 lakhs), Punjab (70.3 lakhs), Orissa (60.8 lakhs) and Haryana (40.9 lakhs). It has earmarked positive note in the last census report. The dimensional shift in the social, political and economic aspects of the Dalits are better in comparison to the previous census. Though not mainstreamed but in the track to be mainstreamed, if the circumstances and situations go side by side.

Findings

Ensuring access to education for the Dalits of India has been the greatest challenge for the Indian government in diminishing the social effects of the caste system, which still remain entrenched in Indian society. There have been many different reasons proposed as to why the Dalits suffer from low rates of literacy and primary education enrollment, but the most realistic one describes history and unequal access as the causes.

Suggestions

Reservations: All the backlogs in reserved seats and posts and in promotions for Dalits which includes SCs, STs and OBCs must be filled forthwith with special recruitment drives. A comprehensive legislation covering all aspects of reservation for SCs/STs in employment and education both public and private institutions should be enacted. A National Commission should be set up to assess the real position of Dalits including reservation in proportionate with population. The state level commissions should be set up to oversee the implementation of all schemes connected with the SCs including reservation. Infrastructure development in the scheduled caste areas like road, water, health, culture and other needs has to be given proper importance by aimimg at Rooting Out Untouchability in all its forms which is deep rooted in Indian society. Strengthening the relevant laws, ensuring their strict implementation for the protection against from

Atrocities, which is vibrant in the major pockets of the country. The Central Government should amend and strengthen the SC and ST (Prevention of Atrocities) Act 1989, providing for special courts with judges, investigating officers and public prosecutors unburdened by any other work. Social and economic boycott and blackmail should be included as substantive crimes. Full economic rehabilitation of victims and their survivors must be ensured. The commercialisation of education should be stopped since the massive fee and donation structure of private educational managements is something that socially and economically backward students cannot afford. For this, the central government must increase its own outlay on education to 6 per cent of the GDP. Steps should be taken to universalise primary education and expand secondary education. Special measures to curb the drop-out rate among SCs should be undertaken.

Agricultural Workers: The Minimum Wages Act for agricultural workers must be stringently implemented throughout the country. The National Rural Employment Guarantee Act must be strictly implemented all over the country by involving the people, their mass organisations and the panchayati raj institutions. It should be extended to all districts and also to urban areas of the country. The public distribution system must be universalised to ensure food to all. Until this is done, BPL ration cards must be issued to all Dalits. Ensure total liberation and full rehabilitation for scavengers (safai karamcharis), ban engagement of contract labour in safai services and other services where SC and ST numerically predominate and instead introduce necessary improvements by involving such Karamcharis; and reactivate the Central Monitoring Committee for Liberation and Rehabilitation of Safai Karamcharis and State, Municipal and District Level communities. Inter-caste marriages should be encouraged by giving special subsidised housing and other facilities to married couples immediately after their marriage. We should consciously try to uphold such inter-caste marriages and make them an event of big social participation and sanction.

Conclusion

Dalits are the marginalised in India but Dalit among the Dalits should get their due space in the society. Elimination of Creamy Layer and preference should be given to the unprivileged among the unprivileged. The other important argument may be put forth that there should be an elite class among the Dalit to carry forward the community. It can create a vista of clear cut vision for their community can be proved to be a boon in mainstreaming the Dalits in India.

References

AIR 1964 SC 737.

Article 37 of the Constitution of India.

Minerva Mills Vs Union of India, Air, 1980, SC 1789.

Article 38 of the Constitution of India.

Article 39 of the Constitution of India.

Article 38 A of the Constitution of India.

Article 41 of the Constitution of India.

Article 42 of the Constitution of India.

Article 43 of the Constitution of India.

Article 43 A of the Constitution of India.

Article 44 of the Constitution of India.

Article 45 of the Constitution of India.

Article 46 of the Constitution of India.

Article 47 of the Constitution of India.

Arjan de Hann (2008). *Social Exclusion: Towards a Holistic Understanding of Deprivation*. Critical Quest: New Delhi.

Away from the Hindus, (1981) Writings and Speeches, Vol. V, Mumbai, Government of Maharashtra, 2003 Writings and Speeches, Vol. 17.3 Mumbai, Government of Maharashtra.

B.R. Ambedkar on "Pakistan or Partition of India" Vol. 8, p. 225.

B.R. Ambedkar on "Pakistan or Partition of India" Vol. 8, p. 226.

Baba Saheb Ambedkar Writings and Speechs. Vol. 17, part-3, p. 283.

CAD Vol. X-XII, p. 456.

CAD Vol. VII, p. 661.

CAD Vol. VII, p. 662.

Ambedkar, B.R. (1916), *Castes in India: their Mechanism, Genesis and Development*, Writings and Speeches, Vol. I, Mumbai, Government of Maharashtra, 1979.

D.C. Ahir (1990), *The Legacy of Ambedkar.* B.R. Publications: Delhi.

Das, Bhagwan (1979), *Thus Spoke Ambedkar*, Vol. I and II, Jullandur, Bheem, Patrika Publications.

Dr Ambedkar on women's emancipation, Dr B.R. Ambedkar series Publications of Ambedkar Peeta, KSOU, Mysore, 2005, p. 5.

Dr B.R.Ambedkar's Exhumation of Cultural Capital and its Dynamics in Indian Society in G.Bhadru Naik 2010a) (ed.), Economic Philosophy of Dr B.R. Ambedkar and its relevance in the Contemporary Society, Warangal.

Dr B.R. Ambedkar (1936), *Annihilation of Caste,* Writings and Speeches, Vol. I, Mumbai, Government of Maharashtra, 1979.

Dr B.R. Ambedkar. (1945), *What Congress and Gandhi have done to the Untouchables,* Writings and Speeches, Vol. I, Mumbai, Government of Maharashtra, 1979.

Extempore speech by Hon'ble Mr. Justice S.H. Kapadia, Judge, Supreme Court of India on the occasion of the Eighth Justice J.K. Mathur Memorial Lecture on 13-12-2008 at Lucknow. Surendrasingh "Dr Ambedkar Contribution to Social Justice". edited by Prof. M. Shabbir, Rawat pub. Jaipur, 2005, pp. 78-81.

Friedman, W. (2002), *Legal Theory 5th Edition*, Universal Law Publication: Delhi.

John Rawl's (2002), *Theory of Justice.* Universal Law Publication: Delhi.

Krishna Iyar (1991), *B.R. Ambedkar Centenary, Social Justice and the Undone vast Justice.* B.R. Publications: Delhi.

Mahbal Ram (2003), *Changing Economic Scenario and Social Justice on India.* Dominant Publications: Delhi.

Many amendments were suggested by the members of Constituent Assembly, viz., Sri L.n. Sahu, Patabi Seeta Ramaiah, Smt. G Durga Bai, Pandith Thakur das Bhargava, Dr B.V. Keshkar, T.T. Krishnamchari, M. Ananthasham Iyengar, K. Shantharam, Aututal Chandra, Upendranath bhraman and Prof. K.T. Shah.

Merunandan, K.B., Naveed Ahmed (2006), *An Introduction to the Constitution of India.* Merugu Publications: Bengaluru.

Mohamed Shabbir (2005), *Ambedkar on Law, Constitution and Social Justice.* Rawat: Jaipur.

Mr Russel and the Reconstruction of Society, (1918) Writings and Speeches, Vol. I Mumbai, Government of Maharashtra, 1979.

Philosophy of Hinduism, (1987), Writings and Speeches, Vol. 3, Mumbai, Government of Maharashtra, 1987.

Prasad, Dr Anirudh (2007), *Outlines of legal language in India,* p. 414.

Purohit, B.R., Sandeep Joshi (2003), *Social justice in India*. Rawat : Jaipur.

Satyapal, P.D. (2010), *From Culture of Reservations to Culture of Representations: Phule-Ambedkarite Agenda for Social Inclusion in India* in V. Subrahmanyam (ed.) Social Exclusion, Integration and Inclusive Policies, Jaipur: Rawat Publications.

Venugopal, P. (1998), *Social Justice and reservation*. Emerald Publications: Chennai.

Wodeyer D. Hegade (2005), *Job reservation for Dalits and Backward classes in Private sector issues and strategies.* Centre for human development studies publications: Mysore.

7

Dr B.R. Ambedkar: A Quest for Social Justice

— *Mrs Jatinder Walia and Mrs Reena Kushwaha*

Abstract

Dr Babasaheb Rao Ambedkar is the man of millennium for social justice since he was the first person in history to successfully lead a trade of securing social justice to vast section of humanity. He believed that root cause of social injustice in India lies in the caste system. He himself being member of low caste was victim of ill-treatment. He argued that a true democracy in India could prevail only when no kind of discrimination would exist in Indian societies. So, he struggled throughout his life for the downtrodden. When he became a member of the drafting committee, he mentioned special provisions in fundamental rights, directive principles and provision to set up constitutional machinery for scheduled castes, scheduled tribes and women. These are considered as some of his great efforts. Today, his ceaseless efforts have brought changes in Indian societies. Educated people are accepting inter-caste marriages and give respect to people of all strata. But still now there is need of awareness because it happens only in metro cities. This present paper investigates the contribution of B.R. Ambedkar in the context of social justice and also measures at what level it achieve success.

[Keywords: *Social Justice, humanity, democracy, discrimination, social justice]*.

Introduction

Dr Bhimrao Ramji Ambedkar (4 April 1891-6 December 1956) was born in Mahar Family in Mhow (Maharashtra) and was popularly known as Babasaheb. He devoted his whole life for the upliftment of the underprivileged of India. He knew very well that India could not achieve success in real sense till the problems existing in Indian Society could not be solved. He wrote number of books and essays on social inequalities. He became the first law minister and chief architect of Indian constitution. He prepared draft of Indian constitution and mentioned all possible provisions by which all forms of discrimination and inequalities existing in Indian society could be abolished. He roused about the humiliation and discrimination of Indian culture to study law in England and became a respected attorney, Indian Jurist, political leader, philosopher, anthropologist orator, editor and prolific writer. He is also considered a pioneer who introduced the concept of reservation policy at the all India level in early 1930's. "He believed that whatever may have been the purpose behind the origin of the Caste system, in its later classical form, it certainly involved an economic motive, the main purpose of which was exploitation rather than economic efficiency of any sort."[1] Indeed, Babasaheb wanted such society which should based on socio-economic and political justice.

What is Social Justice?

First one should understand the meaning of Social Justice. What is Social Justice? The term Social Justice is comprehensive in nature. It, being a multi-dimensional concept, has been explained by scholars, philosophers and Political Scientists differently. According to Utalitarian, "Social Justice relates with one of the dimension of justice which stands for fraternity; with a view to create such human social conditions which ensure free and fair development of all human being.[2] To Rawls, social justice is about assuring the protection of equal access to liberties, rights, and opportunities, as well as taking care of the least advantaged members of society. Thus, whether something is just or unjust depends on whether it promotes or hinders equality of access to civil liberties, human rights, opportunities for healthy and fulfilling lives, as well as whether it allocates a fair share of benefits to the least advantaged members of society.[3] According to Matthew Robinson, Social justice as "... promoting a just society by challenging injustice and valuing diversity." It exists when "all people share a common humanity and therefore have a right to equitable treatment, support for their human rights, and a fair allocation of community resources."

In conditions of social justice, people are "not be discriminated against, nor their welfare and well-being constrained or prejudiced on the basis of gender, sexuality, religion, political affiliations, age, race, belief, disability, location, social class, socio-economic circumstances, or other characteristic of background or group membership" (Toowoomba Catholic Education, 2006). Social justice is generally equated with the notion of equality or equal opportunity in society. According to Miller, social justice deals with the distribution of good (advantages) and bad (disadvantages) in society, and more specifically with how these things should be distributed within society. Further, social justice is concerned with the ways that resources are allocated to people by social institutions (Miller, 2003: 11). Some of the advantages relevant for social justice include money, property, jobs, education, medical care, child care, care for the elderly, honours and prizes, personal security, housing, transportation, and opportunities for leisure. Some of the disadvantages include military service, dangerous work, and other hardships. Keep in mind that Miller's theory applies to both public goods as well as private commodities (Miller, 2003: 10).[4]

The National Pro Bono Resource Centre defines Social Justice as "The concept of Social Justice involves finding of the optimum balance between our joint responsibilities as a society and our responsibilities as individual to contribute to a just society."[5]

Famous Jurist Roscoe Pound expressed his view on Social Justice. He classifies three legally protected interests (a) Public interests, (b) social interests and (c) private interests.[6] He explained the concept of social justice under the sixth principles of 'Social Interests'. According to sixth principles, there is social interest in the individual human life, which is described by him as 'the claim or want or demand involved in social life in civilised society that each individual be able to live a human life there in according to the standards of the society."[7]

Dr B.R. Ambekar Views on Social Justice

Dr B.R. Ambedkar knew very well that without establishing just social order in India, it cannot achieve a real success. He criticised Hindu social system strongly and commented on Vedas etc. Similarly, he reviewed all other societies and religions existed in India and finally he found that a kind of discrimination everywhere that why he followed Buddhism that was according to time. He made several efforts to eradicate all kind of discriminations in societies. He made various committees, commissions and sabhas to express the grievances of the downtrodden classes. "In Ambedkar's view caste cannot exist in a single form. Caste can exist only as plural number, interlinked to each other in unequal measures of social religious and economic relations and rights. In this particular hierarchy, the Brahmins are not only placed at the top but are considered 'superior social beings' worthy of special entitlements, rights, and privileges. At the bottom, untouchables and lower castes are treated as 'sub-human beings or lesser human beings considered unworthy of any rights. In fact, the disabilities they suffer are so severe that they are physically and socially isolated and excluded from the rest of the society. Isolation and exclusion of untouchables is unique feature of Hindu social order. Ambedkar argued that classes or social groups are common to all societies, but as long as the classes or social groups do not practice isolation and exclusion. They are only non-social in their relations towards one another.[8] Education system in Hindu society is not based on justice. It is narrow in nature. He made his all possible effort to reduce inequalities in society. On 20th December, 1946, at the conference of All India Scheduled Caste Student Federation, he sent a message in which he advised them, "Dalit youth, when they get chance, should always prove that they are no less intelligent and capable than anyone else. So also without being self – centred, they should make every effort to liberate community, empower, and dignify it).[9] In this way, Babasaheb put forward the genesis of the caste system and annihilated untouchability legally.

Dr Babasaheb's Contribution towards Social Justice in India

Babasaheb was born in an untouchable family and in unfavourable social ambience, yet the way he revolutionised the social life in India is praise-worthy. He proved that one can born in a low-caste family but through Karma can reach at the top and lead honourable life. Ambedkar's concept of social justice is found in his various activities. There are some examples on the basis of which we can justify that Dr Ambedkar seriously struggled for social justice. It was in 1919 that he, for the first time, intervened in the formulation of British policies with regard to depressed classes by representing a written statement to Southborough Committee appointed to look into the claims of various communities to get franchise rights for representation in legislature.

Dr B.R. Ambedkar introduced the present reservation policy at the all India level in early 1930's. He started Mahad Satyagraha held on 25th December 1927 to take drinking water from Chawdar Tank and Mahad of Kolba District. On 17th June, 1931, Dr Started Dalit movement which gathered force with positive actions like temple-entry, dining together across boundaries. On 28th September 1932 at Worli, he warned, "Temple entry would not help liberate you, the political rights should be used to gain all conveniences for better life."[10] At Calcutta, in September 1944, Dr Ambedkar was felicitated by Dalit community. Dr Ambedkar said he was happy that the Cripps delegation failed. He was surprised that Hindus beg Muslims for conciliation, but ignore Dalits. He referred to the recent correspondence between Gandhi and Viceroy, "Viceroy has clearly mentioned that for the transfer of power Hindu-Muslim unity is not now considered the victory is in sight.' On 20th September 1944 at the meeting of Hyderabad State Scheduled Caste Federation, Dr Ambedkar delivered dynamic speech in which he said, "The goal of Dalits is to gain a share in the political power of the country." Finally being a chairman of the drafting committee, he enumerated special privileges for depressed classes.[11]

During making draft of Indian constitution he incorporated the values of liberty, equality and fraternity, (For example : we the people of India having solemnly resolved to constitute India into a " sovereign, socialist, secular, democratic, republic" and to secure to all its citizens justice, social, economic, political, liberty of thought and expression, belief, faith and worship, equality of status and of opportunity and to promote among them all fraternity assuring the dignity of the nation ....) In the Constituent Assembly on 25th November 1949, "Political democracy can not last unless there lies at the base of it social democracy." On 26th January 1950, he said, "we are going to enter into a life of contradictions. In politics, we will have equality and social and economic life we will have inequality. In politics, we will be recognising the principle of one man one vote and one vote one value. In our social and economic life, we shall by reason of our social and economic structure, continue to deny the principal of one man one vote. We must remove this contradiction at the earliest possible moment or else those who suffer from inequality will blow up the structure of political democracy which this assembly has so laboriously built up."[12.]

Fundamental rights mentioned in the Part III of the constitution pictures about the just society in which each individual does his overall development. For example: "The state shall not deny equality before the law and equal protection of the laws. (Art. 14).[13] In the Article 15, it has been written that there shall be no discrimination on the ground of religion, race, caste, sex or place of birth. It also empowers the state to make positive discrimination in the favour of women and children. Article 16 provides equal opportunity in the matters of public employment and Art. 23 talks about prohibition of traffic in human beings and forced labour. In the same way, some articles mentioned in Directive Principles (i.e. Art. 39 (a) and (d) enjoins the state to provide equal means of livelihood and equal pay for equal work; the state shall make provision for securing just and humane conditions of work and for maternity relief (Art. 42)) proves the efforts of Dr B.R. Ambedkar. Besides these, Article 243D, 243 T(3), 243T(4) provides reservation facilities to Schedule Caste, Schedule Tribes and Women.

Today's Scenario

No doubt, the incredible efforts of Babasaheb has brought colour in Indian society. The provision of reservation policy for the scheduled castes (SC) and scheduled tribes has made a positive impact on their socio-economic condition. A new elite class emerged in lower strata of the society. The spread of education, the pace of urbanisation, the development of means of communication and transport, and so on have been instrumental in loosening somewhat the rigidity and hangover of the caste system, particularly in the urban areas. People living in metro cities no more think about caste system and tie their youngsters in marriage knot happily. If we measure the success of reservation policy we will find that it does not fulfil the dream of Dalit massiha Dr B.R. Ambedker. In this concern Wodeyer D. Hegade writes in his research paper "JOB RESERVATION FOR DALIT AND BACKWARD CLASSES IN PRIVATE SECTORS ISSUES AND STRATEGIES" that reservation policy has not served much purpose to alleviate the poverty and living standard of scheduled Castes because so far hardly 0.5 per cent of Scheduled Castes out of 25 crore of population have got regular jobs, the remaining 99.5 per cent SC masses are still reeling under poverty, hunger, malnutrition and illiteracy because reservation is like a bag of sugar poured in the sea which can not make the brackish sea water sweet. Reservation thus has done little good by providing job opportunities to a handful of educated elites, but political reservation suppressed a great political revolution.[14] It has been also seeing that caste is considered a potent instrument for socio-economic and political empowerment, caste and sub-caste organisations have been being proliferated. There is growing demand by some castes, keeping their caste arrogance intact, to get included in the Other Backward Classes (OBC) category, and by some OBCs to be considered as S.Ts (for instance, Jats in Haryana and Rajasthan).

As per concern to women, they are also improving their standard and empowering day by day. Today, they not only perform duties assigned within four walls but becoming doctor, engineer, professor, singers and so on- have been serving the nation also. Due to Dr B.R. Ambedker's effort, Hindu women enjoy equal rights to inheritance. Section 14 says that any property possessed by a female Hindu shall be held by her as full owner and not a limited owner. But it is irony to say that shattered with the reforms and liberation of women in the Twenty first century, the Indian mindset has not accepted the equality at par with men and hence forcing women to revert their development. Today, marriages are preferred not only within castes, but also within sub-castes.

We absorb that the idea of inter-caste marriage given by him not very effective in rural area. In Haryana and Rajasthan, for instance, the khap (caste council) gives orders to kill young lovers for marrying outside their caste. Such inhuman killings are glorified as honour killings. In such incident women are killed by their parents. News of harassment, molesting, eye-teasing is read every day. As per concern to property share, hardly few parents are ready to offer property to their daughters. In the present era, Indian women instead of upliftment of their mind power are indulging more in sexuality and western lifestyle. We know very well that sheer influence of modern lifestyle and adopting technology does not mean improvement of individual and society.

Conclusion

Dr B.R. Ambedkar pleaded for special privileges for suppressed classes of the society. He proved himself as torchbearer for marginalised classes and through his hard work showed that with his karma one can get respect and change his destiny. Today, we see that most of the youngsters who believe in hardship achieving their goal and reach at height. We heard and read that a milkman' daughter and auto-rickshaw driver's son scored the highest rank in civil administrative exams. Caste system seems no more hurdles for progress in both rural and urban area. He has given a platform on the basis of which a victim can fight for his rights. We can visualise his struggle for social justice in the philosophy of the Indian constitution. The constitution ethos of the social revolution running through the 'preamble', Fundamental Rights and the Directive Principles, provision of the establishment of constitutional authorities expressly emphasise the establishment of an egalitarian social order and based on human values of justice, social, economic and political, equality of status and of opportunity and fraternity assuring human dignity.

Modern education is helping to change the attitude and perceptions. People are becoming more scientific in outlook rather than being blindly superstitious. Laws can maintain social justice if it implements in the right way. Therefore, there is need to bring reform in laws which are not according to circumstances. In the era of the globalisation, India is competing other developed countries. It is Dr B. R. Ambedkar who revolutionised the masses and enlightened the half of Indian population and gave path to reach at the top in each walk of life.

References

1. Friedman, W. (5th Ed.) (2002) *Legel Theory*. Universal Law Publication: Delhi.
2. Frontline, May, 2015.
3. Gupta, R.C. (2013), *Great Political Thinker East and West*. Lakshmi Narayan Agarwal: Agra John Rawls (2002) *Theory of Justice*. Universal Law Publication: Delhi.
4. Mathew, Thomas (1991), *Ambedkar : Reform or Revolution*. Segment Books: New Delhi.
5. Moon, Vasant. *Dr Babasaheb Ambedkar.* National Trust Book of India: New Delhi.
6. *Ibid.,* 90.
7. *Ibid.,* 154-155.
8. Nazeer. H. Khan, *B.R. Ambedker on federation, ethnicity and gender justice*. Deep and Deep Publication: New Delhi.

9. National Pro Bono Resource Centre, occasional paper#1 what is social justicewico41.4server, service.com/vs155205server/cms files.com%20 what%20is social%20India-Final-pdf.

10. *Ibid.,* 338.

11. The Hindu newspaper.

12. Thorat, Sukhadeo and Kumar, Narender (Ed.) (2009), *B.R. Ambedkar Perspectives on Social Exclusion and Inclusive Policies*. Oxford University Press: New Delhi.

13. Uppadhaya, Jai, Jai Ram (2009), *The Constitution of India*. Centre Law Agency, Allahabad: 6.

14. Wodeyer, D. Hegade (2005), Job reservation for dalit and backward classes in private sectors issues and strategies. Centre for human development studies publication, Mysore: 46.

8

Ambedkar Aesthetics: A Creative Inspiration for Dalit Writers

— **Dr Amandeep**

Abstract

The paper analyses the writings and Political activities of Dr Babasaheb Ambedkar who made significant contributions to the anti-caste movement. Ambedkar's thoughts are the sole inspiration for Dalit Literature. Ambedkar stood for the social liberation, economic emancipation and political advancement of the downtrodden. Dalit writers found Self-respect through Ambedkar ideas and agitations. It further analyses how Ambedkar has remained a source of inspiration of Dalit writers. The three cornerstones of Ambedkar aesthetics are – empiricism, constitutionalism and conversion, one succeeding the other in a dynamic continuum. It needs be stressed here that Dalit aesthetics during Ambedkar's time itself undergoes shifts as it strives to seek authentic ways to empowerment.

[**Keywords:** *aesthetics, liberation, emancipation, empiricism, constitutionalism, conversion]*.

Introduction

India has been considered the most stratified of all known societies in human history with its peculiar form of caste system. A number of Indian and foreign sociologists has put forward theories on the class and the caste systems. Dr Ambedkar has traced the development of the caste system in his works Castes in India—Their Mechanism, Genesis and Development (1916), Annihilation of Caste (1936) and who were the Shudras (1948). Since Hinduism is founded on scriptures which sanctioned the caste-based social order the only solution lies is the annihilation of Indian caste system. For this Ambedkar launched several protest movements. The arrival of Ambedkar on the national scene really triggered off dalit writings. His Marathi fortnightly *Muk Nayak* (1920) set the tone for new consciousness. Ambedkar's struggles with pro-British Justice Party (1917) and Self-Respect Movement (1925) launched by Periyar E. V. Ramaswami Naicker brought a new awareness to which contemporary writers across castes responded directly. During Ambedkar's lifetime, dalit discourse was dominated by non-dalit writers, and no division was sought between the dalit and the non-dalit writers as long as the former wrote Sympathetically for the dalit cause. Around 1920, writers S.M. Mate wrote *Asprishyanicar* for Untouchables. Also writers represent the miserable conditions of the dalits to the British government. Among them was Kisan Phagoji Bansood, Gopalbaba Valangkal called pre-Ambedkar leaders. In 1945, Ambedkar started the Siddharth College in Mumbai and his message was to 'unite, educate and agitate'. A brahman writer who was a social reformer Sane Guruji in his book *Shyamci Ai* (1935) shows courage, compassion of true religion. Other important dalit writers of this period were Durga Bhagwat, Vijay Tendulkar, G.T. Madkholkar etc. keep forward the legacy of Ambedkar.

Babasaheb valued literature that was realistic and life-affirming. This is proved by his love of books, his expectation of humanistic ideas in literature, and his literary thought, which is based on the writer's commitment to common humanity. Alok Mukherji rightly says:

> Ambedkar accorded the highest place to humanism. Inspired by him, Dalit literature holds the human being to be its focal point. This literature is a declaration of human freedom. It encourages human liberation, believes in the greatness of human beings, and firmly opposes notions of race, religion and caste. Humanity is the religion of Dalit literature. (Mukherji, 51).

To understand the matrices of Ambedkar's style, a careful reading of his much-debated essay "Annihilation of Caste" would constitute the befitting beginning. The essay carries a "Prologue", which is otherwise very unusual for a prose-tract. What new orientation does Ambedkar lend to the classical 'Prologue'? Obviously, it is not written in the verse form, as is the usual practice in classical theatre. It is rather written in what may be called as 'epistolary form'. A series of letters between some Sant Ram, the Secretary of the Jat-Pat Todak Mandal, Dr Har Bhagwan and Ambedkar himself, in which Ambedkar makes it amply clear that he is not going to participate in any activity undertaken by upper-caste Hindus for the uplift of dalits forms the subject matter of "Prologue". Quite explicitly he writes: "As a rule I do not like to take any part in a movement which is carried on by the caste Hindus. Their attitude towards social reform is so different from mine that I have found it difficult to pull on with them. Indeed, I find their company quite uncongenial to me on account of our differences of opinion" (Ambedkar, Vol. I, 27-28).

"Prologue" sets the tone of Ambedkar's essay. It could also be read as a seminal document on the emerging contours of dalit consciousness and aesthetics. The exchange of letters underlines the essentially dialogic nature of dalit discourse right from Phule to Ambedkar. The counter-content of the letter reveals the non-monologic characteristic of dalit discourse (which often it is described to be). The publication of the private letters itself means that the debate is thrown open into the public realm and those boundaries between the private and the public are no longer sustainable when it comes to the dalit-question. "Prologue" thus heralds a huge drama, an unprecedented action that would be played in the realm of politics, aesthetics and ideas.

Ambedkar takes on the political reformers and socialists – the so-called liberals within orthodox Hinduism. The political reformers, who are otherwise desperate to, enjoy the benefits of freedom, are not eager enough to press for an urgent social re-engineering, similarly socialists "ignore the problems arising out of the social order" as they like their European counterparts seeks to "apply economic interpretation of history." (Ambedkar, Vol. I, 44). What is significant from the point of view of emerging dalit aesthetics is that it does no longer operate within simplified grids or binaries of hardcore upper-caste Hindus *versus* the untouchables? During Ambedkar's time, dalit discourse enters into its subtle phase as it argues with the so-called reformers and the socialists, and other pro-dalit activists.

For an extended Ambedkar-Gandhi debate, we shall now concentrate on his another essay "Gandhism: The Doom of the

Untouchables". Our focus once again is on the aesthetics of it, and its bearings on the emerging dalit aesthetics as a whole. Ambedkar answers back Gandhi's advocacy of caste-system. His replies are pointed and sharp which in a way suggest the utmost focus dalit interrogation had acquired during that period. This is how he counter-reads Gandhi's notion that the caste has provided India some kind of inner security over the centuries:

> The first three arguments call for pity. That the Hindu society has been able to stand while others died out or disappeared is hardly a matter for congratulation. If it is not because of caste but because the foreigner who conquered the Hindus did not find it necessary to kill them wholesale. There is no honour in mere survival. What matters is the plane of survival? One can survive by unconditional surrender. One can survive by beating a cowardly retreat and one can survive by fighting. On what plane have the Hindus survive? (Ambedkar,Vol. IX, 286)

Following his argumentative style through which he constantly exposes the politics of exclusion of the caste Hindus, Ambedkar thinks of the emancipation of fellow dalits in positive terms. Dalit aesthetics consequently undergoes a shift, from criticism of others to constructive empowerment through constitutional means.

In the memorandum, Ambedkar enlists various grievances of the depressed classes under four heads "Political Grievances", "Educational Grievances", "Other Grievances" and Duty of the Government towards "Distressed People" (Ambedkar, Vol. X, 405). There is a clear absence of rhetoric as observations are supported through detailed data in the tabular form. After enlisting grievances, the solutions are suggested thus: "declaring them minority" and "fixing their proportion in the annual vacancies" (423). Ambedkar prefers Buddhism over Marxism for the latter only insists on the economic dimensions of life, while the former is wholesome. Christophe Jaffrelot writes: His conversion was not an escape; nor was it purely an individual step. Collective conversion was also the revolt of a social revolt… it was a strategy of emancipation which went along with the 'separatist' aspect of his approach, although by choosing Buddhism, Ambedkar limited the scope of his break with Hinduism. (Jaffrelot,163). The other reason of his conversion is that he thinks there is no place for a caste system in

Buddhism, which supports egalitarianism and rejects inequality. Buddha rejects casteism and admitted everyone into his religion.

Chander Bhan Prasad says: DrAmbedkar understood Buddha more than any other Indian of his time. When he makes a statement, it becomes a thesis. (Prasad, 20). Not only this Ambedkar mobilised a large number of Dalit women to join in the various phases of his movements like the historic Mahad Satyagraha of 1927, or the Nasik Satyagraha of 1930 or his conversion to Buddhism in 1956. Raj Kumar Rightly says in this context: The Dalit Women who had been privileged to participate in Ambedkar's movements later organised Dalit women from across India under the aegis of Dalit women's movement. (Kumar, 214). In many of Dalit women life stories the condition of women is depicted very painful. These women also suffered from the practice of Dalit Patriarchy. While narrating their stories these women confessed that they had to go back to resume their duties within four weeks of their children's birth. Many of them complained that their husbands took away half of the family income to spend on drinks and if they resisted, they quarreled with them and often beat them. This type of violence against them becomes a symbolic gesture of exploitation and discrimination within communities. Inspite of such a grim scenario these women kept dreaming of a better life. Some of them took refuge in religious life and chose Buddhism for their emancipation from inspiration by Ambedkar.

Ambedkar's commitment to education as a major means for untouchable advancement led him to initiate in the 1920s a Programme for the creations of hostels for untouchable students. This effort resulted in the development of a system of colleges organised by the People's Education society founded by Ambedkar in 1945. Zelliot says in the regard: Ambedkar pronouncements on the need to live clean and moral lives sound very much like Gandhi's. However, Ambedkar's vision of the untouchable's future role went far beyond that of Gandhi, or indeed that of any other untouchable leader. (Zelliot, 159).

In a sequel to his treatise on the shudras, Ambedkar wrote *The Untouchables* in 1948. In the preface of this book, Ambedkar summarised his views on the origin of untouchability in the following manner: there is no racial difference between the Hindus and the untouchables. The distinction between the Hindus and untouchables in its original form, before the advent of untouchability, was the distinction between Tribesmen and Broken Men from alien Tribes. It is the Broken men who subsequently came to be treated as untouchables. Just as untouchability has no racial basis so also has it no occupational. (qtd in Basu, 143). Babasaheb valued literature that was realistic and life-affirming. This is proved by his love of books, his expectation of humanistic ideas in literature, and his literary thought, which is based on the writer's commitment to common humanity. Dr Ambedkar was the essence of social revolution itself and embodied the mythical value structure and ideals of Dalits. Baburao Bagul writes:

> It was for the same reason that writers—of today as well as of tomorrow— whose works have the potential to be placed in the tradition of great literature of the world, call themselves Dalit writers. (Dangle, 289). 'Post-Ambedkarite aesthetics' continues to thrive on the legacy of Ambedkar, and therefore it remains rather self-reflexively Ambedkarite. But the Ambedkar it seeks to recreate or cherish is amply renewed in the sense that it does not directly bring him into the course of narration. As dalit autobiography grows beyond Ambedkar's Maharwada, or Maharasahtra as a region, it begins to derive a lot from local dalit movements or social reform movements. The new dalit aesthetics inspired as it is by Marathi literature written by a battery of neo-Buddhists, is not autonomous enough to merit a nomenclature without any reference to Ambedkar. In the 1980s dalit women's narratives agitated their way into a public sphere in which the stories of dalit movement and women's movement were described under the influence of Ambedkar movement. Later these dalit writers used the autobiographical mode as a sense of assertion of their neglected selves. As a chief architect of Indian constitution, Ambedkar worked hard to fight rights or society based on equality and social justice.

References

Ambedkar, B.R., (1998), *Writings and Speeches*. Vol.1. Ed. Vasant Moon. Mumbai: Education Department. Government of Maharashtra.

——(1991), *Writings and Speeches*. Vol. 9. Ed. Vasant Moon, Mumbai: Education Department. Government of Maharashtra.

——(1991), *Writings and Speeches* Vol.10. Ed. Vasant Moon, Mumbai: Education Department. Government of Maharashtra.

Dangle, Arjun. (1992) (Ed.), *Poisoned Bread: Translations from Modern Marathi Dalit Literature*. Mumbai: Orient Longman Ltd.

Jaffrelot, Christophe (2005), *Dr Ambedkar and Untouchability: Analysing and Fighting Caste.* Orient Longman.

Kumar, Raj (2010) *Dalit Personal Narrative: Reading Caste, Nation and Identity.* Hyderabad: Orient Blackswan PTD.

Limbale, Sharan Kumar (1984), *The Outcaste (Akkarmashi*). New Delhi: OUP.

Prasad Chander Bhan (2006), *Dalit Phobia: Why do they hate us?* New Delhi: Vitasta Publishing House.

Zelliot, E. (1992), *From Untouchable to Dalit: Essays on Ambedkar Movement.* New Delhi: Manohar.

9

Ambedkar's Views on Education for Women Empowerment and Role of ICT in Its Implementation

— *Rohini Arora*

Abstract

Women empowerment is multi-dimensional concept. Dr B.R. Ambedkar had said that education is the key to achieve success. This statement focuses on education as the prime dimension of empowerment for women. This key concept acts as the baseline for women empowerment in India in which Ambedkar had given emphasis on education of women which is the foundation of economic empowerment. Education enhances employment opportunities for women and their ability to make decisions. This paper focuses on Ambedkar's views on education as tool for women empowerment and role of ICT in implementing his views in today's digital era.

[**Keywords:** *Women Empowerment, Information and Communication Technology (ICT), Education, Digital Era*].

Introduction

The operations of caste both at the systemic level and at the functioning of patriarchy, the growing caste / class divide in feminist political discourse makes Ambedkar's view on women's oppression, social democracy, caste and Hindu social order and philosophy, significant to modern Indian feminist thinking (Ambedkar, 1987). Although Ambedkar proved, himself to be a genius and was known as a great thinker, philosopher, revolutionary, jurist – par excellence, prolific writer, social activist and critic and strode like a colossus in the Indian socio-political scene unto his death, his thoughts never received adequate attention in the generality of Indian society just because he was born as an untouchable. However, the contemporary social realities warrant close examination of the wide range of his topics, the width of his vision, the depth of his analysis, and the rationality of his outlook and there essential humanity of his suggestions for practical action. Hence, for Indian women's movement Ambedkar provides a powerful source of inspiration to formulate a feminist political agenda which simultaneously addresses the issues of class, caste and gender in the contemporary socio-political set up, which still keeps conservative and reactionary values in many respects, particularly on gender relations. Ambedkar saw women as the victims of the oppressive, caste-based and rigid hierarchical social system.

Education as Tool for Women Empowerment

Education's unique power to act as a catalyst for wider development goals can only be fully realised, however, if it is equitable. Women must fully benefit from educational opportunities if they have to enjoy the empowerment benefits that come with it (Charmus, Jacques and Wieringa, Saskia, 2003). Education for women and girls has varied benefits towards their empowerment ranging from health, self-defence, political participation, leadership, entrepreneurship, to democracy and governance and employment opportunities (William, Hamlet, 2010). Education empowers women in several perspectives. Some of the perspectives include:

Equal education boosts economic growth for women: Education not only helps women and girls to escape poverty by developing the skills they need to improve their livelihoods, but also generates productivity gains that boost economic growth substantially. For growth to reduce poverty, however, it needs to overcome inequality by improving the lives of the poorest and marginalised women and girls. Education is vital to achieve this goal because it can help ensure that the benefits of growth are fairly shared with women and girls as well.

Health: Women education is critical in helping them with an empowered approach to health issues. Women at times die of health-related diseases which could be preventable upon education. Educated women are more likely to avoid these dangers, by adopting simple and low cost practices to maintain hygiene, by reacting to symptoms, and by making sure a skilled attendant is present at birth.

Education is vital to eliminate malnutrition in the long term: Malnutrition is the underlying cause of more than a third of global child deaths. Educated mothers are more likely to ensure that their children receive the best nutrients to help them prevent or fight off ill health, know more about appropriate health and hygiene practices, and have more power in the home to make sure children's nutrition needs are met.

Education enhances job opportunities, helping women to escape poverty: Educated women are more likely not just to be employed, but to hold jobs that are secure and provide good working conditions and decent pay. By benefiting women in particular, education can help narrow gender gaps in work opportunities and pay. As well as helping lift households out of poverty permanently, education guards against them falling into poverty.

Education empowers women to overcome discrimination: Girls and young women who are educated have greater awareness of their rights, and greater confidence and freedom to make decisions that affect their lives, improve their own and their children's health and chances of survival, and boost their work prospects. Ensuring that girls stay in school or get engaged with education is one of the most effective ways of averting child marriage and early birth. Education is also a key factor in hastening the demographic transition to lower birth and mortality rates.

Education is indispensable in strengthening the bonds that hold women in communities and societies together: Education helps people understand democracy, promotes the tolerance and trust that strengthen it, and motivates women to participate in politics and claim for leadership positions.

Role of Information and Communication Technology in Women Empowerment

The main aim of this ICT-based projects for education of women is to sensitise the community towards the dangers of unemployment leading to poverty and also the neglect of education for girls. According to Lyndsay, the aim is also to solicit their support to lower these levels as much as possible. In achieving this aim we hope to create opportunities for women to use their potential successfully by getting vocational education. Due to lack of knowledge, information and orientation in Vocational Education the grass root level women cannot understand the need of immunisation, importance of growth monitoring or technique. Vocational Education supports career development and social protection of individuals, maintains competitiveness of employed and supports self-employment and entrepreneurship. In India women play a central role in family, community and social development. However, women often remain invisible and unheard. Women more than men have to balance the complexities of surviving in extreme poverty, yet these women are excluded from discussion because they are often illiterate, they lack confidence and they lack mobility. ICT offer the opportunities for direct, interactive communication even by those who lack skills, who are illiterate, lack mobility and have little self-confidence (Plomp, T.; Pelgrum, W. J. and Law, N., 2007). Women can be benefited and get education through and Communication Technology (ICT) simultaneously with their central role and the major area that can be covered under this includes the following:

- Women's increased access to job market and improve entrepreneurship using ICT.
- Increase of average household income in villages.
- Shrinking Information Asymmetry through ICT.
- Improved Governance.
- Indigenous Knowledge.
- Easy-Family communication.
- Increase Social awareness.

Conclusion

Dr B.R. Ambedkar had set many guidelines which are the baselines for empowering women to make them independent in the society. He had given great emphasis on women education in his life and mentioned that education is the key to success. According to his views education make women not only socially independent but economically also. This paper focused on women education and role of information and communication technology in implementing this baseline. Through ICT it is easy for women to get education with no limitation on time and location.

References

Ambedkar, B.R. (1987), "Women and Counter Revolution", "Riddles of Hindu Women" in Dr Baba Saheb Ambedkar: Writings and Speeches, Vol. 3.

Ambedkar, B.R., "The Rise and Fall of the Hindu Woman: Who was Responsible for it?", originally published in the journal, The Mahabodhi (Kolkata), Vol. 59, May-June, 137-51, Reprinted in BAWS, Vol. 17, Part 2, Section 4, (Mumbai: Government of Maharashtra), 109-23.

Charmus, Jacques and Wieringa, Saskia (2003), 'Measuring Empowerment: An Assessment of the Gender Related Development Index and the Gender Empowerment Measure', *Journal of Human Development and Capabilities*, Vol. 4, No. 3, 419-435.

Plomp, T.; Pelgrum, W. J. and Law, N. (2007), 'SITES2006—International comparative survey of pedagogical practices and ICT in education', Education and Information Technologies Vol.12, No. (2), pp; 83- 92.

Lyndsay Green, "Gender-based Issues and Trends in ICT Applications in Education in Asia and the Pacific", UNESCO Meta-survey on the Use of Technologies in Education.

William, Hamlet's (2010), "Blackberry : a practical philosophy for building a good life in the digital age", 1st ed., New York : Harper.

10

Relevance of B.R. Ambedkar in the Renewal of Untouchability and Upliftment of Scheduled Castes

— *Dr Mona Arora*

Abstract

Dr Ambedkar analysed Hindu society before starting his struggle against untouchability and the caste system. He was a scholar as much as a man of action. Ambedkar tried hard to show the mechanisms of the caste system and clarified the origin of untouchability in order to support his fight for equality. For him, if the lower castes were not in a position to overthrow their oppressors, it was because of two reasons: they had partially internalised hierarchy; and because of the very characteristics of caste-based inequality.

(**Keywords:** *Hindu society, caste system, untouchability, hierarchy).*

Introduction

Dr B.R. Ambedkar (1891 – 1956) was a great modern social thinker, a born fighter, a famous lawyer and a humanist. As a contemporary of Gandhi Ji he rendered a yeoman service to the nation by way of his relentless fight against untouchability, inequality, injustice and casteism. He is even remembered for his contribution to the drafting of the Constitution of India.

Since Ambedkar himself had suffered as an untouchable at the hands of caste Hindus, he carried on his battle against untouchability and urged to do away with it. He started a paper called "Mooka Nayaka" and organised Bahishkrita Hitakarini Sabha, a depressed classes union. He endeavoured to convene All India Conference to bring all the untouchable castes under one banner." All India depressed classes Conference". But due to non-co-operation of his own community people, he was not able to achieve it. However, he continued his campaign against untouchability, establishing a political party and a couple of organisations. Pandit Nehru rightly described him as the "symbol of revolt against all the oppressive features of Hindu society."

Even though Gandhi Ji had brought number of ways for the removal of untouchability before the birth of Dr Ambedkar, it was Ambedkar who drew the attention of Congress organisation and entire nation towards the grave problem of untouchables and their deplorable conditions.

Dr Ambedkar's main aim in life was to remove the practice of untouchability and to take "untouchable community" towards socio-economic equality and justice. He tried to insist in minds of untouchables the idea of self dignity, self-confidence and self-respect.

Five Principles of Pancha-Sutra for the Progress of Dalits

To attain respectable status Ambedkar recommended Pancha Sutra for Dalits:

1. *Self-improvement:* To improve oneself without expecting much from others.
2. *Self-progress:* Progressing in life.
3. *Self-dependence:* Learning to lessen one's dependence on other.
4. *Self-respect:* Self dignity and never to sacrifice for it for any reason.
5. *Self-confidence:* Develop confidence in oneself, one's efforts or one's capacities.

Three Principles of Dalit Movement

Ambedkar suggested three principles of Education, Agitation and Organisation to govern "Dalit Movement". He, himself, worked to put these principles into practice. He encouraged education of Dalits through Bahishkrita Shaba, Independent Labours Party, Depressed

Classes Education Society, organised agitations in the direction of searching his goals. His own works "the direct action in respect of Chowder Tank in Mahad, Kalaram Temple at Nasik has done in a few days what million days of preaching by reformers would never have done."

Ambedkar in his efforts to raise the status of untouchables considered caste system one of the greatest obstacles. In his famous book "Annihilation of Caste" (1936), he gave a call to destroy caste system. He wrote in "Harijan" (1933), "The Outcaste is a by Product of Caste System". Nothing can emancipate the outcaste except the destruction of caste system". Ambedkar's disappointment was growing because of the perpetuation of untouchability in Hindu society. Finally, in great despair he renounced Hinduism and became a Buddhist in 1956 with his followers. He, however, died in the very same year.

In first round table conference in London in 1930, Dr Ambedkar on the behalf of depressed classes spoke about the Loath some condition of untouchables and prepared a declaration of fundamental rights of Dalits. He declared abolition of untouchability and the establishment of equal citizenship. He also demanded a separate electorate for the depressed classes. Gandhi Ji opposed this proposal and said, "The political separation of untouchables and the Hindus would be suicidal to the nation". He declared his resolution of "fast-into-death", the conflict between the two leaders was however resolved by famous "Poona Part" (1932). Thus, Ambedkar was able to get some reasonable representation for the untouchables.

Ambedkar was made the chairman of the Drafting Committee to draft the Indian Constitution. Article 17 of the Constitution abolished untouchability. Ambedkar has once declared that he would burn "Manu Smriti for its failure to provide justice to "dalits" the same Ambedkar now could get the opportunity and honour of giving to the people of India their Constitution. He is rightly called "the Abinava Manu" or ["Modern Manu"]. He was awarded the "Bharat Ratna" title posthumously.

Dr Ambedkar's thoughts and ideas are getting greater currency now. The struggle he carried on against inequality is also getting revived and reinforced. Untouchability has not yet become "the thing of the past", its removal requires a basic transformation in the general attitude towards untouchability.

Government attempts to promote the Welfare of Scheduled Castes and Scheduled Tribes can be discussed under:

(a) Constitutional and legislative measures

(b) Other welfare measures and programmes.

(a) Constitutional and Legislative Measures

Government of India has incorporated some special provisions in Constitution for removal of untouchability and to promote Welfare of Scheduled Castes and Scheduled Tribes i.e. Preamble of Constitution declares Equality, Fraternity and ensures Justice to one and all.

- Articles 15, 16, 17, 38 and 46, guarantees no discrimination on the account of caste, religion or class.
- Article 17 abolishes untouchability.
- Article 46 promotes education, agitation and economic interest of Scheduled Castes and other weaker sections.
- Article 334 relates to reservation of seats and special representation.
- Article 335 claims of Scheduled Castes and Scheduled Tribes to societies and posts.

Legislative Measures

In pursuance of provision of Article 17 which declares untouchability a punishable offence, Parliament passed Untouchability Offences Act, 1955 which was later substituted by Protection of Civil Rights Act, 1976. Offences under this Act, includes:

1. Consisting any kind of social injustice, i.e. denying access to any public place shops, parks, hospitals, educational institution, etc.
2. Preventing a person from entering a place of worship or offering prayers.
3. Drinking water from public well.
4. Refusal to sell goods or render services to a person on the grounds of untouchability is an offence punishable with imprisonment for six months or fine up to ₹ 500 or both.

Measures to Check Atrocities against Scheduled Castes and Scheduled Tribes

Scheduled Castes and Scheduled Tribes (Prevention of Atrocities) Act, 1989, came into force in January, 1990 specifies offences, which are considered as atrocities, and provides for deterrent punishments for Commission of the same.

Few Acts as Punishable Crimes

1. Forcibly occupying and cultivating the land of Scheduled Castes/Scheduled Tribes man.
2. Forcing Scheduled Castes/Scheduled Tribes to eat/drink some disgraceful substance.
3. Throwing rubbish or dead animals into the houses of Scheduled Castes/Scheduled Tribes.
4. Sexual harassment of Scheduled Castes/Scheduled Tribes woman.
5. Polluting drinking water used by Scheduled Castes/Scheduled Tribes.
6. Compelling Scheduled Castes/Scheduled Tribes for forced labour or using him as bonded labour.

(b) Other Welfare Measures and Programme for Upliftment of Scheduled Castes

1. *Appointment of National Commission for welfare of Scheduled Castes:* to safeguard the interest of Scheduled Castes/ Scheduled Tribes.
2. *Educational Opportunities:* to extend educational operation to Scheduled Castes/Scheduled Tribes. Special provisions have been made for free education, free distribution of books, uniforms, etc. giving scholarships, banking loan facilities, reserving seats for Scheduled Castes/Scheduled Tribes in Government and non-Government institutions etc.
3. *Expansion of Economic Opportunities:* For benefit of Scheduled Castes/Scheduled Tribes economic programmes include: Providing land to landless Scheduled Castes labourers:
   - Land reforms to bring benefits of land ownership.

- Poor Scheduled Castes farmers supplied with fertilisers, seeds, agricultural implements, interest-free loans, subsidy for developing dairy farming, poultry farming, animal husbandry etc. "Loan-Mela" programme of Rajiv Gandhi Government (1984-89) also provided small loans for poorer Section to earn money through secondary sources – toy making, basket making, shoe making, beedi rolling etc.

4. *Employment Opportunities and Reservation:* To enhance the economic position of Scheduled Castes/Scheduled Tribes 15 per cent and 7.5 per cent reservation is given to Scheduled Castes/Scheduled Tribes respectively.

Other Welfare Programmes

1. Drinking water facility through construction of wells and borewells.
2. Medical Facility: Free medical check ups and financial aid to Scheduled Castes/Scheduled Tribes.
3. Liberalisation of Bonded Labourers: With the help of government assistance about 1.13 lakh bonded labourers (out of total of 1.61 lakh) has been liberated. Report of labour department of Central Government, 1983.
4. Baba Saheb Dr Ambedkar Foundation was set up in March, 1992 as a registered society initially to implement four schemes:

   (i) Dr Ambedkar National Public Library

   (ii) Dr Ambedkar National Award

   (iii) Dr Ambedkar Overseas Fellowships

   (iv) Dr Ambedkar Chairs in Universities.

The foundation has been constituted to include eminent persons in the field of education, social work and development of Scheduled Castes. The scope of foundation has been enlarged to include more activities connected with the life and mission of Dr Ambedkar. These among others include publication of books, foster academic contract; promote research, instituting rewards, etc.

Voluntary Organisations

In addition to governmental schemes, some Voluntary Organisations are also playing an important role in promoting welfare of Scheduled Castes. E.g. Harijan Sevak Sanga (New Delhi), Servants of India Society (Poona), Indian Red Cross Society (New Delhi), Bharatiya Samaja Unnati Mandal (Bhivandi, Maharashtra), etc. Central Government has been giving financial assistance to these organisations for harijan welfare activities.

Evaluation of Welfare Measures

Do the welfare measures really contributed to the upliftment of Dalits? The answer is somewhat disappointing:

- Majority of Scheduled Castes are still illiterate and ignorant to make use of constant provisions given to them.
- Reports of National Commission on Scheduled Castes reveal that crime against Scheduled Castes rather increasing.
- Lack of sincerity on the part of government officials has been the cause of failure of welfare schedules.
- It is unfortunate that in spite of more than 50 years of consistent efforts to elevate the position of Scheduled Castes, expected success has not been achieved. Socially, they have not changed many of their evil customs, economically, more than 30 per cent Scheduled Castes live below poverty line, educationally they are very backward, and politically they are not organised and remain weak in local power structure for asserting their rights.
- The Dalits demand for effective implementation of Scheduled Castes/Scheduled Tribes (Prevention of Atrocities) Act and Rules and to provide full protection to all Dalits who participate in P.R. and other institutions only reveal that they still suffer from a sense of insecurity.
- The Scheduled Castes are still tradition bound. They suffer from a sense of inferiority. They are not well organised. Only in few cities, some organisations are fighting for their rights. Politically also they are not single homogenous entity.

However, younger generation of Dalits is becoming more assertive. Various constitutional provisions that safeguard their interest, on one hand, and continuous exploitation of "Dalits" on the other have led Dalit awareness. This growing awareness in them has led to the emergence of various Scheduled Castes movements.

- They have formed their own political groups e.g. Republican Party of India, Bahujan Samaj Party (Uttar Pradesh, Madhya Pradesh, Punjab, etc.).
- Demanding effective implementation of constitutional safeguards to protect their interests.
- Dalits especially the educated ones are becoming individually conscious of achieving some mobility.

However, this Dalit consciousness arises number of questions like? Will they insist on reservation for all times to come? Will this consciousness help them to forge ahead economically and educationally? What will be the impact of Dalit Consciousness on larger Hindu Society? Will they wind up the practice of untouchability?

It is difficult to find satisfactory answers for these questions. However, answer can be quoted in views of Sachidananda (1976).

The combination of factors like efforts by government, consciousness of dalits and liberal attitude of caste Hindus will diminish the disabilities and discriminations with passage of time.

References

B.R. Ambedkar, "Untouchables or The Children of India's Ghetto"1989.

B.R. Ambedkar, "The Untouchables. Who were they and why they became Untouchables?" in Dr Babasaheb Ambedkar Writings and Speeches, Vol. 7.

B.R. Ambedkar, "The Untouchables", p. 317.

B.R. Ambedkar, The Untouchables (1948).

B.R. Ambedkar, Who were the Shudras?

B.R. Ambedkar, Annihilation of Caste (1936).

12

Women: Understanding Dr Ambedkar's Vision and its Relevance in Contemporary Feminist Discourse

— ***Jasbir Kaur***

Abstract

A woman is full circle, within her is the power to create, nurture and transform- Diane Mariechild

Ambedkar was not only the father of Indian Constitution; he was a great freedom fighter, political leader, philosopher, thinker, economist, editor, social reformer, revivalist of Buddhism and was first Indian to break down the barriers in the way of advancement of women in India. He argued for extensive economic and social rights for women. He stated that women should be given all round development more importantly social education, their well being and socio-cultural rights. He emphasised that each and every section of Indian women be given their due share and it is a must to maintain and protect dignity and modesty of women. He translated many of his ideas and visions into specific policies and institutions during his stint as the architect of Indian constitution and as the law minister of India.

The present paper is an attempt to highlight Dr Ambedkar's views on women problems in pre-and post-independent India and its relevance in contemporary feminist discourse.

[**Keywords:** *Women, dignity, Indian Constitution, policies*].

Introduction

From time immemorial, the women in this land of ours were treated as a sort of thing. Her placing in the society was not at par with other human being. She has no rights. She cannot move nor does anything at her will. In Hindu Shastras, she has been branded just like animals. From the verses of Ramayana as written by Mr. Tulsi Das, "Dhol, ganwar, shudra, pashu, naari- Ye sabtadankeadhikari," one may easily draw inferences as to what status has been granted to our mothers. In 'Manusmriti' the ancient Hindu Code-book, the status granted to women is quite visible and she was put to the lowest rug of humanity as she was treated at par with the animals and slave by the proprietors of Hindu Dharma. All the law books of Hindus have very distinctly written about their degraded status.

"Let a female child be born somewhere else; here let a male child be born" - Atharva Veda 6.2.3

"Women have no right to study Vedas" -Manu Smriti IX 3

"It is the highest duty of the woman to immolate herself after her husband" - Brahma Puran. 80.75

"If a wife, proud of the greatness of her relatives or (her own) excellence, violates the duty which she owes to her lord, the king shall cause her to be devoured by dogs in a place frequented by many" - Manu Smriti VIII 371

But the women in Pre-Manu days enjoyed respectable status in the Hindu society. Women were free and enjoyed equal status along with men in matters of education, divorce, remarriage and economic independence. The deterioration in status of women in the society began with the imposition of severe restrictions on them under the influence of Manusmriti. Manu held a very low opinion about women. Thus, under the influence of Dharamshastras (*Manusmriti*), women was held in bondage lifelong and were deprived of basic human rights like right to education, right to property and right to study religious scripture.

So, today's problem of women has its origin in the vedic times. Women those days were considered inferior to women. They were equated with the Shudras/ati-shudras, the fourth/fifth varnas of the vedic religion. Women were not considered fit for spiritual attainment as they were not allowed to read Vedas. Such was the placement earmarked to our mothers, sisters and even great grand mothers that the heads of humanity bend upon down with shame!

Dr B.R. Ambedkar studied extensively the Hindu *Shastras* and *Smritis* to find out the root cause of degraded status of women in India. Dr Ambedkar was appalled at the low status of women in the Hindu society. Dr Ambedkar points out that *Shastras*, Caste and Endogamy – the three important pillars of patriarchy in Hindu society –were responsible for discriminatory practice against women and their degradation in social status.

That is why Dr Ambedkar was of the firm opinion that until or unless, by applying dynamite, the Hindu Dharma-shastras are not blown up, nothing is going to happen. In the name of sanskaras, the Hindu women are tied up with the bondage of superstitions, which they carry till their death. They are also responsible for inculcating these wrong notions learnt by them through baseless traditions and preaching of the Shastras in the budding minds of their offsprings.

Dr Ambedkar's Efforts to Uplift the Status of Women

In this direction, Dr B.R. Ambedkar has tried to break down the barriers in the way of advancement of women in India. He laid down the foundation of concrete and sincere efforts by codifying the common Civil Code for the Hindus and the principle is capable of extension to other sections of the Indian society. Prior to these efforts of Dr Ambedkar, the destiny of the Indian women depended upon the wrong notions and perceptions chalked out by the proprietors of orthodoxy. The operation of caste both at the systemic level and at the functioning of patriarchy, the growing caste/class divide in feminist political discourses makes Ambedkar's views on women's oppression, social democracy, caste and Hindu social order and philosophy, significant to modern Indian feminist thinking. The Writings and Speeches of Ambedkar show what values India should develop and how they would modernise its social and political institutions.

Through his writings, Dr B. R. Ambedkar unravels the inequality and injustice inherent in Hindu social order that perpetuates inequality and subordination of women in a systemic manner. In his treatises, "**The Rise and Fall of Hindu Women**", "**The Women and Counter Revolution**", "**The Riddle of Women**", and "**Castes in India:Their Mechanism, Genesis and Development**" through the issues of his journals **Mooknayak** (1920) and **Bahishkrit Bharat** (1927),

Dr Ambedkar has analysed the manner in which gender relations are artificially constructed under Hindu social order which not only moulds attitude of Hindus towards their women but also conditions women to confirm to a stereotype feminine behaviour, requiring them to be passive and submissive, suited only to a life of domestic and family responsibilities. He worked hard to challenge the iniquitous gender relations under the Hindu social order so that Hindu society could be reconstructed along the modern democratic ideas of liberty, equality and fraternity.

Ambedkar saw women as the victims of the oppressive, caste-based and rigid hierarchical social system. He believed that socio-cultural forces artificially construct gender relations, especially by Manusmriti and Hindu religion. As Simone De Beauvoir observed, "Women are made, they are not born."

In his paper on "Castes in India: their mechanism, genesis and development," Dr Ambedkar described how women were treated cruelly by the way of *sati*, enforced widowhood and girl marriages just to maintain strict endogamy in a caste. The social evils regarding women in Hindu religion as well as in Muslim society were highlighted by him. As a researcher, Dr Ambedkar extensively studied the position of women in both the religion (and also in the other religions) and thrown light on denial of rights to her and ultimately the status of individual. He stated that the consequences of *purdah* system on Muslim women were that it deprives her of mental and moral nourishment.

"We shall see better days soon and our progress will be greatly accelerated if male education is persuaded side by side with female education..." were the words of young Ambedkar, during his studies at New York which came out while writing a letter to his father's friend. He started fierce propaganda against the Hindu social order and launched a journal Mook Nayak in 1920 and Bahiskrit Bharat in 1927 for this purpose. Through its issues he put due stress on the gender equality and the need for education and exposed the problems of the depressed as well as women.

On December 25, 1927 at a Conference of Depressed Classes held at Mahad, Dr B.R. Ambedkar made a bonfire of Manusmriti in presence of more than fifty women to protest against the discrimination of women and untouchables upheld by it. At the end of the Conference,

Dr Ambedkar also addressed a meeting of about three thousand women of the Depressed Classes, the first meeting of its kind in modern India and urged them to dress well and live a clean life. Do not feed your spouse and sons if they are drunk. Send your children to schools. Education is necessary for females as it is for males. He said, "I measure the progress of community by the degree of progress which women had achieved." He strongly believed in the fact that if "a woman is educated a family is educated". He not only encouraged them to get educated themselves but also encouraged them to educate their children and keep them away from all kinds of vices. He strongly opposed taking of intoxicants that was because he realised that most cases of domestic violence occurred under their influence.

In January 1928, a womens association was founded in Mumbai with Ramabai, Ambedkar's wife, as its president. In the Kalaram Temple Entry Satyagraha at Nasik in 1930, five hundred women participated and many of them were arrested along with men and ill-treated in jails. To face tortures along with their men, women also organised their *Samata Sainik Dal.* The encouragement of Dr Ambedkar to empower women to speak boldly was seen when RadhabaiVadale addressed a press conference in 1931. She said "It is better to die a hundred times than live a life full of humiliation. We will sacrifice our lives but we will win our rights." The credit for this self-respect and firm determination of women goes to Ambedkar. Dr Ambedkar believed in the strength of women and their role in the process of social reform.

In his address at the Depressed Classes Women's Conference held at Nagpur on July 20, 1942 under the presidentship of Mrs Sulochanabai Dongre in which 25000 women attended, Dr B.R. Ambedkar said, "I am a great believer in women's organisations. I know what they can do to improve the condition of society if they are convinced. In the eradication of social evils they have rendered great services". Speaking on marriage and parental responsibilities, he advised women to get married only when they are financially able. They should stand by their husband as a friend and equal and refuse to be his slave. He reminded them that having too many children is a crime. The paternal duty lies in giving each child a better start than its parents had. He concluded his address, "I am sure if you follow this advice, you will bring honour and glory to yourselves".

Dr Ambedkar also championed the cause of women within the Legislative Council as well. As a member of Mumbai Legislative Council, he raised the problems of Indian women in the discussion within the Council and sought their solutions. His arguments on the Maternity Benefit Bill and on Birth Control were quite relevant to recognise the dignity of women. Supporting the Maternity Benefit Bill for women labourers in his speech, he said:

> "It is in the interest of the nation that the mother ought to get a certain amount of rest during the pre-natal period and also subsequently and the principle of the Bill is based entirely on that principle——.That being so Sir, I am bound to admit that the burden of this ought to be largely borne by the government. I am prepared to admit this fact because the conservation of the people's welfare is primarily the concern of the government. And in every country, you will find that the government has been subjected to a certain amount of charge with regard to maternity benefit."

Besides, he highlighted the issues of Muslim women. His secular perspective is known through his thoughts on "Purdah" (Veil) system, religious conversions and legal rights for Muslim women. In short, along with the depressed class women, his thoughts for emancipation of all the women are expressed with same allegiance. Ambedkar's emphasis was on reconstruction of the Hindu society on the basis of equality rather than the social reforms initiated by Brahma Samaj or Arya Samaj because their attempts were limited only to the upper caste. The extent of awakening achieved among the women of downtrodden classes was visible from the fact that the Women's Conference demanded abolition of polygamy and urged institutions of pensions and leave with pay for women workers.

As the first Law Minister of independent India, Dr B.R. Ambedkar introduced Hindu Code Bill in the Parliament in February 5, 1951 so as to codify Hindu laws pertaining to marriage, divorce, inheritance that sought to give equal rights to women vis-à-vis men in these aspects. However, the bill was strongly opposed by orthodox Hindu opinion on the ground that it would lead to break-up of Hindu social order (patriarchy) if the bill was passed in that form. The government lacked political will to pilot the bill through Parliament and decided to withdraw it. To register his protest against government inaction, Dr B.R. Ambedkar resigned from the Union Cabinet.

Dr Ambedkar sought that Buddhism awards women, status equal to men and considered women capable of attaining spirituality. By adopting Buddhism, Dr Ambedkar expelled in just for underprivileged segments including women and accepting the dignified equal status. Dr Ambedkar denied worshipping Hindu deities, ultimately freed women from inhumane customs, rituals and superstitions and made the way for her liberation.

Relevance of his Ideas

Dr B. R. Ambedkar can be regarded as one of the greatest intellectual and social reformer of modern India who struggled throughout his life for the liberation of Indian women (particularly from depressed classes) from the lifelong bondage and slavery under the weight of Hindu social institutions. By conceptualising caste and gender inequality as inseparable constituents of Hindu social order, Dr B.R. Ambedkar laid the foundations for gradual transformation of Indian social consciousness and gender justice in India.

The vision of Dr Ambedkar about women is explicitly depicted in Indian Constitution. Equality of sexes is strongly backed by the constitution through Articles 14, 15 and 16. The principle of gender equality is enshrined in the Indian Constitution in its Preamble, Fundamental Rights, Fundamental Duties and Directive Principles. He laid down the foundation of social justice and there can be no social justice without gender equality.

Dr B. R. Ambedkar not only wrote extensively to counter the orthodox Hindu opinion against women but worked as an activist and social reformer at the grass roots level to organise and empower women of depressed classes so that they could fight to reclaim their social rights such as right to drink water from their source and right to enter temple that were traditionally denied to them by the caste Hindus. It was due to the encouragement by Dr Ambedkar that a large number of women came out openly on the public streets to reclaim their social rights and self-respect.

Since Ambedkar was well convinced about the status of women, as the chairman of the Drafting Committee, he tried adequate inclusion of women's rights in the political vocabulary and Constitution of India. Therefore, by considering women's equality both in formal and sustainable senses he included special provisions for women while all other general provisions were applicable to them, as to men. Hence, there are Articles like 15(3), 51(A), and so on. His key work in the Indian Constitution made it to be known as a New Charter of Human Rights. He looked upon law as the instrument of creating a sane social order in which the development of individual should be in harmony with the growth of society.

As a member of the Mumbai Legislative Council, Dr B.R. Ambedkar was in the forefront in championing the cause of women's empowerment by forcefully arguing for the passage of Maternity Benefit Bill. As the Law Minister in the Union Cabinet, Dr Ambedkar made every effort for the passage of Hindu Code Bill despite staunch opposition from vested interests. This shows the great importance he attached to the cause of gender equality in India.

Although his efforts did not, entirely go waste. Later, the original Bill was split into four different Bills with slight changes. Those were passed as the Hindu Marriage Act,1955; The Hindu Succession Act,1956; the Hindu Minority and Guardianship Act,1956; and the Hindu Adoption and Maintenance Act1956. As Lord Casey said, Ambedkar stands as the "fountainhead of wisdom and knowledge" in modern India.

Constitutional Provisions for the Cause of Women

As the Chairman of Constitution Drafting Committee, Dr Ambedkar made a pioneering contribution in introducing Articles 14, 15, 16, 39, 42 in the Indian Constitution that guarantee protection to women from any kind of discrimination.

Artticle 14-Equal rights and opportunities in political, economic and social spheres.

Article15 prohibits discrimination on the ground of sex.

Article 15(3) enables affirmative discrimination in favour of women.

Article 16 provides for Equality of Opportunity in matters of public employment.

Article 23 prohibits trafficking in human beings and forced labour.

Article39-Equal means of livelihood and equal pay for equal work.

Article 42- Just and human conditions of work and maternity relief.

Article 46-The state to promote with special care, the educational and economic interests of the weaker section of the people and to protect them from social injustice and all forms of exploitation.

Article 47-The state to raise the level of nutrition and the standard of living of its people and the improvement of public health and so on.

Article 51(A) (c) Fundamental duties to renounce practices, derogatory to the dignity of women.

Article 243D (3), 243T(3) and 243R(4) provides for allocation of seats in the Panchayati Raj System.

Various Laws for Protection of Women

There are number of protective laws in India to prevent exploitation of women. To quote few, Sati Prevention Act 1987, Dowry Prohibition Act 1961, the Family Courts Act 1984, Protection of Human Right Act 1993, The Maternity Benefit Act 1961, Immoral Traffic (Prevention) Act 1956, The Child Marriage Restraint Act 1929, The Pre-Natal Diagnostic Technique (Regulation and Prevention of Misuse) Act 1994, The legal Practitioners (women) Act 1923 and so on.

On the direction and guidance of the constitution of India various revolutionary laws giving equal status to women with men have been enacted in order to remove all disparities, dissimilarities against women. The Equal Remuneration Act 1976 and National Commission for Women Act 1990.

Like Ambedkar, The National Policy for the Empowerment of Women 2001, also admits, "The underlying causes of gender inequality are related to social and economic structure...and practices. Consequently, the access of women, particularly those belonging to weaker sections including Scheduled Castes/ Tribes Other Backward Classes and Minorities...to education, health, and productive resources, among others is inadequate. Therefore, they remain largely marginalised, poor and socially excluded". The Policy includes creating an environment through positive economic and social policies for full development of women to enable them to-realise their full potential, Equal access to participation and decision making of women in social, political and economic life of the nation, strengthening legal systems aimed at limitation of all forms of discrimination against women.

The newly enacted Protection of Women from Domestic Violence Act 2005 provides effective relief to women facing violence, such as preventing dispossession from the shared household to them, this act does not make domestic violence a crime. It is only the violation of a court order in case of dispossessions that makes a person guilty of an offence.

"It is the education which is the right weapon to cut the social slavery and it is the education which will enlighten the downtrodden masses to come up and gain social status, economic betterment and political freedom," was the view of Dr Ambedkar. Various steps have been taken by the Government of India for the education of women. To bring girl children, especially from BPL families, into the mainstream of education, government has been providing a package of concessions in the form of free supply of books, uniform, boarding and lodging, clothing, midday meals scholarships, free bicycles and so on.

In order to improve the entrepreneurial ability and skill of women, government has been imparting various types of training designed to promote self and wage employment. Provision of skill training to women in Self help groups has been given recognition so as to enable them to start their own income-generating activities. The duration of the training and cost depends upon the nature of trade selected by the members.

To provide secured accommodation to the working women, Working Women Hostels have been established. The work participation rate indicates to a great extent the economic empowerment of women in the society. The status of women is intimately connected with their economic position, which in turn depends on the opportunities for participation in economic activities. There has been a considerable improvement in the entry of women in all sectors of employment in the country. Political equality to all children regardless of birth, sex, colour, etc. is one of the basic premises of democracy. Political equality includes not only equal right to franchise but also more importantly, the right to access to the institutionalised centres of power. Thus, political participation of women means not only using the right to vote but also power sharing, co-decision making and co-policy making at all levels.

In January 1992, the National Commission for Women was set up by an Act of Parliament with the specific mandate to study and monitor all matters relating to the constitutional and legal safeguards.

Now there is a greater representation in legislature, executive and judiciary. India is one of the few countries in the world, which has had a woman Prime Minister. Various states from time to time have women Chief Ministers. Women have crossed many barriers and head various departments in large multinationals today. A beginning has been made in the Army also, when women are being commissioned as SSC officers. The 73rd and 74th Amendments to the Indian Constitution were brought about in 1993, which served as a breakthrough towards ensuring equal access and increased participation in the political power structure.

But unfortunately, in the present times despite the various Constitutional safeguards and various laws claiming equality to all citizens, women are denied rights enjoyed by a citizen of this country. In fact, she is denied even the basic right to live. She may bring the man into the world by carrying him in her womb for nine months yet she is not allowed to live another day once it is known that it is 'she' and not 'he' there in the womb. It is found that though advances are being made in the field of science and technology, worldwide literacy rates have risen yet old societal norms seem to govern the day.

Most people are literate but not educated. Education by means of access to knowledge and learning played pivotal role the social reforms. Stagnation in process of social reforms and imposing so called divine status of ancient women on today's women there by influencing her development and upliftment. Shattered with the reforms and liberation of women in the era of globalisation and modernisation, the Indian mindset has not accepted the equality at par with men and hence forcing women to revert their development. There are many examples of women harassment in the form of beating, child marriage, acid throwing, domestic violence, female infanticide and sex selective abortion, rape, traffing and the list is endless.

In such a situation when immorality seems to be the order of the day how is a woman expected to get herself educated and contribute to the progress of the country? Dr Ambedkar greatly emphasised on a society based on moral values. Education is incomplete without instructions in moral values. According to Dr Ambedkar, "Morality comes in only when Man comes in relation to Man. It arises from the direct necessity from Man to love Man. It does not require the sanction of God. It is not to please God that Man has to be moral but for the good of the society."

Increasing incidences in women harassment in all way, violence, crime and humiliation insisted on her is only because of political apathy, which failed to kept social dogma. Education system, employment opportunities, tremendous population, inflation and non-availability of resources to strive are the barriers for development among people. Sheer influence of modern lifestyle and adopting technology doesn't mean improvement of individual and society.

The societal framework meant to make women subordinate or subjugated need to be dismantled. Active participation of women from all the strata could make it possible. Many notable women activist are working on issues like environment, health, poverty etc. Those who indulge in social reforms were not supported, not even by women. Women reservation bill is the hottest agenda of the discussion and fact is that a lay woman even doesn't know what it is. The more ridiculous male attitude is that girl's education meant only for her marriage. Today's women are trapped in the circle of insecurity, male domination, lack of awareness about her rights and no decision-making powers.

Much is talked about women empowerment today but it is more economic, political and health related. Moreover, the empowerment of women in urban areas and the metropolises cannot be the indicator of growth in the country, in the country where eighty per cent population is in rural areas. Until the lot of women in these areas is also not improved simultaneously, development will remain an illusion to them. So the issue of social empowerment of women need to be raised higher and given utmost importance then only it could complete phenomena. Moreover, the Constitution Provisions and Acts are not sufficient.

We must concentrate on imparting social education. It will not be prudent on our part to restore the rights of the women belonging to the affluent section of the society only. Therefore, our efforts should be directed towards all round development of each and every section of Indian women by giving their due share. It is a must to maintain and protect chastity, dignity and modesty of women. It is the need of the hour to give due share to each and every section of the Indian women. I am sure, without removing social stigma, no progress or development could be achieved.

Conclusion

To conclude, it can be said that Dr Ambedkar ideas are of great relevance to Indian society to achieve social justice, removal of untouchability, in establishing equality and true Democracy. The role played by Dr Babasaheb Ambedkar, as chairperson of the Drafting Committee of the Constitution, has left imprint on the social tapestry of the country after independence, and shaped the socio-political fabric of the India today. It would have been a different India without him and, in a probability, a much more inequitable and unjust one. He attempted to forge India's moral and social foundations a new and strove for a political order of the constitutional democracy that is sensitive to disadvantaged, inherited from the past or engendered by prevailing social relations. Dr Ambedkar had the highest academic credential for an Indian of his time, and his erudition and scholarship have been widely acknowledged.

References

Ahir, D.C. (1990), *The Legacy of Ambedkar*. Delhi.

Ambedkar, B. R. (1979), "*Castes in India: Their Mechanism, Genesis and Development*", in Dr Baba Saheb Ambedkar: Speeches and Writings, Vol. 1, Education Department, Government of Maharashtra, 1916.

____________(1987), "*Women and Counter Revolution", "Riddles of Hindu Women*" in Dr Baba Saheb Ambedkar: Writings and Speeches, Vol. 3, Department of Education, Government of Maharashtra.

____________(1950), "*The Rise and Fall of the Hindu Women*", The Mahabodhi (Calcutta).

Arya, Sudha (2000), *Women Gender Equality and the State*. Deep and Deep Publications : New Delhi.

Chirakarode, Paul (1993) *Ambedkar: Boudhika Vikshobhathinte Agnijwala*, Dalit Books, Thiruvalla.

Heywood, Andrew (1998) *Political Ideologies: An Introduction.* Macmillan Press, London.

Keer, Dhanjay (2009), *Dr Babasaheb Ambedkar: Life and Mission.* Popular, Prakashan : Mumbai.

Kumar, Vinay (2014) (ed.), Dr B.R. Ambedkar's ideology and its contemporary Relevance – I. 21st Century Publications : Patiala.

Limaye, Champa (1999), *Women: Power and Progress.* B.R. Publishing Corporation: New Delhi.

Mallik, Basant Kumar (1993), "*Ambedkar on Women's Progress*", in Grover, Verinder (ed.) B.R. Ambedkar, Deep and Deep Publications : New Delhi.

Shabbir, Mohammad (1998), (Ed.) Ambedkar on Law, Constitution and Social Justice, Rawat Publication.

Sharma, Sanjay Prakash (2003) (ed.), Dr B.R. Ambedkar- A Cruseder of Social Justice.

Sheetal Sharma (2006), "Educated women empowered women", *Yojana,* October, Vol. 50.

12

Revisiting Ambedkar's Idea of Social Justice in Global Age of India

—*Devinder Kaur*

Abstract

Dr Ambedkar's concept of social justice means a mode of life to give every man his right place in society. Its precepts may be: to live honourably, to give respect to all, to injure no one, and to give every man his due without any artificial discrimination in mind and unnatural classification in society. Ambedkar admits that it is a problem not merely of distributing the material abundance among the people but basically a mode of life based on mutual respect and regard, a feeling of fellowship as equal members of a society. Hence the measure of social justice is not material progress, but the abundance and proliferation of human values among the people. Now-a-days it is a wider and broader concept. We can include linguistic and religious minorities, schedule castes and schedule tribes, deprived and untouchables, mentally challenged, physically disabled and women etc. under the umbrella of social aspect of justice. Due to globalisation the social problems have also became worldwide or global. Privatisation and urbanisation have changed the role of welfare state to maintain and protect the social justice. This paper investigates the enlarged dimensions of social justice with the Ambedkar's idea of social justice in Indian society.

[**Keywords:** *social justice, discrimination, religious minorities, privatisation*].

Introduction

Social justice is a comprehensive and compact phenomenon. Social justice as pointed out **John Rawls** in ***the theory of social justice*** is that a society can be regarded as egalitarian only when it is based on principles of equality and solidarity, where human rights are valued and the dignity of every individual upheld. A just society is one which provides a degree of protection to its weaker, differently able and less gifted members. Provision of human rights in Universal Declaration of Human Rights together with the International Convention on Social and Economic Rights contain progressively the aim of promoting the social justice worldwide. As stated in Article 1 of the Universal Declaration of Human Rights: "All human beings are born free and equal in dignity and rights." In accordance with modern political trend Indian constitution has provided fundamental rights to protect the human rights of Indian citizens. Enlightened citizens are required for the enjoyment of rights, equality and social justice but there was a lack of political consciousness among the people at the time of independence. The constitution provides social justice by which we means to abolish all types of discriminations on the grounds of caste, colour, creed, sex, place of birth or religion etc. and to achieve this proper arrangement have been made in Article 14-18. Since independence governments are making policies and programme to achieve the social justice. After the collapse of USSR, like many developing countries India entered in the age of globalisation. Due to globalisation the social problems have also became worldwide or global. Privatisation and urbanisation have changed the role of welfare state to maintain and protect the social justice. This paper investigates the enlarged dimensions of social justice with the Ambedkar's idea of social justice in Indian society.

Social Justice and Ancient Indian Society

According to K.S. Hegde, the inclusion of fundamental rights in India's constitution had its beginning in the forces that operated on the national struggle during the British rule. They have their roots in the history of the last several centuries. They are mainly the product of history. [K.S. Hegde, 1971: pp. 50-72]. So to understand the place of social justice in society and changing idea of social justice with the passage of time, its compulsory to understand the social structure of Indian society. In ancient India, the individual was subject to the ideological control of the joint family, the caste and the village community and therefore it was obligatory for him to conform to the standards prescribed by these three institutions [D C Chaturvedi, 1992:10]. Social norms for individuals were very strict. Community or individuals had no right to intervene in the affairs of the ruling class. Intervention or any kind of struggle was considered as revolt or serious offence. It was considered injustice. According to Shriram Yerankar. "The ancient Hindus also tried to solve the problem of social justice by dividing the society into four varnas: Brahmana, Kshatriya, Vaishya, and Sudras based on division of duties and occupation, Manu said, in general," it is better to discharge one's own dharma incompletely or imperfectly (vigunah) than to perform completely that of another (na parakyanh Sivanushthitah)". [Shriram Yerankar: Yojana 2011:35]. The right to revolt against the unjust monarch was not granted to Shudras. They were not allowed to bear arms and were left completely defenseless. [B.G. Gokhle, 1961:163-164]. In the name of divine religion, justice and morality, numerous inhuman practices developed among the so called higher strata of society. From Vedavada emanated Brahmanvada and Manuvada, which made the Indian society a hell for most of people, especially the Shudras and the untouchables. [D.R. Jatava,1998:02].

Ambedkar's Social Justice and Constitution of India

Division of society on the basis of duties and occupation and further on the basis of birth in a particular caste or religion was justified as social justice in ancient Indian society. But with the passage of time many social reformers fifteenth to nineteenth century criticized the social discriminations against shudras and women in society. The twentieth century was in influence of socialistic ideology. According to K. Marx, "If man is shaped by his surroundings" he wrote, "his surroundings must be made human." [K. Marx and F. Engles, 1956:176]. Like many other countries the Indian freedom fighters were also against the racial discriminations and social and economic inequalities. For the social reformers in Indian society, social justice means to give equal respect, protection and equal freedom to women, to remove discriminations against Dalits, Poor and the weaker sections of society, to create favourable conditions for labour and also the removal of forced labour and drudgery. Jyotiba Phule, Mahatma Gandhi, Ambedkar and many others have given stress on the inclusion of depressed classes in society. Ambedkar himself belongs to a dalit family so he observed closely the problems and discrimination against depressed classes. Dr Ambedkar was an intellectual who laid emphasis on equality of all Indian citizens as well as the dignity of each individual. Dr Ambedkar was the chairman of drafting committee and thus also an architect of Indian Constitution. Dr Ambedkar, firstly began with the general idea of justice. He was a revolutionary leader and a forceful fighter. His own definition of justice is given in *Writings and Speeches* is very clear and precise that, "justice is simply another name of liberty, equality and fraternity."

Ambedkar expressed his disappointment with the content of the Objective Resolution. He expressed in it a clear enunciation of the doctrine of socialism. (C.A.D) Ambedkar's draft contained an elaborate clause designed to establish state socialism in important fields of economic life by the law of the Constitution itself so that the implementation of the plan would not be left to the will of the Legislature. [Gokulesh Sharma, 1997:26]. There have thus been four main trends in the realm of thought in India- Liberal, Extremist, Gandhian and Socialists. Nehru and Ambedkar were also influenced by socialism. They believe that the solution of many Indian social problems lies in socialism. The contents of Ambedkar's concept of social justice included unity and equality of all human beings, equal worth of men and women, respect for the weak and the lowly, regard for human rights, benevolence, mutual love, sympathy, tolerance and charity towards fellow beings. Humane treatment in all cases of dignity of all citizens, abolition of caste distinctions, education and property for all and goodwill and gentleness. He emphasised more on fraternity and emotional integration. His view on social justice was to remove man-made inequalities of all shades through law, morality and public conscience, he stood for justice for a sustainable society. [Purohit and Joshi, 2003:189].

Dr Ambedkar's concept of social justice means a mode of life to give every man his right place in society. Its precepts may be: to live honourably, to give respect to all, to injure no one, and to give every man his due without any artificial discrimination in mind and unnatural classification in society. Ambedkar admits that it is a problem not merely of distributing the material abundance among the people but basically a mode of life based on mutual respect and regard, a feeling of fellowship as equal members of a society. Hence the measure of social justice is not material progress, but the abundance and proliferation of human values among the people.

Backward classes are presumed to be the important minorities in the country. B.R. Ambedkar, in the Draft Constitution of India, covers special provisions relating to minorities including schedule castes, and scheduled tribes along with religious and other minorities of India. Thus the backward classes in India form an aggregate of closed status groups; they belong to these groups by birth, not because of their individual economic characteristics. [Kuppuswamy: 1986]

On the eve of independence there was little disagreement about the need for pluralism and provision of justice for minorities. In the constitution assembly Dr B.R. Ambedkar made the point clear saying:

To diehards who have developed a kind of fanaticism against minority protection I would like to say two things. One is that minorities are an explosive force witch, if it erupts, can blow up the whole fabric of the state. The history of Europe bears ample and appalling testimony of this fact. The other is that the minorities in India have agreed to place their existence in the hands of the majority. In the history of negotiations for preventing the partition of the Ireland, Redmond said to Carson "ask for any safeguard you like for the Protestant minority but let us have a united Ireland." Carson's reply was, "Damn your safeguards, we don't want to be rule by you." No minority in India has taken this stand. They have loyally accepted the rule of majority, which is basically a communal majority and not a political majority. It is for the majority to realise its duty not to discriminate against minorities. Whether the minorities will continue or will vanish must depend upon this habit of the majority. The moment the majority loses the habit of discriminating against the minority, the minority can have no ground to exist. They will vanish. [A.S. Narang, 2002:63] The constitution of India has provided enough scope for social justice. It promised not only political democracy but also social democracy as explained by Dr Ambedkar in the concluding speech in the Constitutional Assembly:

"Political democracy cannot last unless there lies at the base of it social democracy. What does social democracy means? It means a way of life which recognised liberty, equality and fraternity which are not being treated as separate items in a trinity. They form a union of trinity in the sense that to divorce one from the other is to defeat the very purpose of democracy. Liberty cannot be divorced from equality; equality cannot be divorced from liberty. Nor can liberty and equality be divorced from fraternity."

Why is fraternity essential for social justice? For, as Dr Ambedkar elucidated, "Fraternity is another name for fellow-feeling. It consists in a sentiment which leads an individual to identify himself with the good of others whereby the good of others becomes to him a thing naturally and necessarily to be attended to like any of the physical conditions of our existence.' [Sabine, G.H., 1973:64]. This fellow feeling is very important because only legal and constitutional provisions can never be enough to change the traditional superior mind sets. In India, we have a long history of caste-based and religious conservatives, who were always, involve in dividing people in the name of religion and dogmatism. Feeling of others, fear and lack of trust factor or mistrust are the main enemies to which equality and fraternity can kill, but it is not so easy in a fragmented society which is divided on the basis of caste, religion, race creed, and gender. Thus, social justice seems to be an endless process. Feeling of fraternity is a practice of 'Humanity' which is the best religion. People should believe on the inner strength of individuals.

The Preamble of Indian constitution uses the term social justice-social, economic and political. India has opted for liberal democratic model. The Part III and IV of our constitution laid emphasis on the concept of social justice. The Part III is a separate chapter on fundamental rights in Indian constitution. It also explains the scope and methods of social justice. Article 38 directs the state to promote the welfare of the people by securing and protecting, as effectively as possible, a social order in which justice- social, economic and political- shall inform all the institutions of national life. Article 17 lies down:

"Untouchability" is abolished and its practice in any form is forbidden. The enforcement of any disability arising out of 'untouchability' shall be an offence punishable in accordance with law".

Article 42 enjoins the state to secure just and humane conditions of work, and to provide for material relief. Many directive principles of state policy are socialistic principles.

B.C. Chaturvedi concludes that the economic rights conceded by the directive principles are based on the ideas which have been borrowed from the twin concepts of socialism and welfare state.

Prof. Kameshwar Choudhary on the occasion of Parinirvan Diwas of Dr B.R. Ambedkar said, "Ambedkar's Idea of social justice was based on our indigenous historical, social and cultural roots" [Times of India, 2010].

Changing and Broadening the Concept of Social Justice in Global Age

On the 26th January 1950, we are going to enter into a life of contradictions. In politics we will have equality and in social and economic life we will have inequality...we must remove this contradiction at the earliest possible moment or else those who suffer from inequality will blow up the structure of political democracy which this assembly so laboriously built up.

–Dr B.R. Ambedkar

Now-a-days, it is a wider and more broader concept. We can include linguistic and religious minorities, schedule castes and schedule tribes, deprived and untouchables, mentally challenged, physically disabled and women etc under the umbrella of social aspect of justice. As D.R. Jatava accepts that it is therefore, not possible to contain social justice in one formula, or it cannot be defined strictly in fixed terms. [D.R. Jatava,1998: p. 62]. Social justice provides an improved environment and favourable conditions for human rights. Post independent India accepted the concept of a welfare state with socialistic and mixed economic system with a view of upbringing the deprived classes. Government launched and implemented many policies for the inclusion of socially excluded groups in society. Efforts were continue to remove the inequality and poverty which are the main obstacles in the path of social justice achievement but the expected results were not achieved and with the fall of USSR, fell into a financial crunch in eighties. Social justice and harmony were still in its childhood. To cope with this situation India adopted the new economic policy based on western model suggested by IMF and the World Bank.

Broadly speaking, social justice stems from the idea that all human beings are entitled to the fulfillment of certain basic needs and rights, regardless of their social differences such as economic disparity, class, gender, race, ethnicity, religion, age, sexual orientation, disability or health. (Neo Simutanyi, 2008). Similarly, another scholar Bajwa, G.S. defines human rights as a dynamic concept, "In earlier usage the word 'right' had a legal connotation. For example, the individual had an inalienable right to life and he could not be deprived of that right by the state without due process of law. Today the word 'right' has also the connotation of a goal: for example, the individual has the right to free education, free legal aid, pollution free environment, free medical care etc. which the state is expected to provide. [Bajwa, G.S., 1995]. These statements put light on the wider canvas of social justice which introduced many new dimensions of fundamental rights as right to pollution free air, right to pure water, right to mental hygiene, right to good governance, basically social justice means to create an environment in which individual can enjoy his right to life in a dignified manner.

Conclusion

To sum up we can say that Bharat Ratna Dr Bheem Rao Ambedkar was a very intellectual social thinker who has given a visionary and dynamic shape and nature to our Constitution. People of India love him as Baba Saheb and Masiha. Basically it is Ambedkar's idea of social justice which is flourished and nourished in the global age. The idea of social justice which was implemented in ancient india is now looking as hundred years of injustice in society. As Bajwa, G. S., says that understanding of human rights depends much upon the conditions and opinions prevailing in the given society, at a given time and it attains new dimensions with the march of history.

Its really true because Manu has made social system of his own times. How it can be totally accepted after 2000 years? Social justice in our Constitution is a legal and written documentation. But as earlier said social justice is an endless movement, after more than 67 years of Indian constitution enactment, governments have a lot to do in the era of globalisation. social justice has generated the idea of social inclusion and financial inclusion where each policy and programme should be in reach of the every individual in the society.

References

K. Marx and F. Engles (1956), *The Holy Family or critique of critical critique,* Foreign language pub. House Moscow: 176.

B.G. Gokhle (1961), *Indian thought through the Ages*. Asia Publications House, Mumbai: 163-164.

D.C. Chaturvedi (1992), *Indian Fundamental Rights*. Saru Publishing House, Meerut (Uttar Pradesh): 10.

K.S. Hegde (1971), *Directive principles of state policy in Constitution of India* S.C.J: 50-72.

Gokulesh Sharma (1977), *Human Rights and Social Justice,* Deep and Deep Publications: New Delhi.

Dr Ambedkar, *Writings and speeches,* Vol. 3: 25.

A.S.Narang (2002), Ethno-Nationalism and minorities in India", in Akhtar Majeed, ed. *Nation and Minorities*, Kanishka Publishers: New Delhi: 63.

Kuppuswamy, B. (1986), *Social change in India*, New Delhi: Vikas Publishing House.

D.R. Jatava (1998), *Social Justice in India,* Ina Shree Publishers: 62.

Sabine, G.H. (1973), *A History of Political Theory*: 64.

Purohit, B.R., Sandeep Joshi (2003), *Social Justice in India*, Rawat Publications: Jaipur : 189.

Times of India, December 07, 2010.

Bajwa, G.S. (1995), Socio-political Dimensions of human rights in India: A Retrospective Study, in Sehgal, B.P.S. (Eds), *Human rights in India: Problems and Perspectives.* Deep and Deep Publications: New Delhi.

Neo Simutanyi (2008), "The African Debate on Social Justice." Paper presented to the Friedrich Ebort Stiftung- Tanzania/Chama Cha Mapinduzi Youth Leage Regional Forum on *youth perspective and social justice,* Dar es Salaam, Tanzania, 23-27 November.

Rawls John (1971), *"A Theory of Justice*", Oxford: Clarendon Press.

Shriram Yerankar (2011), "*Social justice in the Indian context*", Yojana, April: 35-37.

12

Ambedkar's Vision of a Mere Democratic India

— Nirmal Singh

Abstract

The encounter of democracy with caste is a historical process accommodating two sets of opposed values. There is a common understanding that caste is antagonistic to democracy. Indeed, the hierarchical universe of the caste system is theoretically at odds with the equalitarian requirements of substantive democracy. The political culture of Indian society is leading to more and more social contradictions. On one hand we aspire to become egalitarian society and, on the other, the caste culture negates this very aspiration. And what is more problematic we cannot become egalitarian without the help of this very caste culture, at least in economic sense. The present paper is an attempt to understand Ambedkar's views on caste system and Indian democracy. Paper has two-fold objectives, first, to understand and analyse caste system in India, and second, to explore Ambedkar's vision of social democracy.

[**Keywords:** *Democracy, caste system, egalitarian society, caste culture*]

Introduction

Basic root of Ambedkar's philosophy was to establish a mere democratic India. Inequalities could not be the bases of this very system and in Indian context; he articulates a casteless society based on the principles of liberty, equality and fraternity. When Ambedkar tried to explore the hierarchical nature of Hindu Social orders, it did not mean that he was merely criticising the orders without any further planning.

Ambedkar interrogated the caste ridden Hindu society on the criterion of democracy and observed that "Caste system is a grave impediment in the path of democracy. The roots of democracy lie not in the form of the government but in the social relationships and the terms of association between the people who form the society. Community of purpose, desire of welfare, loyalty of public ends and mutuality of cooperation are essential hallmarks of the democratic society. A scheme of government does not exist in vacuum, it operates within the society. Its usefulness depends upon its relationships with the other sphere of society. Elections, parties and participation are, after all formal institutions of democracy. They cannot be effective in an undemocratic atmosphere. Political democracy means the principle of "one man one vote" which indicates political equality. But if oppression and injustice exists, the spirit of political democracy would be missing. Democratic government therefore, should be an expansion of a democratic society. Democratic society is characterised by absence of stratification of society into classes and the social habit on the part of individuals and groups which ready for the continuous readjustment of recognition of reciprocity of interests. Looking from this perspective, the purpose of democracy is not so much to put a curb on an autocratic king but to bring about the revolutionary changes in the social and economic life of the people without any bloodshed.

Ambedkar viewed democracy as an instrument of bringing about change peacefully. Democracy does not merely mean rule by the majority or government by the representatives of the people. This is a formalistic and limited notion of democracy. We would understand the meaning of democracy in a better fashion if we view it as a way of realising drastic changes in the social and economic spheres of society. Ambedkar's idea of democracy is much more than just a scheme of government. According to Ambedkar, Democracy is a way of life which requires everyone to respect the rights of every human being to be a person, a unique entity. Democracy is not an attempt at uniformity, which is impossible, but an integrated verity. He viewed that all men are not equal in their capacity but all men are equally necessary for society. We must begin by acknowledging the fact that there is a complete absence of two things in Indian society. One of these is equality. On the social plane, we have…a society based on principles of graded inequality which means elevation for some and degradation for others. On the economic plane, we have a society in which there are some who have immense wealth as against many who live in abject poverty.

Dr Ambedkar's View on Caste System

Caste is undoubtedly an all India phenomenon in the sense of that they are hereditary, endogamous groups which form a hierarchy, and that each of these groups has a traditional association with one or two occupations. This is in fact, a regression from Ambedkar's analysis of the place of labour in the caste system........ Caste system is not merely division of labour; it is also a division of labourers..... It is a hierarchy in which the divisions of labour are graded one above the other. For Dr Lohia, it is meaningless to talk of equality while maintaining separate castes. Castes have to be abolished. In 1935, at *Yevla* in Nasik district, Maharashtra, B.R. Ambedkar had declared his firm resolves to change his religion. He said that "To reform the Hindu society is neither our aim nor our field of action. Our aim is to gain freedom. We have nothing to do with anything else (Ambedkar, 1987: 263-64)." The struggle for the emancipation of the depressed classes from the thralldom of untouchability and casteism has been in continuation for a pretty long time. However, the Dalit liberation movement got an impetus during the British period. With the dawn of democratic institution in India, the Dalit liberation movement steadily became more vocal, assertive and effective.

Dalit as a socio-political concept appears frequently in the contemporary discussion on Indian politics. It has become a form of academic violence which promotes casteist myths. Thus, Dalits become a static community. The term Dalit is referred to broken, ground downtrodden people who become subject to deliberate act of exploitation by those above them in a hierarchical social system. The term "Depressed classes" was mentioned in the Census report 1921, but since the enactment of the Government of India Act 1935, the Dalits are consistently referred to as "Scheduled Castes".

Mahatma Jyotirao Phule could properly realise the importance of education in improving the lot of the untouchables and backwards castes. He stated very categorically that, "For want of education intellect deteriorated. For want of intellect morality decayed. For want of morality progress stopped. For want of progress wealth vanished. For want of wealth the *Shudras* perished. All these sorrow sprang from illiteracy (Mahatma Phule, 1980: 189). The principle of graded inequality has been carried into the economic field. "From each according to his ability, to each according to his need" is not the principle of the Hindu Social order. The principle of the Hindu Social order is: From each according to his need to each according to his nobility (The illustrations given above are merely drawn from imagination. They are facts of the history).

Phule strongly attacked the exploitation of peasants by the bureaucracy, Ambedkar and Periyar both supported and helped the organised movements of peasants against landlords. The denial of temple entry to Dalits by status quo and conservative caste Hindu is seen as a part of the social oppression that is still intertwined with class oppression as most of the Dalits are poor farm workers. Dalits have been denied entry into temples. Ambedkar's scathing comment on Hindu scripture culminated in a public burning of *Manusmriti* in 1927 and in 1935 Ambedkar announced his vow to leave Hinduism entirely and to convert to some other religion (Eleanor Zelliot. 2008: 193). Mehar satyagraha and *Kalaram* satyagraha were also an attempt to gain entry in the temples. The main figures of this larger anti-caste movement, Jyotirao Phule, B.R. Ambedkar, and E.V. Ramaswami 'Periyar' with many others throughout India attacked the system of exploitation at all levels, culturally, economically and politically. They asserted that Hinduism, had not been the religion and culture of the majority but rather it was an imposed religion. Phule tried to formulate a new theistic religion, Periyar promoted atheism, Ambedkar turned to Buddhism.

Through conversion movement, Dalits offer a new alternative religion, Buddhism, in negation of Hinduism. It started with Ambedkar's personal conversion announcement in 1935 which was followed by a *Mahar* conference in 1936 where Ambedkar declared, if you want to make the world in which you live, happy, change your religion; if you want independence, change your religion. The conversion movement made an immense appeal to the Dalits, through its benefits are mostly limited to mental relax but other size impact is remarkable (B.R. Ambedkar, 1987: 192). If the Dalit question could be answered by religion, i.e., if the problem is somehow the bane of

Hinduism alone, non-Hindu religion should have solved the problem a long time ago. What is the condition of Dalits, for example, in a state like Punjab where Sikhism, as egalitarian and non-Hindu religion has had to sway for three centuries? The charge is equally placed at the doorstep of Christianity (Shyam D. Babu and Chandra Bhan Prasad, 2009: 23).

Ambedkar asked that: Can a leopard change its spots? No, never. "Hinduism is like the leopard there can be no "Hindu" without a caste...... untouchability is a part and parcel of Hinduism. If you become Muslims, you will get the political rights as Muslim; if you become Christian, you will get the political rights as Christians; if you become Sikhs, you will have your political safeguards as Sikhs. In short, our political rights will accompany us (B.R. Ambedkar, 1987). Through sanskritisation movement, a section of untouchables who could improve their economic condition, either by abandoning or continuing their traditional occupations. A low caste was able, in a generation or two, to rise to a higher position in the hierarchy by adopting vegetarianism or teetotalism, and by sanskritising its rituals and pantheon (M.N. Srinivas, 1952: 32). They tried to justify their claims to a higher social status in caste hierarchy by inventing suitable mythologies. Ambedkar had famously declared that the untouchables had two enemies: Brahminism and capitalism. His first political party, the Independent Labour Party (ILP), was fashioned on the lines of the British Labour Party, which followed the Fabian line of peaceful transition to socialism but abhorred capitalism. Ambedkar's ILP was then the true leftist party of India, with the communities then going the Congress party. The ILP, on the other hand, demonstrated in practice how to embed caste and class in the struggle for social justice.

Ambedkar's Vision of Social Democracy

Ambedkar emphasises the need for bringing about an all-round democracy. Ambedkar's vision of social democracy emanates from his quest for a "just society" which is based on the idea of a casteless society. He not only provided a ruthless criticism of the existing social order but also came up with an alternative vision and alternative model of social order based on liberty, equality, fraternity and annihilation of caste. Dr Ambedkar says: "Democracy is not a form of government, but a form of social organisation. After India's independence for dispensing social justice in the wake of emerging democracy in a hierarchically arranged society, Ambedkar discussed the operationalisation of principles of equality, liberty and fraternity, which were considered to be cardinal principles of any democracy. For social justice, he tries to find a creative combination of democracy and modernity. He looked at democracy as an initial condition or the sphere which could be used for converting opportunity into an asset. For him conversion could be achieved only through modernity. Ambedkar tends to treat democracy as an initial condition of social justice both as consciousness and also as a material possibility.

John Rawls developed the following principles of justice: (a) each person is to have an equal right to most extensive basic liberty compatible with similar liberty for others, (b) social and economic inequities are arbitrary unless they are reasonably expected to be to the advantage of the representative man in each income class, (c) inequalities are to attach to positions and offices equally open to all. Similarly, taking a leaf from Rawl's theory of social justice argues that, "the fundamental issue in distributive justice is equality; a more equal or at least a less unequal distribution of the benefits and of social co-operation". He opines that:

Rawl, concept of social justice would mean giving every man his due. The basic aim of social justice is to remove the imbalances in the social, political and economic life of the people to create a just society. "In that sense distributive justice to go beyond equality in the purely formal sense: equality before the law, seeks to go beyond equality in the purely, formal sense: equality before the law, the equal protection of the laws, or even formal equality of opportunity. Its central concern is, in the language of Rawls 'to address the bias of contingencies in the direction of equality'...Any attempt to promote distributive justice must begin with a consideration of the existing inequalities in society...it is essential to keep in sight both inequalities between individual and disparities. Disparities between groups have been historically go great significance in Indian society".

John Rawls idea of distributive justice opposed that "all social values are to be distributed equally unless an unequal distribution of any or all of these values is to everyone's advantage". Ambedkar's idea of social justice is tantamount of the concept of justice propounded by John Rawls, who includes in his theory of distributive justice an "element of the difference principles, in Ambedkar's case, it is the principle of special treatment. Both these principles of justice require a distribution of resources that will most effectively satisfy the needs of worst off (Gopal Guru, 2001). In terms of culture-specificity, the term social justice has a different meaning in Indian society. It means dispensing justice to those to whom it has been systematically denied in the past because of an established social structure. Ambedkar's Quest for social justice can be visualised in the philosophy, policy and ideals of the constitution of India. On the basis of these, it can easily argue that Ambedkar has mentioned multiple principles for the establishment an open and just social order in general and Indian society in particular. Ambedkar was of the opinion that social justice can be dispensed in a free social order in which an individual is end in itself. Similarly, the term of associated life between members of society must be regarded by consideration founded on liberty, equality and fraternity. In a way these principles of social justice are similar to the principles of social justice as mentioned in Rawl's theory.

To Ambedkar "A democratic form of the government presupposes a democratic form of society. The formal framework of democracy is of no value and would indeed be a misfit if there was no social democracy. The political leaders never realised that democracy was not only a form of government; it was essentially a form of society. To Ambedkar, the aim of democracy is essentially the practical interests of society as a whole, and not of any class group or community. Democracy as a social organisation is meant that it includes all members of society. For this purpose, Ambedkar had to fight against tyranny, injustice and false tradition in order to release the suffering people from bondage. He vigorously struggled against injustice, social slavery, inequality and poverty. To him, true socialism would not tolerate ill-treatment and oppression, because these are opposed to socialism. The present social orders are not suited to create a socialist spirit among the people.

State socialism is not based on bloody revolution as Marx argued. Ambedkar believed that bringing socialism is the duty and the responsibility of the state. State shall provide protection against economic exploitation and shall work towards making equalitarian society. Ambedkar said that "Caste is the monster that crosses your path, you cannot have political reforms, and you cannot have economic reforms, unless you kill this monster. Ambedkar said that political democracy cannot last unless there lies at the base of it social democracy. What does social democracy mean? It means a way of life, which recognises liberty, equality and fraternity as the principles of life. The Indian state needs to be reformed and reinvented are manifestly clear. The question is: do we have the state which can finally redeem the pledges made by the framers of the constitution which can make India, in Ambedkar term, a social democracy rather than a mere political democracy?

References

A.M. Shah. (2002), "The 'Dalit' Category and its Differentiation". *Economic and Political Weekly,* Vol. 37, No. 14, 6 April: 1317-1318.

Ambedkar, B.R. (1987), *Why Go For Conversion?* Bengaluru: Dalit Sahitya Akademy.

Ambedkar, Dr Babasaheb. (1990), *Yanche Bahishkruit Bharat ani Muknayak (Marathi) [translated to mean the Depressed India or Front runner].* Education Department. Government of Maharashtra.

Ambedkar, B.R. (1945), *What Congress and Gandhi have done to the Untouchables.* Mumbai:Thacker and Co.

Anand, Mulk Raj and Eleanor Zelliot. (1992) (eds.), *An Anthology of Dalit Literature.* New Delhi: Gyan Prakashan.

Anand, Mulk Raj. (1990) (ed.), *Annihilation of Caste: Undelivered Speeches of Dr B.R. Ambedkar*. Delhi: Arnold Publishers.

B.R. Ambedkar. (1987), *Go For Conversion*, Bengaluru: Dalit Sahitya Acadamy.

B.R. Ambedkar. (1987), *"Why Go For Conversion*?" Bengaluru: Dalit Sahitya Akademy, p.192.

D.N. (1991), "Ambedkar and Separate Electorates Issues". *Economic and Political Weekly,* Vol. 26, No. 21, 25 May: 1328-1330.

Eleanor Zelliot. (2001), *From Untouchable to Dalit*, New Delhi: Manohar Publishers and Distributors.

Eleanor Zelliot. (2008), "Gandhi and Ambedkar: A Study in Leadership". In Ishita Banerjee (ed.), *Caste in History*. New Delhi: Oxford University Press, p. 193.

Emanual Nahar. (2007), Minority Politics in India. Chandigarh: Arun Publishing House Pvt. Ltd.

G.K. Karanth. (2004), "Replication or dissent? Culture and Institutions among Untouchable' Scheduled Castes in Karnataka". In Dipankar Gupta (ed.), *Caste in Question.* New Delhi: Sage Publication, p. 161.

Ghanshyam Shah. (2001), *Dalit Identity and Politics*, New Delhi: Sage Publications.

Guru, Gopal and Geetha, V. (2000), "New Phase of Dalit-Bahujan Intellectual Activity". *Economic and Political Weekly,* XXXV, No. 3: 15-21 January.

Guru, Gopal. (2001) "The Language of Dalit Bahujan Political Discourse" in Ghanshyam Shah (ed.), *Dalit Identity and Politics.* New Delhi: Sage Publications.

John Rawls. (1971), A Theory of Justice. Harvard University Press.

Kalpana Kannabira. (2009), "Sociology of Caste and the Crooked Mirror: Recovering B.R. Ambedkar's Legacy", *Economic and Political Weekly,* XLIV, No. 4, 27 January, p. 37.

Lajpat Rai. (1909), Speeches and Writings, *Modern Review*, Vol.1, July.

Lata Murugkar. (1991), *Dalit Panther Movement in Maharashtra*. Mumbai: Popular Prakashan, pp. 54-55.

Louis Dumont. (1999), *Homo Hierarchicus: The Caste System and its Implications.* New Delhi: Oxford University Press, pp. 66-67.

M.N. Srinivas. (1952), *Religion and Society among Coorgs of South India.* Delhi: Oxford University Press, p. 32.

M.N. Srinivas. (1972), *Social Change in Modern India*, Delhi: Orient Longman.

Mahatma Phule. (1980), *Samagra Vigmaya*. Mumbai: Maharashtra Rajya Sahitya and Sanskriti Mandal, p. 189.

Nandu Ram. (1995), *Beyond Ambedkar*. Delhi: Har Anand Publications, p. 87.

Nirmal Singh. (2011), "Dr Ambedkar and the Renewing Scenario of Dalit Identity". In Dr S.S. Randhawa and Sardool Singh (eds.), *Dr Ambedkar's Philosophy of Social Justice.* Chandigarh: Salaria Publication House.

Nirmal Singh. (2012), "Insight of Caste System in India: Its Reflection in 21th Century" International Research Analysis and Evaluation, International Indexed & Referred Research Journal, December: Vol. IV, Issue- 39.

Nirmal Singh. (2014), "BSP in Punjab: Analysing its Failure" *Economic and Political Weekly* (EPW), November 29: Vol. XLIX, No. 48.

Rajni Kothari. (1994), "Rise of Dalits and the Renewed Debates on Caste". *Economic and Political Weekly*, Vol. 26, No. 26. 25 June: 1590.

Ronki Ram. (2001), "From Servitude to Assertion: Ambedkar's Subaltern Approach to Nationalism and Dalit Liberation". *Social Sciences Research Journal* (Chandigarh). Vol. 9, No. 2: 146-170.

Ronki Ram. (2004), "Untouchability in India with a Difference: Ad-Dharm, Dalit Assertion and Caste Conflict in Punjab". *Asian Survey*, XLIX, No. 6, November-December: 895-912.

Ronki Ram. (2004) 'Limits of Untouchability, Dalit Assertion and Caste Violence in Punjab". In Harish K. Puri (ed.), *Dalit in Regional Context*, New Delhi: Rawat Publications.

Ronki Ram. (2009), "Regional Specificities and Caste Hierarchies in Punjab". *Indian Journal of Politics,* Vol. 43, No. 2: 15-29.

Ronki Ram. (2009a), "Bhakti and Social Protest: Guru Ravidass and the Rise of the Dalit Consciousness in Punjab. *Indian Journal of Politics*. Vol. 43, No. 4: 43-64.

Ronki Ram. (2010), Dalit Chetna: Sarot te saroop, Chandigarh: Lokgeet Prakashan.

Rudolph Lloyd I and Susanne Hoeber Rudolph. (1967), *The Modernity of Tradition*, Delhi: Orient Longman Limited.

S.R. Bharati. (2002), "Dalit, a Term Asserting Unity". *Economic and Political Weekly,* XXXVII, No. 42, 19 October, pp. 4339-40.

Shyam D. Babu and Chandra Bhan Prasad. (2009), "Six Dalit Paradoxes", *Economic and Political Weekly*, XLIV, No. 23, 6 June, p. 23.

Surinder S Jodhka. (2003) "Caste Tension in Punjab", *Economic and Political Weekly,* Vol. 37, No. 28, July 12: 2923-26.

Surinder, S. Jodhka. (2007), "Internal Classification of Scheduled Castes: Punjab Story" *Economic and Political Weekly*, Vol. XLII, No. 43, October 27, 2007.

Susan Bayly. (1999), *Caste, Society and Politics in India*. Cambridge: Cambridge University Press, p. 14.

13

Women Empowerment in India and Dr B R Ambedkar

— *Kanchan Chandan*

Abstract

Dr Ambedkar the determined fighter and a deep scholar has made significant efforts to lead the society on the path of Liberty, Equality and Fraternity. He was first Indian to brake down the barriers in the way of advancement of women in India. He laid down the foundation of concrete and sincere efforts by codifying the common Civil Code for Hindus and other sections of the Indian society. The present paper is an attempt to highlight Dr Ambedkar's view on women problems in pre-and post-independent India and its relevancy in present scenario. Dr Ambedkar started his movement in 1920. He started fierce propaganda against the Hindu social order and launched a journal Mook Nayak in 1920 and Bahiskrit Bharat in 1927 for this purpose. Through its issues he put due stress on the gender equality and the need for education and exposed the problems of the depressed as well as women. The encouragement of Dr Ambedkar to empower women to speak boldly was seen when Radhabai Vadale addressed a press conference in 1931. He strongly advocated for family planning measures for women in Mumbai Legislative Assembly. Dr Baba Saheb spent his life for the betterment of women even involved in bad practices and professionals like prostitutions. Ambedkar created awareness among poor, illiterate women and inspired them to fight against the unjust and social practices like child marriages and devdasi system. Dr Ambedkar tried an adequate inclusion of women's right in the political vocabulary and constitution of India. He insisted on Hindu Code Bill suggesting the basic improvements and amendments in assembly. He also insisted and evoked all the parliamentary members to help to pass the bill in parliament. Eventually, he resigned for the same. Thus, his deep concern and feelings for all round development of women is expressed from his each sentence and word.

Introduction

Dr B.R. Ambedkar was among the most outstanding intellectuals of India in the twentieth century in the word. Paul Baran, an eminent Marxist economist, had made a distinction in one of his essays between an "intellect worker" and an intellectual. The former, according to him, is one who uses his intellect for making a living whereas the latter is one who uses it for critical analysis and social transformation. Dr Ambedkar fits Baran's definition of an intellectual very well. Dr Ambedkar is also an outstanding example of what Antonio Gramsci called an organic intellectual, that is, one who represents and articulates the interests of an entire social class. Dr Ambedkar the determined fighter and a deep scholar, secured the highest academic honours from some of the most prestigious universities of the world. He made significant efforts to lead the society on the path of Liberty, Equality and Fraternity. It is proved by a recently conducted survey by History TV 18 and CNN IBN in June 2012. Who is the greatest Indian after Mahatma Gandhi? Is the question asked from the people of India? The contestants include, First PM Jawahar Lal Nehru, Singer Lata Mangeshkar, Industrialist J.R.D.Tata, A.P.J.Abdul Kalam, Indira Gandhi and Vallabhbhai Patel etc. The final cumulative ranking was conducted following the three ways poll; ranking by jury (online and on ground), ranking by popular votes and ranking by market research. Finally, Dr B.R. Ambedkar declared as winner. Historian Ramchandra Guha stated on the declaration of results "Dr Ambedkar's legacy has been distorted to suit particular interests. He was a great scholar, institution builder and economic theorist" Prof. A. K. Sen has also said, "Ambedkar is my Father in Economics. He is true celebrated champion of the underprivileged. He deserves more than what he has achieved today. However, he was highly controversial figure in his home country, though it was not the reality. His contribution in the field of economics is marvelous and will be remembered forever." Ambedkar was not only the father of Indian Constitution; he was a great freedom fighter, political leader, philosopher, thinker, economist, editor, social reformer, revivalist of Buddhism and was first Indian to break down the barriers in the way of advancement of women in India.

He laid down the foundation of concrete and sincere efforts by codifying the common Civil Code for Hindus and other sections of the Indian society. He stated that women should be given all round development more importantly social education, their well being and socio-cultural rights. He emphasised that each and every section of Indian women be given their due share and it is a must to maintain and protect dignity and modesty of women. Dr Babasaheb Ambedkar always believed in movements led by women. He also added that if the women from all walks of life are taken in to confidence, they may play a significant role in the social reforms. They have played very massive and active role to eradicate the social abuses. He insisted that every married woman must participate in her husband's activities as a friend. But she must show the courage to deny the life of slaves. She should insist on the principle of equality. If all the women follow it, they will get the real respect and their own identity.

Objectives, Methods and Materials

The present paper is an attempt to highlight Dr Ambedkar's view on women problems in pre-and post-independent India and the relevancy of his ideas in present political and social scenario of India. Secondary data collected from internet, published papers, books and speeches delivered by Dr Ambedkar in Parliament, various conferences and meetings in pre-and post-independent India.

Analysis and Discussion

Dr Ambedkar started his movement in 1920. He stated, "We shall see better days soon and our progress will be greatly accelerated if male education is persuaded side by side with female education." He started fierce propaganda against the Hindu social order and launched a journal Mook Nayak in 1920 and Bahiskrit Bharat in 1927 for this purpose. Through its issues he put due stress on the gender equality and the need for education and exposed the problems of the depressed as well as women. Ambedkar's perception of women question, emphasising their right to education, equal treatment with men, right to property and involvement in the political process resembled the global feminists demand. As J. S. Mill expressed in the Subjection of Women, the legal subordination of one sex to the other is wrong in itself and one of the chief hindrance to human development; and ought to be replaced by a principle of perfect equality, admitting no privilege or power on the one side, nor disability on the other, Ambedkar also holds the same views on work for women. In January 1928, a women's association was founded in Mumbai with Ramabai, Ambedkar's wife, as its president. In the Kalaram Temple Entry Satyagraha at Nasik in 1930, five hundred women participated and many of them were arrested along with men and ill treated in jails. The encouragement of Dr Ambedkar to empower women to speak boldly was seen when Radhabai Vadale addressed a press conference in 1931. She said "It is better to die a hundred times than live a life full of humiliation. We will sacrifice our lives but we will win our rights." The credit for this self-respect and firm determination of women goes to Ambedkar. Dr Ambedkar believed in the strength of women and their role in the process of social reform. The historic Mahad Satyagraha witnessed participation of three hundred women along with their male counterparts. Addressing another meeting of about 3000 women, he said, "I measure the progress of community by the degree of progress which women had achieved. Let every girl who marries stand by her husband, claim to be her husband's friend and equal, and refuse to be his slave. I am sure if you follow this advice, you will bring honour and glory to yourselves."

He strongly advocated for family planning measures for women in Mumbai Legislative Assembly. In 1942, being a Labour Minister of Executive Council of Governor General, he introduced a Maternity Benefit Bill. He provided several provisions in the constitution for protecting the welfare and civil rights of women. He introduced the Hindu Code Bill in the Parliament and highlighted the issues about women's property right. The bill received strong opposition from many political leaders. In turn, Dr Ambedkar resigned from the cabinet expressing his discontent over non-acceptance of woman's right by the parliament. Besides, he highlighted the issues of Muslim women. His secular perspective is known through his thoughts on Purdah system, religious conversions and legal rights for Muslim women. In short, along with the depressed class women, his thoughts for emancipation of all the women are expressed with same allegiance. Ambedkar's emphasis was on reconstruction of the Hindu society on the basis of equality rather than the social reforms initiated by Brahmo Samaj or Arya Samaj because their attempts were limited only to the upper strata of the society. His in-depth study of Smritis and Shashtras and his experience from the response of upper castes during the temple entry movement crystallised his conclusions on Hindu philosophy and society. Gaining inspiration from Ambedkar, many women wrote on various topics. And Tulsibai Bansode started a newspaper Chokhamela. This shows how Ambedkar created awareness among poor, illiterate women and inspired them to fight against the unjust and social practices like child marriages and devdasi system.

Dr Babasaheb Ambedkar exclaimed, "I strongly believe in the movements run by women. If they are truly taken in to confidence, they may change the present picture of society which is very miserable. In past, they have played a significant role in improving the condition of weaker sections and classes. He always honoured women for their work and hardships. While addressing in conferences to women he could easily communicate with them as a homely person and conversation. He evoked women in the following words. "Never wear such clothes which will degrade our personality and character. Avoid wearing the jewellery on your body everywhere. It is not fare to make hole on nose and wear nath." In this he condemned all the bad traditions, habits and ways of life which made life difficult and complex. And to the surprise, even the illiterate women followed his advice from the bottom of their heart.

Dr Ambedkar spent his life for the betterment of women even involved in bad practices and professionals like prostitutions. The greatest example of it was seen in Kamathipura. There was a person named David who was the mediator working in brothel. He left his profession persuaded by the thoughts and teachings of Dr Babasaheb Ambedkar. He evoked the entire prostitute to give up their profession and lead the life of honour. In the Manu Smriti, Manu not only shows contempt for women but goes on to degrade them as slaves, devoid of intellect; denies them the right of education and the right to property; and forbids them from performing sacrifices. Being India's first Law Minister and chairman of Drafting Committee of the Constituent Assembly, Dr Ambedkar thought it appropriate, rather his duty, to free women from the age old thralldom by reforming the Hindu social laws created by Manu. He, therefore, took initiative to draft and introduce the Hindu Code Bill in the Constituent Assembly.

Dr Ambedkar tried an adequate inclusion of women's right in the political vocabulary and constitution of India. i.e. Article14 - Equal rights and opportunities in political, economic and social spheres. Article 15 prohibits discrimination on the ground of sex. Article 15(3) enables affirmative discrimination in favour of women. Article 39 – Equal means of livelihood and equal pay for equal work. Article 42 – Human conditions of work and maternity relief. Article 51 (A) (C) – Fundamental duties to renounce practices, derogatory to the dignity of women. Article 46 – The state to promote with special care, the educational and economic interests of weaker section of people and to protect them from social injustice and all forms of exploitation. Article 47 – The state to raise the level of nutrition and standard of living of its people and the improvement of public health and so on. Article 243D (3), 243T (3) and 243R (4) provides for allocation of seats in the Panchayati Raj System.

The Hindu Code Bill, the most formidable legislative measure of modern India, sought among other reforms, to put an end to a variety of marriage systems prevailing in India and legalise only monogamous marriages. The Code also sought to confer on women the right of property and adoption which had been denied by Manu. It put men and women on an equal level in all legal matters. Dr Ambedkar said, "I should like draw attention of the house to one important fact. The great political philosopher Burke who wrote his great book against the French Revolution said that those who want to conserve must be ready to repair. And all I am asking this House is: If you want to maintain the Hindu system, Hindu culture and Hindu society, do not hesitate to repair where repair is necessary. This Bill asks for nothing more than to repair those parts of the Hindu system which have become dilapidated." In his letter of resignation dated the 27 September, 1951 to the Prime Minister, he wrote "For a long time I have been thinking of resigning my seat from the Cabinet. The only thing that had held me back from giving effect to my intention was the hope that it would be possible to give effect to the Hindu Code Bill before the life of present Parliament came to an end. I even agreed to break up the bill and restricted it to Marriage and Divorce in the fond hope that at least this much of our labour may bear fruit. But even that part of Bill had been killed. I see no purpose in my continuing to be a Member of your Cabinet".

The Hindu Code Bill was later split in to four Bills and the same were put on the Statue Book by Parliament. The Hindu Marriage Act, 1955; The Hindu Succession Act, 1956; The Hindu Minority and Guardianship Act, 1956 and The Hindu Adoption and Maintenance Act, 1956 are the four enactments which incorporate the ideas and principles of Hindu Code Bill formulated by Dr Ambedkar. They give independent status to women and endow them with the right of adoption, succession and property, so completely denied by Manu. Therefore, it is truism to say that it is due to Dr Ambedkar that a large part of the Hindu social law is now on par with the legal system prevailing in advanced western countries.

Conclusion

In the condolence message, on Ambedkar's death in parliament, Prime Minister Jawaharlal Nehru said, "Dr Babasaheb Ambedkar was a symbol of revolt against all oppressive features of Hindu society". His dream of society, based on gender equality is yet to be realised and therefore his thoughts are important for the social reconstruction that favours women empowerment. Dr Babasaheb expressed his views on the state of life of all women. He stated that women must be treated equally and given equal prestige. He insisted on Hindu Code Bill suggesting the basic improvements and amendments in assembly. He also insisted and evoked all the parliamentary members to help to pass the bill in parliament. Eventually, he resigned for the same. The teachings and thoughts of Dr Ambedkar are useful not only women but also all the Indian even today. His deep concern and feelings for all round development of women is expressed from his each sentence and word. In his last speech in Indian Parliament we can know his feelings and respect showed towards women. He quoted the famous thoughts of an Irish Patriot Daniel O Connal as, "No man can be grateful at the cost of his honour, no woman can be grateful at the cost of her chastity. And no nation can be grateful at the cost of his liberty." In his famous book 'Pakistan and partition of India' he expressed his views about Muslim women and their religious traditions, about wearing veil, their marriages and so on. Muslim women were suppressed under various religious traditions. Towards all the women, irrespective of their religion, caste and class, Babasaheb had a particular humanitarianism view. He frequently raised his voice against all sorts of injustice towards women.

References

Ahir, D.C. (1990), "The Legacy of Dr Ambedkar" B.R. Publishing Corporation, New Delhi.

D. Keer, 1987, Dr Ambedkar: Life and Mission, Mumbai.

Gunjal, V.R. 2012, Dr Babasaheb Ambedkar and Women Empowerment, Social Work, Vol. XI (1), pp. 84-85.

Ambedkar, B.R. (1987), "Women and Counter Revolution" Riddles of Hindu Women" in Dr Baba Saheb Ambedkar: Writings and Speeches, Vol. 3, Department of Education, Govt. of Maharashtra.

Arya, Sudha, Women Gender Equality and the State, Deep and Deep Publications, New Delhi.

14

Dr B.R. Ambedkar-A Saviour of Indian Women

— ***Manjinder Kaur***

Abstract

Dr Ambedkar – the determined fighter and a deep scholar has made significant efforts to lead the society on the path of Liberty, Equality and Fraternity. He was first Indian to break down the barriers in the way of advancement of women in India. He laid down the foundation of concrete and sincere efforts by codifying the common Civil Code for Hindus and other sections of the Indian society. The present paper is an attempt to highlight Dr Ambedkar's view on women problems in pre-and post-independent India and its relevancy in present scenario.

*[**Keywords:** society, liberty, equality, fraternity, women]*

Introduction

Dr Ambedkar- the great fighter and a deep thinker has made significant efforts on the path of liberty. He was the first Indian reformer who roots out the barriers in the way of advancement of Indian society in general and of women in particular. Above all he was a pioneer of social justice. To secure all these goals he laid down the foundation of social justice by incorporating many factors or issues into Indian constitution through its various articles for the Hindus and other sections of the society; specially for backward communities and for under privileged classes. He started his movement in 1920. He raised his voice against the Hindu social order and social system through his renowned journal Mook Nayak in 1920 and Bahiskrit Bharat in 1927.

Almost through its all issues he spoke on the gender equality, women education and exposed the problems related to women and other depressed class. He was also a strong advocate of family planning measures for women in Mumbai Legislative Assembly. Ambedkar was an example of inspiration of many classes of society. He spent his whole life for the betterment of Indian society as well as women and other under privileged sections. He was also involved to root out the evil practices like prostitutions. He worked for the welfare of the people for his whole life. He builds up awareness among poor, illiterate women and inspired them to fight against the unjust and social practices like child marriages and devdasi system. As a result of that finally he added and incorporated many rights of women in the constitution of India. It is to be noted here that Ambedkar was not only the father of Indian constitution, he was a freedom fighter, political leader, philosopher, thinker, economist, editor, social reformer, revivalist of Buddhism and above all he was the pioneer of backward classes. He stated women of Indian society should be given equal opportunity and equal share with their male counterpart.

The encouragement of Dr Ambedkar to empower women to speak boldly was seen when Radhabai Vadale addressed a press conference in 1931. He strongly advocated for family planning measures for women in Mumbai Legislative Assembly. Dr Babasaheb spent his life for the betterment of women even involved in bad practices and professionals like prostitutions. Ambedkar created awareness among poor, illiterate women and inspired them to fight against the unjust and social practices like child marriages and devdasi system. Dr Ambedkar tried an adequate inclusion of womens, right in the political vocabulary and constitution of India. He insisted on Hindu Code Bill suggesting the basic improvements and amendments in assembly. He also insisted and evoked all the parliamentary members to help to pass the bill in parliament. Eventually, he resigned for the same. Thus, his deep concern and feelings for all round development of women is expressed from his each sentence and word.

Status of Women in Vedic Period

In the Vedic period women enjoyed all the necessary rights which are common for a human being. The women had access to all branches of learning. In Brahadaranika Upanishad (III, 6-8) we are told that in the king Janaka's Court, the maiden scholar Gargi was examined in her knowledge by Yaghavalkya (Tikoo, P.N.). The women enjoyed equal position on par with men. Even in a religious ceremony, women played an important role. No religious ceremony by men was complete without participation of his wife. For instance, Rama had to get statue of Sita made to carry on with ceremonies for Ashwamedh Yagna. In that period, the girls were free to choose their husband in open "Sayambars".

Status of Women in Later Vedic Period

The status of women in later Vedic period had been downgrading and enslaving through sexual discrimination. The socio-economic status of the women was decreasing day by day. Many orthodox principles were imposed upon them and they had been deprived of basic human rights and opportunities. They were treated as slaves. They had no choices or freedom. They had been discriminated by men and orthodoxy structure of the society; even the minority suffered at the hands of majority. They were considered as one of the three,W's- the wine, women and wealth (T. Bharathi). The women were expected to show their obedience to men. They had no property rights but they were treated as the property of men. Consequently, the women in later Vedic period had thrown in complete darkness.

Manusmriti and Gender Discrimination

The women in Pre-Manu days enjoyed respectable status in the Hindu society. Women were free and enjoyed equal status along with men in matters of education, divorce, remarriage and economic independence. The deterioration in status of women in the society began with the imposition of severe restrictions on them under the influence of Manusmriti. Manu held a very low opinion about women. According to Manusmriti, women are not to be trusted for it is in their nature to seduce men. Men are forbidden to sit in a lonely place even with one's mother, sister or daughter. Women are not to be free under any circumstances, day and night women must be kept in dependence by the males of their families; her father protects her in childhood, her husband protects her in youth and her sons protect her in old age; a woman is never fit for independence. Though devoid of virtues, yet a husband must be worshipped as a god by a faithful wife. Manu did not give right to divorce to women under any circumstance while allowing man to give up his wife at the same time. Indeed man was allowed to abandon and even sell his wife. Even after repudiation by her husband, she was not released from her husband and could not become legitimate wife of another. A wife could be subjected to corporal punishment by her husband reducing her status to that of a slave. Like Shudras, a woman was forbidden by Manu to study Vedas. Offering sacrifices, the very soul of religion, was forbidden to be performed by women. In matters of property, a wife was reduced to the level of a slave as she was not allowed to have any dominion over property. Thus, under the influence of Dharamshastras (Manusmriti), women was held in bondage lifelong and were deprived of basic human rights like right to education, right to property and right to study religious scripture. Dr Ambedkar points out that Shastras, Caste and Endogamy – the three important pillars of patriarchy in Hindu society – were responsible for discriminatory practice against women and their degradation in social status.

Ambedkar and Justice to Women

Dr B.R. Ambedkars approach to women's right is exclusively different from other social reformers like Jyotiba Phule, Raja Ram Mohan Roy, Ishwar Chandra Vidyasagar and Mahatma Gandhi who tried to reform the Hindu society of certain outdated customs and practices without questioning the hierarchical social order. But Ambedkar made his own view for the women rights and that has been reflected in Indian constitution. His goal was to make a society based on social justice. To secure this goal, Ambedkar has given equal status to women on par with men by providing many provisions in the Indian constitution. To him, sexual discrimination should be root out from the society and everybody should get equal opportunity in the society. The Preamble of Indian Constitution guarantees social and economic justice to women and that is because of Ambedkar contribution. In the Preamble it is mentioned: (i) social, economic and political justice, (ii) freedom of thought, expression, belief, faith and worship, (iii) equality of status and opportunity and (iv) fraternity assuring dignity of the individual and national unity to all the citizens of India without any discrimination of caste, creed or sex.

Constitutional Rights and Women

In Indian Constitution, there are few articles exist that help the women of Indian society to improve their position and to compete with their male counterparts. For example,

Article 14 – All are equal in the eyes of law and equally protected by the law. It means equal rights and opportunities in political, economic and social spheres.

Article 15 prohibits discrimination on the ground of sex. Article 15(3) enables positive discrimination in favour of women.

Article 16 mentions there shall be equality of opportunity for all citizens in matters relating to employment or appointment to any office without any discrimination on the basis of religion, caste, creed and sex.

Article 24 prohibits the employment of children below the age of 14 years in factories, mines or in any other hazardous employment.

Article 39 and 39(d) state Equal means of livelihood and equal pay for equal work.

As per **Article 41** the state shall guarantee within its economic limits to all the citizens, the right to work, to education and public assistance in certain cases.

Article 42 the state makes provision for Human conditions of work and maternity relief.

Under **Article 44,** the state provides a Uniform Civil Code to all the citizens throughout the territory of India.

Article 46 – The state to promote with special care, the educational and economic interests of weaker section of people and to protect them from social injustice and all forms of exploitation.

Article 47 – The state to raise the level of nutrition and standard of living of its people and the improvement of public health and so on.

Article 51 (A) (C) – Fundamental duties to renounce practices, derogatory to the dignity of women.

Article 243D (3), 243T (3) and 243R (4) provides for allocation of seats in the Panchayati Raj System.

The Hindu Code Bill

Ambedkar not only ascertain constitutional gurantees to women but also introduced and got passed four Acts which strengthened the position of women in the society. These were incorporated in the Hindu Code Bill. These are:

(i) The Hindu Marriage Act, 1955.
(ii) The Hindu Succession Act, 1956.
(iii) The Hindu Minority and Guardianship Act, 1956.
(iv) The Adoption and Maintenance Act, 1956.

If we look at the provisions of those Acts, we can easily make out that Ambedkar was a great thinker of women rights and emancipation. Provisions that have been enshrined in the Acts are as follows:

The Hindu Marriage Act, 1955

The Hindu Marriage Act, 1955 was amended in 1976 made the following provisions for women:

1. The legitimisation of illegitimate children (Sec.16).
2. Punishment-bigamy (Sec.26).
3. Custody of children (Sec. 26).
4. Marriageable age of females raised to 18 years.
5. Provision for alimony (Sec. 25). The Act abolishes the difference between a maiden and a widow.

The Hindu Succession Act, 1956

This Act contains the following provisions for women:

1. A widow has a right to adopt a son or a daughter which was not there in the Hindu Law.
2. It also provided an opportunity to be independent and dispose of her property by will as she wishes and desires (Sec. 14).
3. A uniform scheme of succession to the property of a Hindu female who dies, intestate after commencement of the Act, was made in Section 15. Previously under the uncodified law the succession to stridhan varied according to the marital status of a woman.

The Hindu Minority and Guardianship Act, 1956

Following provisions are come under the purview of this Act:

1. The mother is empowered to change the guardian, appointed by the father and may appoint a new guardian by will.
2. The fathers right to appoint a guardian for the minor by will during the life time of the minors mother is prohibited under this Act.

The Adoption and Maintenance Act, 1956

This Act has the following provisions:

1. This Act accepts adoption of a male and a female child without any difference, whereas under the uncodified law a daughter could not be adopted.
2. This Acts permits a wife to adopt a child on her own right even during her husbands life time. She had no such right prior to this enactment.
3. In the uncodified law a spinster or a widow had no right to adopt whereas this Act grants them the right to adopt.
4. Under the old Hindu Law a wife need not be consulted while adopting a child or while giving a child for adoption, whereas this Act made it essential to consult her in both the cases.
5. Section 11 lays down that, a father should adopt a daughter atleast 21 years younger to him.

Relevance of his Ideas

Dr B.R. Ambedkar was a great champion of gender equality is clear from his various writings on Hindu social order. In order to find out the root cause of degraded status of women in Hindu society, he studied Shastras, Smritis, Buddhist literature, Kautilya'sArthshastra and so on. Through his critical appraisal of these historical and religious texts, Dr Ambedkar clearly establishes the fact that while women in Pre-Manu days enjoyed equal social status vis-à-vis men and even were economically independent, their status declined in the post-Manu period under the influence of Manusmriti. That is to say, the social institutions of caste and endogamy upheld by Manusmriti were largely responsible for decline in the social status of women in the Hindu society.

The inseparability of caste and gender inequality in the conceptualisation of Hindu social order by Dr B.R. Ambedkar is an important theoretical input in understanding the hurdles to empowerment of women in the Indian social milieu and needs to be taken note of by the Indian feminists. In other words, any feminist discourse/agenda for the empowerment of Indian women must take into account the realities of Shastras (Manusmriti), Caste and Endogamy –the three important pillars of Hindu social order –that moulds Hindu minds and deny equal social status to women in matters of entitlement of rights, property, and inheritance. Dr B.R. Ambedkar not only wrote extensively to counter the orthodox Hindu opinion against women but worked as an activist and social reformer at the grass roots level to organise and empower women of depressed classes so that they could fight to reclaim their social rights such as right to drink water from their source and right to enter temple that were traditionally denied to them by the caste Hindus. It was due to the encouragement by Dr Ambedkar that a large number of women came out openly on the public streets to reclaim their social rights and self-respect. As a member of the Mumbai Legislative Council, Dr B.R. Ambedkar was in the forefront in championing the cause of women's empowerment by forcefully arguing for the passage of Maternity Benefit Bill. As the Chairman of Constitution Drafting Committee, Dr Ambedkar made a pioneering contribution in introducing Articles 14, 15, 16, 39, 42 in the Indian Constitution that guarantee protection to women from any kind of discrimination. As the Law Minister in the Union Cabinet, Dr Ambedkar made every effort for the passage of Hindu Code Bill despite staunch opposition from vested interests. This shows the great importance he attached to the cause of gender equality in India. While Dr B.R. Ambedkar has made a notable contribution towards the emancipation of Indian women through his rich and illuminating interpretations of Hindu social order (based on graded system of Caste hierarchy and gender inequality), the contemporary feminist discourse in India has largely ignored this rich classic literature. However, it needs to be realised that any feminist discourse on gender equality in India in isolation of social institution of caste would be a futile exercise as women as a category undifferentiated by caste does not exist for feminists to mobilise. Unless this social reality dawns on Indian feminists, they would be devoid of any concrete agenda that truly empowers common women. There is, therefore, a need for Indian feminists to turn to Dr B.R. Ambedkar to understand the complex matrix of caste and gender so as to build a counter narrative that challenges the hegemony of patriarchal Hindu social order which reproduces gender inequality and violence in a systematic manner.

Conclusion

Dr Ambedkar's impassioned love for the 'fallen' women as a whole community and his advice to recue thenselves from the despised and disgraceful life were quite meaningful. Dr Ambedkar accorded equal status to women and men in every sphere and he also warned the women against the misuse of their rights. Therefore, it would be appropriate to regard Dr Ambedkar as one of the saviours of Indian women. His contribution is unique and cherishable by the women of India. It should be the foremost duty of women's associations, groups and organisations to actively participate in the processes of social change and welfare. The women's movement needs to be strengthened to overcome the artificial divisions and boundaries created by geography, economy and ideology.

References

1. Ahir, D.C. (1990), *The Legacy of Dr Ambedkar*. B.R. Publishing Corporation: New Delhi.
2. Ambedkar, B.R. (1987), 'Women and Counter Revolution: Riddles of Hindu Women" in *Dr Baba Saheb Ambedkar: Writings and Speeches,* Vol. 3, Department of Education, Goverment of Maharashtra.
3. Arya, Sudha, (2001), Women Gender Equality and the State. Deep and Deep Publications: New Delhi.
4. Barnwal, Bijay K (2014), 'Dr B.R. Ambedkars Quest for Gender Equality: It's Relevance in Contemporary Feminist Discourse', *Online International Interdisciplinary Research Journal,* [Bi-Monthly], Volume-IV, Issue-II, Mar-April.
5. Bharati, T. (1992), 'Ambedkar and Uplift of Women', in *Ambedkar and Social Justice* (ed.),Volume II : 264.
6. D. Keer (1987), Dr Ambedkar: Life and Mission, Mumbai.
7. Tikoo, P.N. (1985), *Indian Women: A Brief Socio-Cultural Survey*. B.R. Publishing Corporation : Delhi.
8. Vasant Moon (ed.), *Dr Babasaheb Ambedkar: Writings and Speeches*, Vol. II, Government of Maharashtra: 166-167.

15

Emancipation of Dalit Women *vis-à-vis* Ambedkar's Perspective

—*Sucheta Singh*

Abstract

Dr B. R. Ambedkar proved, himself to be a genius and was known as a greater thinker, philosopher, jurist-par excellence, prolific writer, social activist and critic and strode like a colossus in the Indian Socio-political scene unto his death, his thoughts never received adequate attention in the generality of Indian society just because he was born as an untouchables. He provides a powerful source of inspiration to formulate a feminist political agenda which simultaneously addresses the issues of class, caste and gender. Ambedkar had deep faith in the fundamental rights-in equal rights of man and women, in the dignity of the individual and in the social and economic justice. In India, basically a women are oppressed and are not treated on par with men. Moreover dalit women are oppressed among oppressed and slaves of slaves. The present paper tries to throw lights on Ambedkar's view on the problems of women and its relevancy in present scenario with special reference to Dalit women.

*[**Keywords:** Dalit women, Human Rights, Castes, Oppressed]*

Introduction

"Women are made, they are not born". —Simone De Beauvoir

Dr B.R. Ambedkar raised question "Why Manu degraded Women?" He attacked Manusmriti as a major source, which legitimises the denial of freedom, self-respect, right to education, property, divorce etc, to women by attributing a very lofty ideal to them. Ambedkar suggest some strategies for emancipation from oppression that he found in Buddhism. According to him, Buddhism is the only religion that promotes equality, self-respect and education. He was the first Indian to break down the barriers in the way of advancement of women in India. He laid down the foundation of concrete and sincere efforts by codifying the common civil code for Hindus and other sections of the Indian Society (Singariya, 2013).

Ambedkar actually showed sincerity of purpose, devotion to duty, fearlessness and self-less confidence in human values that can go a long way in fulfilling the task of emancipation of the weak and down-trodden. He writes, "Expressing one's unbound admiration is one thing and to obey the hero blindly is another. There is nothing wrong in the former, while latter is pernicious thing. It is a positive danger to the state. Irrational hero-worship, is against the spirit of democracy.

He stated that women should be given all round development more importantly social education, their well being and socio-cultural rights. He emphasise that every section of Indian society should give due share of rights to women and it is a must to maintain and protect dignity and modesty of women (Shudha, 2011).

Women were socially discarded for a long period of time; they are compelled to live a vulnerable life, be it economic, education, health and all other areas that fall under basic needs. The word 'Dalit' itself connotes the lowest strata of the society in all the aspects, a term which is condemnable itself (Sharma, 2012). If we will see the status of women in historical perspective, one has to go back to its history to understand the situation of Dalit women. According to the Hindu caste system, the total social system is divided into hierarchies that constitute four *varnas*, since long; where people are divided into various castes and ethnic groups. In this background the position of Dalit women is one of the lowest from all these aspects. *Shudras* which was placed at the bottom of the ladder in the caste hierarchies is termed as "Dalit' those days they were considered as untouchable group of society. Within this untouchable group dalit women have to bear both social humiliation as well as the male dominance in the family.

The Dalit women are discarded and pushed away in the name of their caste and creed. They are not left with much choice of occupation but to become scavengers in the upper-caste houses, sweepers the *Bai's* or maid servants: or given into body trade or prostitution for the sake of their livelihood.

In 'The Mahan Kosh' Dalits have been defined as one who belongs to the lowest caste or *Hini Jati* and has been trampled down by or broken under the feet of the Upper Castes or *Uchi Jati* (Nabha, 1930). According to Gangadhar Pantwane, Dalit is not a caste, but he is a man exploited by the social and economic traditions of his own country. He does not believe in God, rebirth, soul, Holy books teaching separation, fate and heaven because they have made him slave. He does not believe in humanism. Interestingly the category Dalit was used by Ambedkar himself. Ambedkar in his fortnightly *Bahiskrit Bharat* defines it comprehensively. Dalithood is a kind of life condition which characterises the exploitation, suppression and marginalisation of Dalits by the social, economic, cultural and political domination of the upper caste Brahmanical order (Guru, 1998). If one takes this view all the exploited and downtrodden producers who have been deprived from the ownership of the means of production, denied basic right of a dignified social life and livelihood, discriminated through biased socio-economic and political decisions taken in favour of non-producers and privileged classes and kept deliberately away from the mainstream of advantages of progress are to be considered *Dalits* (Diwakar, 1999). The recent use of the term *Dalit* has been developed in the manifesto of Dalit Panther Movement in 1975. Who is *Dalit*? In this regard this manifesto says members of *Scheduled Castes, Scheduled Tribes, Neo-Boddhists*, the working people, the landless and poor peasants, women and all those who are being exploited socially, politically, economically and in the name of religion (Guru, 1998). So *Dalits* are exclusively the socially and economically marginalised people in India. Now the term Dalit has become a symbol of change and revolution (Zellot, 1992).

Women in Historical Perspective

Dr Ambedkar made historical study of the women's status in ancient India and the factors that led to a decline in their status in later years. He pointed out that during that period, women enjoyed all sorts of necessary rights which are essential for a human being. The women had access to all branches of learning. The women enjoyed a position on par with men. They played important role in religious ceremonies.

The girls were free to choose their own life partners by *swayamvara* system and they married after attaining puberty (Jatava, 2001).

The condition of women started deteriorating through sexual discrimination in later vedic period. They were treated as a bonded labour many restrictions were imposed on them and deprived of basic human rights. Although the women were in majority in society they were discriminated, humiliated and ill-treated by men as the minorities suffered at the hands of majority. They were considered as one on the three 'W's- the wine, women and wealth and are expected to show complete obedience to men. The women were denied property rights and were treated as a property of men.

Further, Manu clearly enunciated that a widow should never dream of remarriage (Manu Smiriti, V 157). The *Artha Shashtra* stated the sole aim of women is to get married and bear children. *Katha Upanishad* strictly warns men not to follow they strut about within the periphery of ignorance. They lead us as blind men lead the blind (Tikoo, 1985). The Golden Age of Guptas had been the Dark Age for women they advocated early marriages- even the pre-puberty marriages. The Gupta kings strictly practised the *Brahminical* law by upholding certain rules and roles for women- like *sati* and celibacy of widows. In the medieval period, Muslims invaded Indian and introduced the *purda* system. It can be observed from the above discussion that initially the condition of women enjoyed their all human rights but in the later period their sufferings, suppression and enslavement increases. Many social workers like Rajaram Mohan Roy and Jyotiba Phule scarified their lives for the causes of women.

Dr Ambedkar Mission for the Upliftment for Dalit Women

Dr Ambedkar is one amongst the few Indian social and political thinkers, who has done original thinking on the Hindu social order and the status of women within the Hindu society. Exposed to the Western ideas of humanism and rational thinking, he was appalled at the low status of the women in the Hindu society. He not only worked hard at the grassroots level to raise awareness about the degraded status of women in India but also wrote extensively to counter the views on gender relations sanctioned by *shastras* and upheld by tradition (Barnwal, 2014).

In his writings, Dr Ambedkar unravels the inequality and injustice inherent in Hindu social order that perpetuates inequality and subordination of women in a systemic manner. He analysed the manner in which gender relations are artificially constructed under Hindu social order which not only moulds attitude of Hindus towards their women but also conditions women to confirm to a stereotype feminine behaviour. He worked hard to challenge the iniquitous gender relations under the Hindu social order so that Hindu society could be reconstructed along the modern democratic ideas of liberty, equality and fraternity.

The text prepared by Ambedkar provided constitutional guarantees and protection for wide range of civil liberties for individual citizens. He incorporated several Articles in the Indian Constitution for the upliftment of Dalits and women which included the provision of equal status to Dalits with other segments of society, abolishment of untouchability and discrimination against them, provisions of fundamental rights to all, equal protection of laws, voting rights and reservation in education, jobs, promotion and political fields to them.

Justice to Women

Ambedkar has given equal status to women on par with men by providing many provisions in the Constitution. "The Constitution quickened by social conscience has added invincible legal missiles for women's liberation" (Iyer, 1996). The Constitution in the Preamble guarantees:

(a) Social, economic and political justice,
(b) Freedom of thought, expression, belief, faith and worship,
(c) Equality of status and opportunity, and
(d) Fraternity assuring the dignity of the individual and national unity to all the citizens of India without any discrimination of caste, creed or sex.

A few articles in the Constitution may help women to improve their status and to compete with their male counterparts in our society. Besides providing Constitutional guarantees to women, Ambedkar introduced and got passed four Acts which strengthened the position of women in the society. There were incorporated in the Hindu Code Bill. These Acts are:

1. The Hindu Marriage Act, 1995.
2. The Hindu Succession Act, 1956.
3. The Hindu Minority and Guardianship Act, 1956.
4. The Adoption and Maintenance Act, 1956.

By the implementation of these Acts that pertaining to marriage, divorce, inheritance that sought to give equal rights to women vis-à-vis men in these aspects. However, the bill was strongly opposed by the orthodox Hindu opinion on the ground that it would lead to break-up of Hindu social order (patriarchy) if the bill was passed in that form (More, 2011).

By having equal rights, women have achieved a lot through they are still suffering from the social evils like dowry, eve-teasing, rape, etc. In the era of postmodernism, women have entered into all professions including the police departments and airlines. Dr Ambedkar states that "Unity is meaningless without the accompaniment of women. Education is fruitless without educated women, and agitation is incomplete without the strength of women". He also gave timely shock treatment to the complacent Hindu psyche and society. He castigated and exposed evils of untouchability, graded system of inequality and inhuman aspects Hinduism, particularly its *chaturvarna*. (ibid)

Ambedkar unravels the genesis, mechanism and spread of caste system in India and its consequences for gender relations on the Hindu society. He stated that endogamy is the only characteristic that is peculiar to caste the superimposition of endogamy and exogamy means the creation of caste. He perceived education as a catalyst for accelerated change. He began to raise his voice for the liberation of women through his newspapers *Mook Nayak* launched in 1920 and *Bahishkrit Bharat* in 1927. Main turning point came that made a bonfire of *Manusmriti* in presence of more than fifty women to protest against the discrimination of women and untouchables on 25th December 1927 during a Conference of Depressed Class at Mahad. After the Conference Dr Ambedkar addressed a meeting of about three thousand women of depressed class and urged them to dress well and live a clean life.

Send your children to schools. Education is necessary for females as it is for males (Mallik, 1993).

Dr Ambedkar championed the cause of women within the Legislative Council as well. His arguments on the Maternity Benefit Bill and on Birth Control were quite relevant to recognise the dignity of women. Dr Ambedkar observed that he had love for the principle of non-violence but had differentiated non-violence from abject surrender. He told the volunteers that it did not befit a man to live a live of surrender, servitude and helplessness. He declared that he believed with saint Tukaram that destruction of the wicked was also a form of non-violence (More, 2011).

Relevance of Dr Ambedkar Ideas at Present

Dalits represents a community of about 170 million in India constituting about 17 per cent of the total Indian population (Census, 2011). Dr B.R. Ambedkar main aim was to uproot the evil of deep-rooted caste system, uplift the status of downtrodden society, create honour amongst so called upper castes and to transform this country from uncivilised state to civilised state. Before independence the social, economic and political conditions of dalits and women were very grim. At present some development has been observed among the disadvantage groups in India (Michael, 2007).

Dr B.R. Ambedkar's mission in life was to challenge the ideological foundations of graded system of caste hierarchy that denied equality, freedom and human dignity to women in Hindu Society. He believed that society should be based on reason and not on atrocious tradition of caste system. Therefore, in order to reconstruct Hindu Society along modern democratic ideas of liberty, equality and fraternity to struggle in "**The Annihilation of Caste System**", that Hindu mind should be purged from the tradition of the *Shastras*. He found education, inter-caste marriages and inter-dinning as methods by which caste and patriarchy maintained through endogamy can be eliminated. (Ambedkar, 1935).

He was a great champion of gender-equality that is clear from his various writings on Hindu social order. Through his critical appraisal of various historical and religious text he conclude that the social institution of caste and endogamy upheld by *Manusmriti* were largely responsible for decline in the social status of women in the Hindu society.

Untouchability has reduced, their socio-economic and political status have improved. Today Dalits have become a powerful political force in India and enjoy greater access to education and economy than ever before. They are exercising their voting rights. Their political consciousness and awareness about political activities and participation in these activities have increased very much. Due to these facts now-a-days the government is also making various decisions relating to their rights and privileges. Efforts are still going on to remove different discriminatory practices against them (Kumar, 2012).

Now votes of the Dalits have become one of the major deciding factors for winning of a candidate or a political party in elections. The honours for Dalits in high caste society have also increased. Today we do not ask the person seating besides us which caste he belongs to? Today at least in towns both Dalits and non-Dalits enjoy the same tea stall, hotel and cinema hall but usually nobody bothers about knowing the caste identity of a person. This is all due to the un-tired and intelligent efforts of Dr Ambedkar. But it does not mean that the untouchability has totally abolished. Still it is maintained in offices, colleges, ceremonies etc. Today's tragedy is that the rulers of our nation do not want the effective implementation of constitution (Lakshmi, 2014). There is a far gap in between their sayings and workings. Manu introduced caste system in India. Dr Ambedkar introduced caste annihilation system in India. Indian Hindu orthodoxy stood by Manu. Ambedkar stood for Dalits and women developments in India (Karthik, 2012).

Dr Ambedkar not only wrote extensively to counter the orthodox Hindu opinion against women but worked as an activist and social reformer at the grass root level to organise and empower women of depressed classes so that they could fight to retain their social rights such as right to drink water from their source and right to entre temple that were traditionally denied to them by the caste Hindu. It was due to the encouragement by Dr Ambedkar that large number of women came out openly on the public streets to reclaim their social rights and self-respect (Barnwal, 2014).

Conclusion

Dr B.R. Ambedkar expressed his views on the state of life of all women. He stated that women must be treated equally and given equal prestige. By conceptualising caste and gender inequality as inseparable constituents of Hindu social order, Dr Ambedkar laid the foundation for gradual transformation of Indian social consciousness and gender justice in India. The teachings and thoughts of Dr Ambedkar are not only useful for women but also for all the sections of the society. His deep concern and feeling for all round development for women is expressed from his each sentence and word. The Dalits also will have to come forward and to labour hard in all social, economical, educational and political fields to compete with the other members of the society. They should avoid power demonstration and enjoy their rights properly.

People from the mainstream of the society will also have to change their mentality and thought process towards these excluded people. They will have to be more munificent towards the Dalits regarding untouchability and the upliftment of their socio-economic, educational and political status etc. by accepting them as equal humans like themselves. The social structure of our society is based primarily on them because they are the people who perform all types of menial works which are usually avoided by the people of elite class. Without them no society has run previously, not running now and will not run in future. So it can be said that Dr B.R. Ambedkar can be regarded as one of the greatest intellectual and social reformer of modern India who struggled throughout his life for the liberation of Indian women particularly depressed classes from the lifting bondage and slavery under the weight of Hindu Social institutions. Dr Ambedkar laid foundations for gradual transformation of Indian social consciousness and gender justice in India.

References

Ambedkar, B.R. (1935), "The Annihilation of Castes", text of the Presendiantional Address to Jat-Pat-Todak Mandal Annual Meeting Lahore.

Arya, Sudha (2011), *Women Gender Equality and the State*, New Delhi: Deep and Deep Publication.

Barnwal, B.K. (2014), "Dr B.R. Ambedkar's Quest for Gender Equality It's Relevance in Contemporary Feminist Discourse", *Online International Interdisciplinary Research Journal*, Vol.IV, Issue-II, pp. 393-399.

Census (2011), *Census of India*. Government of India, Ministry of Home Affairs, Office of the Registrar General and Census Commissioner, India.

Diwakar, D.M. (1999), Dalit Question of Inequality, Exploitation and Mobilisation: A Micro View of Ground Realities. *Man and Development*, Vol. XXI, No. 3, September, p. 63.

Guru, Gopal (1998), "The Politics of Naming", *Seminar*, No. 471, Nov., p. 16.

Iyer, Krishna. V.R. (1996), Constitutional Challenges and Democratic Response.

Jatava, R.D. (2001), *Dynamics of Ambedkar Ideology*. Jaipur: Sublime Publications.

Kumar, Lalan (2012), Political Participation of Dalits in Punjab: A Comprehensive Study of Nawanshahar and Patiala districts. *Introduction, Ph.D. Thesis*.

Lakshmi, Jay (2014), "Relevance of Ambedkar's Contribution in The Upliftment or Modern Days Dalits and Women", *Journal of Humanities and Social Sciences*, Vol.19, Issue.2, pp. 62-66.

Manu Smriti, V 157.

Mallik, B.S. (1993), "Ambedkar on Women's Progress", In Grover, V., (ed.), *B.R. Ambedkar*, New Delhi: Deep and Deep Publications.

Michael, S.M. (2007), *Dalits in Modern India: Vision and Values*. New Delhi: Sage Publication.

More, Vijay., G (2011), "Dr B.R. Ambedkar's Contribution for Women's Rights", Variorum, *Multi-Disciplinary e-Research Journal*, Vol. 2, Issue I, August.

Nabha, Bhai Kahan Singh (1930), *Mahan Kosh*, (Encyclopedia of Sikh Literature). Language Department, Patiala, Punjab, p. 468.

Navayan, Karthik (2012), Dr Ambedkar Contribution in Law and Justice for the Upliftment of the Disadvantaged. *National Seminar on Ambedkar's Contribution for the Upliftment of the Disadvantaged*. 2nd and 3rd September, 2010, Seminar Hall, MGNIRSA.

Sharma, Nandita (2012), "The Status of Dalit Women in India-From Deprivity to Supremacy", *International Literary Journal*, Vol. II, Issue I.

Singariya, M.R. (2013), "Dr B.R. Ambedkar and Women Empowerment in India", *Journal of Research in Humanities and Social Science*, Vol. 2 Issue 1 (2014) pp. 01-04.

Tikoo, P.N. (1985), *Indian Women: A Brief Socio-Cultural Survey*, New Delhi: B.R. Publishing Corporation.

Zelliot, Eleanor (1992), *From Untouchable to Dalit : Essay on the Ambedkar Movement*, New Delhi: Manohar Publications, p. 268.

16

Ambedkar's Conversion to Buddism:The Quest for Equality

—*Archana Thakur*

Abstract

The influence of Babasaheb Ambedkar on nationalist India are well-known. He all through his entire life wanted total freedom and upliftment of the Indian masses. Dr Ambedkar's thought that Hinduism in practice would be an obstacle to healthy social developments and political democracy in India. The idea of converting to another religion in order to escape from the caste system logically ensued from Ambedkars analysis of Hinduism, whose originality and strength laid in its demonstration that in this civilisation social hierarchy was consubstantial to religion. To leave it was thus the only means to attain equality. So,he thought of Buddhism which he rightly considers was very modern in its to way of thinking and would be an answer to social disparities created by Hinduism. In this article my hypothese is Why did Ambedkar choose Buddhism to liberate his Depressed Classes, not other religion? Was his failure in politics leading him to Buddhism? Lastly, after a thorough analysis, I will conclude that he converted to Buddhism because of his failure and frustration with politics in finding a way to uplift the life of the untouchable people.

Introduction

Dr B.R. Ambedkar, the chief architect of Indian Constitution may be regarded as one of greatest intellectual and social reformer of modern India for his pioneering contribution in reforming Hindu social order. He not only struggled throughout his life for the emancipation of social status of the underprivileged. In fact, Ambedkar, regard as the father of the Indian Constitution and liberator of the Depressed Classes in

India, is one of the most remarkable men in Indian history. Ambedkar was a politician, writer, revolutionist, and advocator of the neo-Buddhist movement in India. The story of his life is the story of how exceptional talent and outstanding force of character succeeded in overcoming some of the most formidable obstacles that an unjust and oppressive society has ever placed in the way of the individual. Born in Mhow in central India in 1891, he was the fourteenth child of parents who belonged to the very lowest stratum of Hindu society.[1]

In this paper, I am going to write about Ambedkar's advocacy for the right of the untouchable people and his frustration in politics. Afterwards, I will discuss about how he looked for a religious solution to help the untouchable people through conversion of Hindu religion and at last I will discuss his path to Buddhism.

According to orthodox Hindu tradition, he was not entitled to receive education or to acquire property, he could engage only in the most menial and degrading work and he could not come into physical contact with members of the higher castes. There are several reasons why Ambedkar fought for equal rights in Hindu society for the Depressed Classes. Mainly and personally, he was mistreated seriously by other caste people where later on, he stood up to fight for the cause of the untouchable people. Since he was born in the Depressed Classes, he encountered several prejudical incidents during his youth. At school at Satara, he was made to sit outside the class room on a piece of gunny mat, which he had to carry the school. He had to go without water, not because there was no water, but because he was an untouchable, who had no right to drink from a public source. Second, at Satara again some teachers would not touch his note-books for fear of being polluted. Third,—Touch me not || was a common theme for him outside of the school. Fourth, even when people recognised him as a man of learning and high official in the Baroda State in 1917, he was treated in an inhuman ways; no drinking water was available in his office; his subordinates kept a distance from him; low-paid workers threw files and papers on his desk from a distance due to the fear of being polluted. Fifth, at Baroda, he was thrown out from a public hotel without any accommodation.

Hence, he had to resign in frustration and returned to Mumbai. Sixth, even when he taught at the college level as a professor, he was treated as a Pariah by the Hindu professors and was not allowed to drink water from the pot kept in the Professors' common room.[2] Seventh, while he practiced as a barrister in a High Court of Mumbai, the solicitors would not condescend to have any business with him on the ground of untouchability. Even a humble canteen boy would not serve him tea.[3]

Turned Away from Hindu Society

Ambedkar explained that the Brahminical system denies the right to existential dignity to the Bahujans and relegates them a subhuman existence. They are denied their essential rights, viz., their *Right to Identity*. All the identities that are attached to the Bahujans are not given by themselves, but are called by others. They are forbidden to exercise any *right to Access or Claim over Resources* of the society in which they live. On the whole, the caste system clamps social oppression, economic exploitation and political suppression which are worse than slavery.[8] The main culprit of this degeneration of Indian society is Brahminism. Hence, Ambedkar uses the terms Brahmanism and Hinduism interchangeably in his writings, especially in his polemical ones. He writes, "Hinduism is a religion which is not founded on morality. Whatever morality Hinduism has is not an integral part of it. It is not imbedded in religion. It is a separate force which is sustained by social necessities and not by injunction of Hindu religion".[4]

There was another reason why Dr Ambedkar turned away from Hinduism. In his view the very core of Hinduism was Varnashrama Dharma i.e. Religion based on caste and stages in life viz.1. Celibacy 2. Married life 3 Retreat to forest and 4. Complete retirement from worldly life. So far as wrong about them: but the concept of caste was completely opposed to the democratic principles of liberty, equality and fraternity. And what was the justification for retaining caste in modern democratic society. They were not based on any distinctions in nature at all. It may be that they were a living force in a certain state of Hindu society and serve men's interest at that stage. But like several other institutions which do not keep pace with a changing environment and consequent social change conscious or unconscious, they have become mere fossils now and are indeed a dead weight on more progressive forces and mere hurdles on the path of the development of a healthy society.[5]

It was an attempt to make the Hindu society aware of its defects shortcomings. Ambedkar says: I do not care for the credit, which every progressive society must give to its rebels. I shall be satisfied if I make the Hindus realise that they are the sick men of India and that their sickness is causing danger to the health and happiness of other Indians.[6] Ambedkar stood firmly in the midst of storms, and continuously thought of the Untouchables and fought for their equality and social freedom in the Indian society. For him, the Hindu society was nothing but a collection of castes, which is based on labourers than the labour. He criticised the caste system by saying, "Hindu society gives more importance to the division of people and not the work. In other words, there is no place for the individual in the Hindu society."[7]

In India, he analyses that there is no society at all. We have multitudes of societies based on caste. People are not born as humans. They are born into castes and imbibe such notions of mind which do not allow humane interaction among them. "The first and foremost thing that must be recognised is that Hindu Society is a myth…That is the reason why the Hindus cannot be said to form a society or a nation." He squarely blames "Brahmanism in instituting caste system has put the greatest impediment against the growth of nationalism "Unless the social order is changed, no progress could be achieved. The community cannot be mobilised either for defense or for offence. Nothing can be built on the foundations of caste. No nation, no morality.[8] Ambedkar in a clear cut way enumerated the evils of Hindu religion:

1. It tends to deprive moral life, freedom, spontaneity and to reduce it to a more or less anxious and servile conformity to externally imposed rules.
2. There is no loyalty to ideas, there is only conformity to commands.
3. The laws are iniquitous in that they are not the same for one class as for another. The laws are prescribed to be the same for all generations.
4. The laws are not made by certain persons called prophets or law-givers.
5. This code has been invested with the character of finality and fixity.

He concluded that this religion must be destroyed and there is nothing wrong in working for the destruction of such a religion. He emphasised that people must be enabled to realise that what they are told was not religion but that it was really law and its abolition and amendment must be urged.[9]

Call for Social Change

However, Dr Ambedkar perceived the problems of Dalits in an altogether different perspective. He believed that any effort to improve the lot of the Dalits should be directed towards uprooting the very caste system itself. Dr Ambedkar was of the view that as long there would be a caste system, there would also be outcaste. He fought against the tyranny of the caste system in all possible ways. He mobilised the Dalits under the banner of "educate, agitate and unite." He inculcated in their minds the value of self-respect, dignity, and an urge to fight for their rights.

This struggle led to his decision to quit Hinduism. The first reference made by Dr Ambedkar to a conversion of the Untouchables dates back to 1927. During the Mahad Conference, he had indeed declared: "We want equal rights in society. We will achieve them as far as possible while remaining within the Hindu fold or, if necessary by kicking away this worthless Hindu identity. And if it becomes necessary to give up Hinduism it would no longer be necessary for us to bother about temples.[10] From then onwards he was on the search to find a religion, which could serve as a means for the upliftment of the Untouchables. On 13 October 1935, a provincial conference of the depressed classes was held at Yeola in Nasik district. In his presidential address he announced his decision to leave Hinduism and said, "The disabilities we have suffered, and the indignities we had to put up with, were the result of our being the members of the Hindu community. Will it not be better for us to leave that fold and embrace a new faith that would give us equal status, a secure position and rightful treatment? I advise you to severe your connection with Hinduism and to embrace any other religion. But, in doing so, be careful in choosing the new faith and see that equality of treatment, status and opportunities will be guaranteed to you unreservedly. Unfortunately for me I was born a Hindu Untouchable. It was beyond my power to prevent that, but, I declare that it is within my power to refuse to live under ignoble and humiliating conditions. I solemnly assure you that I will not die a Hindu."[11]

He mapped out the evil practice of caste Hinduism. In a way he was conscientising not only the oppressed but also the oppressors. More than sympathy, equality and liberty are needed for the well-being of the Untouchables. And it was not possible unless this Hindu religion be discarded. Ambedkar said, "If you have to get rid of this same shameful condition, if you have to cleanse this filth and make use of this precious life, there is only one way and that is to throw off the shackles of Hindu religion and the Hindu society in which you are bound."[12]

After his failure to secure the basic right and equal status for the Depressed Classes in the Hindu society at a conference for the Depressive Classes in Mahad of Mumbai, he had burned some portions of the classic Hindu law book, the *Manusmriti*, that discriminated against low castes.[13]

Search for True Religion Based on Equality

A simple understanding of religion is believing in God as the centre of all reality. It helps individual to build up a relationship between God and oneself. However, Ambedkar, while explaining the meaning of religion, did not mention God in his understanding of religion. He further added that material comfort was by no means the solvent of all human ills. Religion to him was the driving force of human activities. He remarked, "Man cannot live by bread alone. He has a mind which needs food for thought" and added, "Religion instills hope in man and drives him to activity.[14]

In general, man needs both material and spiritual life. Otherwise, according to Ambedkar, communist philosophy is to—fatten the pigs, as though men are no better than pigs. He emphasised further that between man and animal, there is the difference of developing sentient mind.[15]Ambedkar has given four characteristics of religion:

(1) "Religion in the sense of morality must, therefore, remain the governing principle in every society.
(2) Religion if it is to function must be in accord with reason which is merely another name for science.

(3) Its moral code must recognise the fundamental tenets of liberty, equality and fraternity. Unless a religion recognises these three fundamental principles of social life, religion will be doomed.

(4) Religion must not sanctify or ennoble poverty.

This way Ambedkar defined religion as something that offered you prosperity or elevation first in this world and then salvation. In his view, the belief in soul was far better than the belief in God.[16]

Ambedkar was not satisfied with the untouchable youth conference at Poona. In order to have of his an estimation of the real support of his people for the conversion movement, he organised conference on May 30 and 31, 1936, at Dadar, Mumbai. In this conference Ambedkar said that so long as they remained in the Hindu fold, there was no salvation for them. They had to go out of the Hindu fold to secure true freedom for their activities such as wearing dress, eating food, securing jobs, receiving education and living in the midst of the civilised society, you have nothing to lose, expect your chains and everything to gain by changing your religion.[17]

The declaration reiterated by the leaders of the depressed classes made the months of the heads of different faiths water and whetted their appetite. They began to press Ambedkar to embrace their own religion and win equality and freedom. He tried to understand religion from a social perspective. Keeping this in mind, he examined and analysed the different major religions of the world.

Views about Islam

In all his writings and speeches, Ambedkar has maintained the importance and necessity of religion. According to him, religion is a part of once inheritance. He further added that material.

In terms of social strength, Islam was no doubt a viable alternative for consideration. Take the caste system. Islam speaks of brotherhood. Everybody infers that Islam must be free from slavery and caste. Regarding slavery nothing needs to be said.

But if slavery has gone, caste among Musalmans has remained. Dr Ambedkar then quotes the 1901 census report for Bengal to show that Muslims there have several castes, including Arzal or untouchable castes with whom no other Mohamedan would associate and who are forbidden to enter the mosque to use the public burial ground. He also quotes from the same Report about the panchayat system of each caste which extends to social as well as trade matters resulting in castes which are as strictly endogamous as Hindu castes. He concludes, "The Mohamedans observe not only caste but also untouchability."[18]

Ambedkar said, "There are many sects among them and the bond of one single religion has hardly helped forge any unity among them. Many have been killed in the Shia-Sunni riots in Lucknow, though both are Muslim. Religion, even if it is Islam, has never been a unifying force. More wars have been fought in the name of religion."[19]

Another point about Islam was according to Ambedkar "what the consequences of conversion will be the country as a whole" he continued "is well worth bearing in mind, conversion to Islam will denationalised the depressed classes. If they go over to Islam, the number of Muslim would be doubled and the danger of Muslins domination also be becomes real. "There can thus be no manner of doubt that the Muslim Society in India is afflicted by the same social evils as afflict the Hindu Society. Indeed, the Muslims have all the social evils of the Hindus and something more.[20]

His Views about Christianity

Ambedkar loved Christian teaching. He was a devoted student of the Bible and possessed large collection of biblical literatures. In his comparative study of religions, he confessed that Christ captivated him with his love towards the poor and marginalised. Christianity always took side of the oppressed, downtrodden. It helped people, especially the Dalits, the Untouchables; to find an identity and live a better life. All these services to humanity by Christianity influenced Ambedkar. Ambedkar believed in the teachings of Christ and the message of liberation. He said, "It could be a dynamic, strong enough, to lift us up out of our present degraded position". With this sentiment, he came very close to Christianity yet moved so far from it due to various other factors.[21] Christianity has always accepted the principle of hierarchy in both church and society, while at the same time holding the doctrine of equality to be relevant only in terms of eschatological promise.[22]

Ambedkar found that Christian missionaries wanted to convert upper castes and to establish educational institutions. He also saw that the Christianity of south India observed the caste system in the churches. Though Ambedkar liked Christ's teachings of love and compassion, yet he rejected Christianity as a solution for caste system.

Ambedkar and Sikhism

Ambedkar had a positive attitude towards Sikhism. He examined whether Sikhism could assure the dignity of the Untouchables. He met many Sikh leaders. They thought that Ambedkar would convert into Sikhism. Therefore, Sardar Dilip Singh Doabri, the vice-president if the Golden Temple Managing Committee, wired to Ambedkar, saying that, "Sikhism fulfills the requirements of Ambedkar in view of conversion. The Sikh religion is monotheistic and all loving and provides for equal treatment of all its adherents"[23]At one time, B.R. Ambedkar seriously consider conversion to Sikhism. The Sikh belief in meeting oppression with a love for the cause of martial Sikhism, and fighting back to defend one's interests held great attraction for him and other scheduled caste leaders.[24]

Explaining in detail why he chose Sikhism, Ambedkar further observed 'the second question is, looking at these alternative faith purely from the standpoint of the Hindus, which is the best Islam, Christianity they not only go out of the Hindu religion, but they also go out of Hindu culture. On the other hand, if they become Sikh they remain within Hindu culture. This is by no means a small advantage to the Hindus." According to Ambedkar, "what the consequences of conversion will be the country as a whole "he continued" is well worth bearing in mind, conversion to Islam or Christianity will denationalised the depressed classes if they go over to Islam, the number of Muslim would be doubled and the danger of muslins domination also be becomes real if they go over to Christianity, the numerical strength of the Christian becomes five to six cores. It will help to strengthen the hold of Britain on the country. On the other hand, if they embrace Sikhism, they will not only not have the destiny of the country but they will help the destiny of the country."[25]

In spite of opposition sponsored by Gandhi and other, Ambedkar took one more step in respect of the conversion movement. He deputed on September 18, 1936, a group of his followers to the Sikh mission at

Amritsar to study Sikh religion. Ambedkar was now coming into closer contact with the Sikh mission and its leaders, and there was some understanding between them and the mission to start a college in Mumbai in the interest of depressed classes, who were expect to be coverts to Sikhism.[26]

In November, he went to England to sound out the British leaders about the guarantees which they would be ready to grant in the new Constitution to the Untouchables who would have converted to Sikhism.[27] The British authorities replied that these provisions would apply only to the Sikhs of Punjab, which, in his views, was an irrelevant proposition. At the beginning of 1937, negotiations continued between Dr Ambedkar and the Sikh leaders but meetings became less frequent and by the end of the year Dr Ambedkar ceased to mention the idea of conversion. Accordingly, the Sikhs established the Khalsa College for the Depressed Classes and honoured Ambedkar as the chairman of the College Committee. However, within a year Ambedkar was frustrated with Sikhism. His association with the Sikh mission came to an abrupt end, because according to Ambedkar's assessment, the Sikhs were no better than the Hindus so far as caste distinctions were concerned.[28]

Conversion to Buddhism, the Ultimate Strategy

Addressing the Maharashtra Untouchable Youths' Conference at Poona in January 1936, he declared that even if God himself was produced before him to dissuade him from leaving the Hindu fold, he would not go back on his resolution. Similarly, in his 'Reasons for Conversion' speech in Mumbai three months later, in which he related some incidents from his own life which had led him to decide in favour of the renunciation of Hinduism and conversion to some other religion, he told his audience, 'If you continue to remain in the fold of Hinduism, you cannot attain a status higher than that of a slave. For me, personally, there is no bar. If I continue to remain an Untouchable I can attain any position that a Hindu can…But it is for your emancipation and advancement that conversion appears to be very necessary to me. To change this degraded and disgraceful existence into a golden life conversion is absolutely necessary.…I have to start conversion to improve your lot. I am not at all worried about the question of my personal interest or progress. Whatever I am doing today, it is for your betterment and in your interest.' Then, in words reminiscent of the vows taken by the Bodhisattvas in the great Mahayana sutras, he concluded, 'You look upon me as a "God" but I am not a god. I am a human being like you all. Whatever help you want from me, I am prepared to give you. I have decided to liberate you from your present hopeless and degrading condition. I am not doing anything for my personal gain. I will continue to struggle for your uplift and to make your life useful and meaningful. You must realise your responsibility and follow the path which I am showing you. If you follow it earnestly, it would not be difficult to achieve your goal.'[29]

So great an effect did Ambedkar's address have on the conference that the delegates passed a resolution declaring that they were ready to change their religion *en masse* and that the Mahar community should, as a preliminary step in this direction, refrain from worshipping Hindu deities, from observing Hindu festivals, and from visiting Hindu places of pilgrimage.

Ambedkar was always in search of a religion, which could really shoulder the responsibility for the betterment of the depressed classes. Buddhism was the best option for him. In one of his talks, which was broadcasted in May 1956, by the British Broadcasting Corporation, he said: "Buddhism gives three principles in combination which no other religion does. Buddhism teaches prajna (understanding) as against superstition and supernaturalism, karuna (love) and samata (equality). Neither God nor soul can save the society". To him Buddhism was a revolt against "parasitic luxury", and prepared the foundations of a prosperous and glorious civilisation.[30]

According to Ambedkar, Buddhism was a true religion because it led to a life guided by the three principles: knowledge, right path and compassion. In Buddhism, he discovered a ray of hope and light for all communities. He contended that the Buddha sought to raise the social status of the servile classes and he believed in the necessity and urgency of the social and religious reforms, which the poor, the fallen and the weak needed. The creed of Buddha was not only a protest but a challenge to the whole Hindu society's unfair behavior-patterns. And for the individual he said, "Buddhism teaches social freedom, intellectual freedom, economic freedom and political freedom…equality not between man and man only but between man and woman.[31]

The Buddhist way of life, thus, aimed at the moral regeneration and social emancipation of human beings; each member of society had to strive for his own moral progress as well as that of other individuals. The Buddhist way of life was further divided into two parts: the Buddhist way for the laity and the Buddhist way for the *Bhikkus*; these included the whole range of moral behaviour patterns in Buddhist society.

The fact that Buddhism was perceived by him as an alternative to the Hindu social hierarchy is clearly reflected in the speech he made during the ceremony of his conversion in Nagpur on 14 October 1956: "By discarding my ancient religion which stood for inequality and oppression today I am reborn. I have no faith in the philosophy of incarnation; and it is wrong and mischievous to say that Buddha was an incarnation of Vishnu. I am no more a devotee of any Hindu god or goddess. I will not perform Shraddha (the Hindu funeral rite). I will strictly follow the eightfold path of Buddha. Buddhism is a true religion and I will lead a life guided by the three principles of knowledge, right path and compassion."[32]

These words reflected the anti-Hindu social motives of Dr Ambedkar's conversion. All the more so as they were followed by 22 oaths of which the first six, the eighth and the nineteenth were directly pointed against Hinduism.

Oaths taken by Dr Ambedkar

1. I shall not recognise Brahma, Vishnu and Mahesh as gods, nor shall I worship them. 2. I shall not recognise Ram and Krishna as Gods, nor shall I worship them. 3. I shall not recognise Gauri and Ganapati as gods nor shall I worship them. 4. I do not believe in the theory of incarnation of god. 5. I do not consider Buddha as the incarnation of Vishnu. 6. I shall not perform Shraddha [a Hindu rite that one carries out for the safety of the deceased] nor shall I give offerings' to god. 7. I shall not do anything which is detrimental to Buddhism. 8. I shall not perform any religious rites through the agency of a Brahmin. 9. I believe that all human beings are equal. 10. I shall endeavour to establish equality. 11. I shall follow the eight-fold path of the Buddha. 12. I observe the ten *Paramitas* (observances) of the Buddha [the virtues in which a follower of the Buddha has to restrain himself].13. I shall be

compassionate to all living beings and I shall nurture them with care. 14. I shall not steal. 15. I shall not lie. 16. I shall not commit adultery. 17. I shall not drink liquor. 18. I shall lead my life striving to cultivate a harmonious blend of the three basic principles of Buddhism [Enlightenment, Precept and Compassion]. 19. I thereby reject my old religion, Hinduism, which is detrimental to the prosperity of human kind and which discriminates between man and man and which treats me as inferior. 20. I fully believe that Buddhism is Saddhamma. 21. By my embracing Buddhism I am being reborn. 22. I hereby pledge to conduct myself hereafter in accordance with the teaching of the Buddha.[33] Hundreds of thousands of Dalits – mostly Mahars – got converted along with Dr Ambedkar on 14 October 1956 in Nagpur.

Conversion had become necessary for Ambedkar because his people's strength had been taken away. Ambedkar knew that in any struggle one who holds strength becomes victorious, and one who has no strength loses. Therefore, he recommended conversion as the only solution to the problem of untouchability. Ambedkar said: To reform the Hindu society is neither our aim nor our field of action. Our aim is to gain social freedom. We have nothing to do with anything else. If we can gain our freedom by conversion, why should we shoulder the responsibility of reforming the Hindu religion? And why should we sacrifice our strength and property for that? None should misunderstand the object of our movement as being Hindu social reform. The object of our movement is to achieve social freedom for the Untouchables. It is equally true that the freedom cannot be secured without conversion.[34]

The revolt which Ambedkar mobilised culminated in Buddhist movement. It was indeed a liberating force. Conversion, therefore, has become the first step in the long march of Untouchables towards social freedom. Ambedkar makes a clarion call to the oppressed classes: The Untouchables will remain Untouchables as long as they remain within "Hinduism". Conversion is not the lasting solution but it certainly is a step towards solution—the first step to destroy the caste. Therefore, we call upon all Untouchables to get out of Hinduism as urgently as possible.

Conclusion

After a thorough examination of Ambedkar's life, political and social activities, and his views of religious and secular paths to liberate the untouchable people, I come to the conclusion that Ambedkar turned to Buddhism as a liberated path due to its doctrines of equality, liberty, and fraternity for his untouchable people. Dr Ambedkar was a many-sided genius. He was a distinguished economist, a professor, a brilliant lawyer, a reputed author and a great political leader. But above all he showed us to how one could attain the heights of glory through hard work and faith in oneself. He was one of the highly gifted and qualified Untouchables ever born in India. At a very early stage of his career, he realised the pitiable plight of Untouchables. He made up his mind to devote his whole life for their socio-economic upliftment. Nevertheless, those selfless works were in vain because of the rigid and traditional Hindu social system. People belonging to the higher castes made the social system their weapon to dominate over the lower castes. Ambedkar stood firmly in the midst of storms, and continuously thought of the Untouchables and fought for their equality and social freedom in the Indian society. Ambedkar also asserted, along with the need of social reform, the urgency of political awakening for the servile classes. As an Untouchable, Ambedkar experienced material suffering and intellectual agony. After a careful and deep consideration of other religion like Hindu, Islam, christianity, Sikhism and Buddhism, he believed that religious conversion was essential to rouse the rational consciousness of the Untouchables. Thus, he found refuge in the Buddha's *Dhamma* as a real remedy for the ills of Untouchables. In Buddhism, he found equality, liberty, fraternity and a ray of hope and light for all the communities. How far has this conversion to Buddhism helped in changing the condition of the Untouchables. Despite decades of struggle and conflict, the scheduled castes in India continue to face widespread discrimination and inhumane treatment from a society even today. Call them Untouchables, Harijans or Dalits; the plight of these 200 million continues to challenge our credential as a democratic society which claims to be concerned about the well being of all its citizens. Even today the high castes continue to exploit the lower castes, psychologically, economically, socially and politically. There were some early attempts made for the upliftment of the Untouchables.

For the Hindus, the social system is divinely ordained and part and parcel of their tradition, it cannot be destroyed. Upper caste Hindus have a vested interest in maintaining and perpetuating caste. If caste goes, Hinduism will die. With the Untouchables it is just the opposite. Caste is the greatest obstacle in the way of their progress and social freedom. If they do not destroy caste, caste will destroy them. Human beings are essentially social animals. They are by nature interrelated and interdependent. A person can develop his or her personality only in the human society. For this purpose every human being, above all, needs the recognition that befits a human being. Caste society cannot provide the atmosphere and space required for authentic human development.

References

Ambedkar (1987), *Why go for Conversion*? Bengaluru: Dalit Sahitya Academy, p. 5.

Ibid., p. 8.

Ambedkar (1987), *Annihilation of Caste*. Bengaluru: Dalit Sahitya Academy.

Ambedkar, *Why go for Conversion*? Bengaluru: Dalit Sahitya Academy, 1987. P.D. Satya Pal, Dr B.R. Ambedkar and his Vision for Recostruction for Indian Society, International Journal of Multi disciplinary Educational Research, Vol. 1, Issue. 2, June 2, 2012.

Ambedkar, *Writings and Speeches.* Vol. 5. Maharashtra: Mumbai Government Central Press, 1989.

Babasahb Ambedkar, *Writings and Speeches* BA WS, Vol. 17.

C.D. Naik (2009), *Ambedkar's Perspective on Buddhism and other religion.* Delhi, India: Kalpaz Publication.

D.C. Ahir, Dr Ambedkar's Pilgrimate to Buddhism, in *Dr Ambedkar, Buddhism and Social Change,* ed. By A.K. Narain and D.C. Ahir (Delhi, India: B. R. Publishing Corporation, 1994), pp. 1-2.

Das, B. (1969), "Thus spoke Ambedkar", Jalandhar: Bheem Patrika Publications, Vol. 4, p. 108.

Das, B. (1969), "Thus spoke Ambedkar", Jalandhar: Bheem Patrika Publications, Vol. 4, pp. 71-72.

D. Keer, Dr Ambedkar, op. cit., p. 500.

Francis M. Wilhoit (1979), *The Quest for equality in freedom.* New Brunswick, NJ: Transaction, Inc.

G.S. Lokhande, Bhimrao Ramji Ambedkar, New Delhi, Intellectual Publishing House, 1977 [1982], pp. 255-6.

Keer, Dhananjay (1954), *Dr Ambedkar Life and Mission.* Mumbai: Popular Prakashan.

Ibid., p. 284.

Ibid., p. 285.

Kuber, W. N. (1978), *Dr Ambedkar – A Critical Study.* New Delhi: People's Publishing House, p. 92.

Ibid., p. 94.

M.S. Gore., The Social Context of an ideology: Ambedkar's political and social Thought", New Delhi: Sage Publications, p. 91.

N. Appaj Rao (1998), *The Indian human heritage, Hyderabad.* India: University Press Limited, p. 54.

Paķistan or The Partition of India, Dr B. R. Ambedkar, Vol. 8, Education Dept, Government of Maharashtra, Mumbai, 1990, pp. 228-230.

P.D. Satya Pal, *Dr B.R.Ambedkar and His Vision For Reconstruction of Indian Society,* International Journal of Multidisciplinary Educational Research, Volume 1, Issue 2, June 2012.

Rajshekar, V. T. (1980), *Ambedkar and His Conversion.* Bengaluru: Dalit Sahitya Academy: 71.

Sangharashita (1986), *Ambedkar and Buddhism* (Glasgow, UK: Windhorse Publications.

Satyapal, P.D. 2010, *From Culture of Reservations to Culture of Representations: Phule-Ambedkarite Agenda for Social Inclusion in India* in V. Subrahmanyam (ed) Social Exclusion, Integration and Inclusive Policies. Jaipur: Rawat Publications.

Thich Hang Dat, "Why did Ambedkar choose Buddhism to liberate his depressed classes"<http:thichhanngdat.com/files/Ambedkarpdf>

Wilkinson, S. and M. M. Thomas (1972), *Dr B. R. Ambedkar: The Neo-Buddhist Movement*, Madras: Park Town, p. 60

Zelliot, E. (2004) "Dr Babasaḥeb Ambedkar and the Untouchable Movement", New Delhi: Blumoon Book, p. 225.

17

Constitutional Obligations and Empirical Implications: Understanding Ambedkar *vis-à-vis* Right to Food

— *Tejinder Pal Singh*

Introduction

Food is the first and foremost human need for existence and is central to the discussion of human rights. The Indian State prescribes a list of offences: if a person attempts to commit suicide for lack of food; if a person steals some food or other articles for getting food; begging is also an offence. All such acts for getting food are punishable under the law. Further, if a person is sentenced for committing such an offence, he/she is provided with the minimum basic necessities, that is, food, shelter and clothes, in the prison. Should society encourage the commission of such offences or should it provide food as a concomitant to the right to life, which is a fundamental right? Food security is a basic human right, indeed it is a pre-condition for the full enjoyment of the Right to Food. The 1996 World Food Summit (WFS) declared, "Food security at the individual, household, regional, national and global levels exists when all people, at all times, have physical and economic access to sufficient, safe and nutritious food to meet their dietary needs and food preferences for an active and healthy life" (FAO, 1996).

The Right to Food is much more than having two-square meal. The International Covenant on Economic, Social and Cultural Rights (ICESCR) recognises the "right to an adequate standard of living, including adequate food", as well as the "fundamental right to be free from hunger". The "right to adequate food" is a much higher standard, including not only absence of undernutrition, but to the full range of qualities associated with food, including safety, variety and dignity, in short all those elements needed to enable an active and healthy life. The right to adequate food is defined by the United Nations Special Rapporteur as a human right to have a regular, permanent and unrestricted access directly or indirectly to qualitatively and quantitatively adequate food. The food should be culturally acceptable. It should fulfill the individual and collective needs of the people and enable them to lead a dignified life free from fear (FAO, 2004). Furthermore, as human rights are interdependent, indivisible and interrelated, therefore, the right to food is correlated with the enjoyment of other human rights, such as the right to live life with dignity, health, water, adequate housing, property, education and information, work and livelihood, social security, freedom of association and right to take part in public affairs, freedom from the worst forms of child labour etc. Any discrimination in terms of food availability, accessibility, adequacy, utilisation and stability, on the grounds of caste, ethnicity, religion, gender etc., is inextricably linked to the poverty, hunger and undernutrition, thereby violating the right to food, particularly of the marginalised and vulnerable sections.

There is no shortage of international legal documents enshrining the Right to Food to which Indian State is a party – the Universal Declaration of Human Rights (UDHR), the International Covenant on Economic, Social and Cultural Rights (ICESCR), the International Convention on the Elimination of All Forms of Racial Discrimination (ICERD), the Convention on the Elimination of Discrimination against Women (CEDAW), the Convention on the Rights of the Child (CRC), and the 2006 Convention on the Rights of Persons with Disabilities (CRPD). Further, India is also committed to the several non-legally binding international human rights instruments, including recommendations, guidelines, resolutions or declarations. Such soft-law instruments are accepted by States and serve as guidance for the implementation of Right to Food. For instance, Voluntary Guidelines to Support the Progressive Realisation of the Right to Adequate Food in the Context of National Food Security (or Right to Food Guidelines), adopted by consensus in 2004 by Council of FAO.

Objective of the Study

The Right to Food forms one of the basic social and economic rights essential to realise democracy. Even more than six decades of establishment of Constitutional democratic framework, this right is far away from realisation in Indian society. Though this right, to an extent, has been translated into legal entitlements with the enactment of the National Food Security Act (NFSA), 2013, yet poverty, hunger and undernutrition levels in India are among the highest in the world. The unequal access to and control over power and livelihood resources is central to the violation of this right. The present paper has attempted to highlighted the "paradoxical" reality while analysing the right to food from the perspective of the Indian Constitutional Obligations, especially, manifested in the 'Directive Principles of State Policy' (DPSP) on the one hand, and on the other hand, to what extent the B.R. Ambedkar's visionary conception of democracy has been put to effect even after six decades of independence.

Ambedkar's Visionary Conception of Democracy

Bhimrao Ramji Ambedkar (1891–1956), popularly also known as Babasaheb, was an Indian jurist, political leader, philosopher, thinker, anthropologist, historian, orator, prolific writer, economist, scholar, editor, a revolutionary and one of the founding fathers of independent India. He was also the Chairman of the Drafting Committee of Indian Constitution. He was widely claimed as the champion of human rights and the messiah of the deprived and marginalised sections.

Human rights in the Constitutional framework of Indian State are divided into two separate, but interdependent, parts. Part III of the Constitution contains the 'Fundamental Rights', including the right to life, which in conventional human rights parlance may be termed as civil and political rights (CPR), while Part IV of the Constitution contains the 'Directive Principles of State Policy' (DPSP), which include all the economic, social and cultural rights (ESCR) such as the right to food.

The Directive Principles are chiefly due to Ambedkar, and build on his visionary conception of democracy. This vision, in turn, was intimately related to his notion of the "good society" as a society based on "liberty, equality, and fraternity" (now manifested in the form of

Preamble, which reflects the guiding philosophy as well as fundamental values of Indian Constitution). Democracy, as he saw it, was both the end as well as the means of this ideal. It was the *end* because ultimately democracy was considered as synonymous with the realisation of liberty, equality and fraternity. At the same time, democracy was also the *means* to attain this ideal. Indeed, in his perspective, democracy was intrinsically geared to social transformation, justice and human progress. He viewed democracy as an instrument of bringing about change peacefully. In other words, for him, democracy is a form and method of government whereby revolutionary changes in the economic and social life of the people are brought about without bloodshed. Further, he went beyond the formalistic and limited notion of democracy in the terms of rule by the majority or government by the representatives of the people. Democracy, rather merely a form of government, is primarily a mode of associated living, of conjoint communicated experience. It is essentially an attitude of respect and reverence towards fellowmen. Thus, he visualised democracy as a way of life and for this to happen, it was essential to link political democracy with economic and social democracy. "Social and economic democracy are the tissues and the fibre of a political democracy. The tougher the tissue and the fibre, the greater the strength of the body…" This was one of the main objectives of the Indian Constitution, and particularly of Directive Principles. As observed by him, political justice is of no consequence, unless a democracy assures economic and social justice as well. He argued that, "we must...not...be content with more political democracy. We must make sure our political democracy a social democracy as well." Social justice means a way of life which recognises liberty, equality and fraternity, and economic justice broadly means equitable distribution of wealth and avoidance of concentration of wealth in few ever hands. Ambedkar himself argued that, "Our object in framing the Constitution is really two-fold: (i) To lay down the form of political democracy, and (ii) To lay down that our ideal is economic democracy and also to prescribe that every government whatever is in power shall strive to bring about economic democracy. The Directive Principles have a great value, for they lay down that our ideal is economic democracy".

Ambedkar's idea of democracy was based on bringing about an all-round democracy, which was much more than just a scheme of government. A scheme of government does not exist in vacuum, rather operates within the society. Its usefulness depends upon its relationship with the other spheres of society.

Political democracy means the principle of 'one man one vote' which indicates political equality. But if oppression and injustice exist, the spirit of political democracy would be missing. Democratic government, therefore, should be an extension of a democratic society. In the Indian society, for instance, so long as caste-based inequalities exist, real democracy cannot operate. In this sense, democracy means a spirit of fraternity and equality and not merely a political arrangement. Success of democracy in India can be ensured only by establishing a truly democratic society. Establishing democracy in such a society would be nothing short of a revolution. This would be a revolution in the social structure and attitudes of the people. In the place of hereditary inequality, the principles of brotherhood and equality must be established. Therefore, Ambedkar supported the idea of all-round democracy. However, soon after Independence, this revolutionary conception of democracy fell into oblivion.

Constitutional Obligations *vis-à-vis* The Right to Food

This aspect is universally accepted and it is common view that society must ensure adequate food supply. The Constitution of India provides for the explicit as well as implicit provisions to ensure food security for all and realize the Right to Food. Article 21 provides that "No person shall be deprived of his life or personal liberty except according to procedure established by law". The expression 'Life' in this Article has been judicially interpreted to mean a life with human dignity and not mere survival or animal existence. In the light of this, the State is obliged to provide for all those minimum requirements which must be satisfied in order to enable a person to live with human dignity, such as education, healthcare, just and humane conditions of work, protection against exploitation, etc. Later, the Supreme Court of India (in PUCL case) recognised Right to Food as an integral part and inherent to a Right to life with dignity, and Article 21 should be read with Articles 39(a) and 47 to understand the nature of the obligation of the State in order to ensure the effective realisation of this right.

The Constitution of India prohibits any forms of discrimination based on caste. Similarly, Article 23 gives protection against exploitation. It prohibits traffic in human beings and beggars and other similar forms of forced labour and makes any contravention to this an offence punishable in accordance with the law. Apart from the Fundamental Rights under Part III enshrined in the Constitution, Part IV of the Constitution provides for Directive Principles of State Policy which are required to be issued by the State while evolving its policies. Article 39(a) provides that "the State shall... direct its policy towards securing that the citizen, men and women equally, have the right to an adequate means of livelihood..." Article 47 creates a duty of the State that "the State shall regard the raising of the level of nutrition and the standard of living of its people and the improvement of public health as among its primary duties..." Therefore, given the aspirational and non-justiciable nature of the Directive Principles, however, most of the development of the right to food has occurred within the context of Article 21, which includes a fundamental Right to Life and is located within the enforceable and justiciable Fundamental Rights section of the Constitution. For instance, the National Human Rights Commission (NHRC), dated 17th January 2003, clearly stated that "there is a fundamental right to be free from hunger."

The Directive Principle calls upon the Nation State for establishment of a Welfare State. The purpose of Directive Principles is to secure a truly Welfare State by bringing social and economic democracy in Indian society. Directive Principles provide the framework, based on the ideals of justice, liberty, equality and fraternity, which guides the State in the formulation of its policy. A Welfare State promotes a just socio-economic order and thereby aids the realisation of the right to food of the people. It also directs the Nation State to ensure to its people in course of time a social order based on justice social, economical and political. Though, unlike Fundamental Rights, Directive Principles are not enforceable in a Court of Law. Nevertheless, according to Ambedkar's perspective, they are fundamental in the governance of the society. The root of the violation of Right to Food can be seen in his argument for linking political democracy with economic and social democracy. "On the January 26, 1950," he said, "we are going to enter into a life of contradictions. In politics we will have equality and in social and economic life we will have inequality". The contradiction is still with us today, and in some respects at least, the problem is even intensifying at this time of growing inequality, poverty and hunger due to elitist (top-down) approach, development-induced displacement, centralised corporate model, capitalist mode of production, land commodification and forcibly encroachment, loss of livelihood opportunities, and even loss of control over destinies due to unregulated free-market and globalisation forces.

Understanding Nutritional Status in a Food Surplus Indian State

While conceptualising the right to food, some issues are to be taken into consideration for realising this right. *Firstly*, broadly speaking, the right to food can be interpreted as a claim of individuals on society (starting but not ending with the state). It is an entitlement to be free from hunger, which derives from the assertion that the society has enough resources, both economic and institutional, to ensure that everyone is adequately nourished. However, difficulties arise as soon as we try to flesh out this broad definition and translate it into specific entitlements and responsibilities. *Secondly*, the term 'freedom from hunger', for instance, lends itself to several interpretations: getting two square meals a day, meeting specific calorie norms, avoiding nutrition-related ailments, and so on. Ideally, the right to food should be seen as a right to 'nutrition', as in Article 47 of the Constitution. However, good nutrition itself depends in complex ways on a wide range of inputs: not just adequate food intake but also clean water, basic healthcare, good hygiene, and so on. Even if we confine our attention to food intake, the constituents of good nutrition are a matter of debate among nutritionists. For instance, there is some controversy about the importance of various 'micronutrients' for good nutrition. For all these reasons, it is hard to translate the right to food into a specific list of entitlements. *Thirdly*, there are some difficulties in clarifying the responsibilities associated with the right to food. The primary responsibility is surely with the State, because the State alone commands the resources (economic and institutional) required to protect everyone from hunger, and because the state is generally responsible for safeguarding constitutional rights. Thus, whether the right to food is the responsibility of the State alone? or the responsibility for protecting the right to food is a shared responsibility, involving not only the state, but also other institutions or individuals? To illustrate, suppose a girl is undernourished because she does not get a fair share of food within the family. Clearly, her right to food would be violated.

But who is responsible? At some level, State responsibility would be involved, since the State has an overarching duty to eradicate social discrimination. But surely, the girls' parents (or whoever controls the distribution of food within the family) would also bear a substantial part of the responsibility for this situation. Here again, there is a difficulty in apportioning responsibilities for protecting the right to food.

To attain the obligations under the international law and constitutional ethos, the government launched various anti-hunger schemes and food related programmes, such as Public Distribution System (PDS), Midday Meal scheme, Targeted PDS, Integrated Child Development Services, Antyodaya Anna Yojana, Mahatma Gandhi National Rural Employment Guarantee Act, National Food Security Mission, etc. The recent avatar to realise the right to food is the National Food Security Act (NFSA) 2013, which covers about two-third of India's population with the objective of providing food and nutritional security by ensuring access to adequate quantity of quality food at affordable prices. This Act: provides for coverage of up to 75 per cent of the rural population and up to 50 per cent of the urban population; stipulates an entitlement of 5 kg of foodgrains per person per month for priority households and 35 kg per household per month for Antyodaya Anna Yojana (AAY) households at subsidised prices of ₹ 3 per kg of rice, ₹ 2 per kg of wheat, and Re 1 per kg of coarse grains; has special focus on nutritional support to women and children. Pregnant women and lactating mothers during pregnancy and six months after the childbirth will also be entitled to maternity benefit it of not less than ₹ 6000. Children up to 14 years of age will be entitled to nutritious meals or take-home rations as per prescribed nutritional standards; in case of non-supply of entitled foodgrains or meals, the beneficiaries will receive a food security allowance; also contains provisions for setting up of grievance redressal mechanisms at district and state levels; has separate provisions have been made in the Act for ensuring transparency and accountability; also contains measures for reforms in the TPDS, to be undertaken progressively by central and state governments etc.

While being a Welfare State, Indian Constitutional and democratic ethos guarantee justice, liberty and equality, yet various forms of discrimination and exclusion still persist. India transformed from being a food deficient to food surplus nation. Earlier we faced the problem of scarcity, but now there is problem of plenty where the millions of tonnes of wheat rot because warehouses are overflowing and huge quantities of wheat and rice are stored in open spaces, risking decay. Consequently, the Supreme Court, in 2010, urged the government to distribute grain free to the hungry but the government failed on its part. In 2013-14, total foodgrain production has been estimated at 265.6 million tonnes, which is highest ever in the country. Despite the constitutional obligations of Indian State, the empirical investigations have highlighted that there are "paradoxical" situations in realising the Right to Food in Indian Society:

- The 2014 Gross Hunger Index (GHI) ranked India at 55 among 76 emerging economies, still trailing behind countries like Thailand, China, Ghana, Iraq, Sri Lanka and Nepal.
- The 2014 Human Development Index (HDI) estimated 55 per cent of India's population is suffering from multidimensional poverty. India's HDI value for 2013 is 0.586, positioning the country at 135 out of 187 countries in terms of three basic parameters: to live a long and healthy life, to be educated and knowledgeable, and to enjoy a decent standard of living. India's HDI is also below the average of countries in both the medium human development group (0.614) and in South Asia (0.588).
- According to the UNICEF, malnutrition is more common in India than in Sub-Saharan Africa, and one in every three malnourished children in the world lives in India.
- The "HUNGAMA" (Hunger and Malnutrition) Survey Report 2011 highlighted that 42 per cent of children are underweight and 58 per cent are stunted by the age of 24 months. The awareness among mothers about nutrition is low as 92 per cent mothers had never heard the word 'malnutrition'. The rate of child underweight and stunting is proportional with mothers' levels of education.
- India is home to the largest number of poor with one-third of the world's 1.2 billion extreme poor living here. It also had

the highest number of under-five deaths (1.4 million) in the world in 2012, according to the UN MDG report 2014.

- The nutritional performance of adult women in India, at present, parallels a situation referred to famously as *The Asian Enigma*. Ramalingaswami, Jonsson and Rohde (1996) deployed this term to refer to the prevalence of higher levels of child undernutrition in South Asia, despite its much better performance in economic and social spheres, than Sub-Saharan Africa. The low birth weight of babies relates essentially to the poor nutritional status of women (mothers, to be specific). Prevalence of under-nutrition among adult women in India is among the highest in the world. About 36 per cent of adult women (15-49 years) in India had chronic energy deficiency (CED, i.e., body mass index (BMI) below 18.5) in 2005-06. This is much higher than the prevalence in most countries of Sub-Saharan Africa (for which comparable data exist).
- Based on the recommendations of the Tendulkar Committee using Household Consumer Expenditure Survey 2011-12 data of the National Sample Survey (NSS) 68th round, the NITI Aayog (earlier Planning Commission) estimated the poverty ratios for 2011-12 to be 21.9 per cent (25.7 per cent in rural areas and 13.7 per cent in urban areas) in 2011-12, but the NFSA covers about two-thirds of the population (75 per cent in rural areas and 50 per cent in urban areas). So the question arises why to bear an additional burden of 45 per cent? Further, the States/UTs are to complete identification of eligible households under the Act and the beneficiaries are yet to be identified as States have delayed specifying fresh criteria and completing verification. All the figures cited so far are national averages. It goes without saying that the situation gets worse – far worse – as we consider the poorer states (for instance, Jharkhand, Chhattisgarh, Odisha), and the more deprived regions within these poorer states (for instance, Palamau in Jhakhand, Sarguja in Chhattisgarh, Kalahandi in Odisha), not to speak of the poorer communities within these deprived regions.

- The politics of poverty and hunger may develop strong tendencies towards kleptocracy that can undermine food security even when harvests are good. Even the Supreme Court-appointed vigilance committee, headed by former Supreme Court judge Justice D.P. Wadhwa, had already slammed PDS for "rampant corruption, black marketing and diversion involving a vicious cartel of bureaucrats, fair price shop owners and middlemen". In addition, the poor management and maintenance of available foodgrain produce are left to rot in the storage facilities. The Court, in this context, had asked the government to distribute the food free to the needy rather than letting it rot in warehouses. The recent report submitted by the High Level Committee (HLC) on restructuring of Food Corporation of India (FCI) highlighted that the food management system has not been able to deliver on its objectives very efficiently; only six per cent of total farmers in India have gained from selling wheat and paddy directly to any procurement agency; diversions of grains from PDS amounted to 46.7 per cent in 2011-12; the benefits of procurement have not gone to larger number of farmers beyond a few states, and leakages in TPDS remain unacceptably high etc. Further, it recommended bringing down the coverage of population under NFSA to around 40 per cent from the present 67 per cent etc.

The causes of hunger and undernutrition are often not a scarcity of food but an inability to access available food in a caste stratified society. Being relegated to the bottom of the caste hierarchy, dalits lack access to and control over productive resources. The caste designation of a community in rural India, still, has a significant impact on the ability of members of that community to access and control critical productive resources like land, water, credit, livestock, agricultural inputs, training and extension services, technology, market information and access. The caste based discrimination can be described as the 'hidden apartheid', which is manifested in the form of percentage of malnourished children under five years of age (2005-06):

State	*National Average*			*Average for SC/ST children*	
	Total	*Male*	*Female*	*Scheduled Castes*	*Scheduled Tribes*
Stunted	48.0	48.1	48.0	53.9	53.9
Severely Stunted	23.7	23.9	23.4	27.6	29.1
Wasted	19.8	20.5	19.1	21.0	27.6
Severely Wasted	6.4	6.8	6.1	9.3	6.6
Underweight	42.5	41.9	43.1	47.9	54.4
Severely Underweight	15.8	15.3	16.4	18.5	24.9

These nutritional deficiencies have devastating consequences for the well-being and future of a nation like India which is claiming to reap the benefits of the demographic dividend. It severely diminishes the quality of life. Undernutrition is associated with reduced learning abilities, greater exposure to disease and other impairments of individual and social opportunities. Undernutrition in children is not affected by food intake alone, it is also influenced by access to health services, quality of care for the child and pregnant mother as well as good hygiene practices. Girls are more at risk than boys because of their lower social status. Further, a direct relationship exists between water, sanitation, health, nutrition, and human well-being. Consumption of contaminated drinking water, improper disposal of human excreta, lack of personal and food hygiene, and improper disposal of solid and liquid waste are major causes of diseases in developing countries like India.

Conclusion

The Constitution of India and its underlying ideas (chiefly due to Ambedkar) provide a sound framework for thinking about the right to food. In this framework, the right to food is one of the basic social and economic rights that are essential to achieve "social and economic democracy", without which political democracy is at best incomplete. Indeed, there is an obvious sense in which mass hunger and food insecurity is fundamentally incompatible with democracy in any meaningful sense of the term. Further, the realisation of the right to food can be analysed in terms of the improvement of nutrition indicators over time which is slow. There is also evidence of disparities in nutritional achievements (in terms of regions, i.e., between rural and urban areas; gender; and caste). In addition, the nutrition situation in India is a sort of 'silent emergency'. Little attention is paid to it in public debates and democratic politics but more verbalisation is made during elections for vote-bank gimmicks.

Food should not be used as a tool for political and economic pressure. Government should promote and safeguard a free, democratic and just society in order to provide a peaceful, stable and enabling economic, social, political and cultural environment in which individuals can feed themselves and their families in freedom and dignity. Governments, both Union and States, should promote all-round democracy, sustainable development and good governance, and promote and protect human rights and fundamental freedoms in order to empower individuals and civil society to make demands on their governments, devise policies that address their specific needs and ensure the accountability and transparency in decision-making processes and implementing such policies firmly.

Thus, if the right to food is to be achieved, it needs to be linked with other social and economic rights, such as the right to education, the right to work, the right to information, the right to health etc. These economic and social rights complement and reinforce each other. Taken together, however, they hold the promise of radical change in public priorities and democratic politics. Dr Ambedkar said very categorically that political democracy cannot be successful unless we have social and economic democracy. In other words, there is imperative need for linking of political democracy with social and economic democracy to gear towards social transformation, and for an inclusive and sustainable food security for all.

References

Dr Babasaheb Ambedkar: Writings and Speeches, Vol. 13, Education Department, Government of Maharashtra, Mumbai, 1994. p. 216.

Dreze, Jean, *Democracy and Right to Food*, Economic and Political Weekly, April 24 2004, pp. 1723-31.

Economic Survey 2013-14, 2014-15, GoI.

International Covenant on Economic, Social and Cultural Rights 1966: article 2(1), 11(1) and 23; Ziegler 2012: "What is the right to food?"

Jose, Sunny, *Adult Under-Nutrition in India: Poverty or Ethnicity?* Economical and Political Weekly, May 3, 2014, Vol. XLIX, No 18, pp. 72-74.

Proceedings of a hearing held on 17th January 2003; reprinted in Gonsalvez, C., P.R.Kumar and A.K. Srivastava (eds.) (2005), *Right to Food*, second edition, New Delhi: Human Rights Law Network, pp. 404-421.

Proceedings of the constituent assembly of India, Friday November 19, 1948; available at http://www.parliamentofindia.nic.in/debates/vol17p9.htm.

Special Rapporteur on the Right to Food 2012a: "Right to Food."

http://www.ifpri.org/publication/2014-global-hunger-index. Retrieved 20 January 2015.

http://www.naandi.org/CP/HungamaBK Dec11LR.pdf. Retrieved 21 January 2015.

http://timesofindia.indiatimes.com/india/India-ranks-135-in-human-development-index-UNDP/articleshow/38959685.cms. Retrieved 21 January 2015.

18

Dr B.R. Ambedkar's Propensity for Sikh Religion: A Path towards Salvation

— ***Parambir Brar***

Abstract

Bhim Rao Ambedkar had experienced various discriminations in his early life by virtue of being born in an untouchable family. He wanted to get rid off from such ill-treatments which make him suffer intellectually as well as socially. For this, he sorted to convert into another religion which will act as substitute to Hinduism for the simple reason that the Hindu religion does not recognise the principles of equality on the basis of social status and also, it fosters inequality by insisting upon grading people on basis of Chaturvarna system. So, he started looking towards Sikhism because this religion would not alienate the converts from Hindu culture as Sikhism is an offshoot of Hinduism only but due to some differences with Sikh leaders of contemporary period and prevalence of untouchability among Sikhs, this conversion could not take place and as a result, Ambedkar, along with his followers sought for Buddhism instead of Sikhism as an alternative way towards salvation.

[**Key Words:** *Sikhism, Discrimination, Untouchability, Conversion, Depressed classes, Salvation*].

Introduction

Bhim Rao Ramji Ambedkar, also known as Babasaheb, was an Indian nationalist, jurist, political leader, activist, philosopher, scholar, revolutionary and also revivalist of Buddhism in India. He was also known as the father of Indian Constitution. He was born to Ramji Subedar on April 14, 1891 in military cantonment of Mhow

(Military headquarters of war) in Central Provinces (now Madhya Pradesh). As he was born into a poor untouchable family, Ambedkar spent his whole life fighting against social discrimination, the Indian caste system and the system of Chaturvarna- the Hindu categorisation of human society into four Varnas. Being a member of Dalit (Mahar) community, he surely underwent the humiliation of being one, as a student, as an individual growing up in a caste ridden society. It influenced his intellectual and social life in more than one way. He was obsessed with casteism to his very end and it especially depicted during the time when he was a member of Jawahar Lal Nehru's Catholic cabinet and formulator of Indian Constitution at the time of Independence.

After his father's retirement, his family settled in Kap-Dapoli in Ratnagiri district. Around 1894, Dapoli municipal education department decided not to admit untouchables in their schools. After this incidence, his family moved to Mumbai and his father got posted as storekeeper in PWD office at Satara. During this phase, he experienced hardship because of being an untouchable. Once, he, along with his siblings is travelling to Goregaon on a train. On reaching the station, no one was ready to take them to interior. One driver offered them the cart but was not ready to drive for untouchables. So, Ambedkar had to drive and the regular bullock driver rested in backseat. For complete journey of one and a half day, they had to go without water because the untouchables were not allowed to drink water from village wells. Many such events took place in Bhim Rao's early life.

In the wake of coming back to India in 1927, after completing his education at University of Columbia, he opted to battle against the caste discrimination which is prevalent in each and every corner of country. He started to discover approaches to reach to the individuals and make them comprehend the disadvantages of the predominating social injustice. He also propelled a daily paper called "Mooknayaka" (pioneer of the quiet). He protested the choice of Congress and Mahatma Gandhi to call the untouchable group as 'Harijan'. He would say that untouchable people are not separate from general public, rather they all are parts of same society.

Reasons for Opting Sikhism as an alternative

Ambedkar declared at Yeola in 1935: "I was born a Hindu, I had no choice. But I will not die a Hindu because I do have a choice." Ambedkar and his followers had to convert as the religion they were born in was not a religion but a form of slavery. But the religion they wanted to follow must had everything that the modern society would need for better social, mental, economical, communal and other aspects of development. In the words of Ambedkar: ***"I like the religion that teaches liberty, equality and fraternity***." So, Ambedkar, after this famous conversion announcement of 1935, was determined to seek alternatives to Hinduism. Around 1936, we can see the evidences of Ambedkar's attraction to Sikhism. There were reasons for this attraction. Sikhism was an Indian religion, and one with traditions of equalitarianism which he thought important. It was also "close enough" to Hinduism that he felt would not so much alienate Hindus who were afraid of conversion that would increase the powers of an alien religion. In 1936, he met Dr Moonje of the Hindu Mahasabha, with a statement of conversion of lower caste Hindus to another religion (Sikhism) that was later given out on a wider basis to other leaders like M.R. Jayakar, M.C. Rajah and others. Interestingly, Dr Moonje gave a qualified approval while Gandhi unequivocally condemned a conversion to Sikhism.

It was at this time, in April 1936, that Ambedkar went to Amritsar for a conference of the Sikh Mission. He addressed the meeting, before huge crowds; some Dalits from Kerala converted to Sikhism at this time. Dr Ambedkar told the group that he had decided to renounce Hinduism, but not where to go as yet. However, his attendance at the conference alienated the Jat-Pat Todak Mandal, which had given an invitation for him to speak in Lahore, and they wanted him to expunge some passages critical of the Vedas from his address. Ambedkar refused, and had the speech printed on his own – "Annihilation of Caste." In it, he makes the statement, "the political revolution of the Sikhs was preceded by the religious and social revolution led by Guru Nanak." In contrast to what he saw as the "reform" of the Bhakti Movement in Maharashtra, Sikhism was revolutionary. Ambedkar's argument was that emancipation of the mind had to precede social and political revolution: "political revolutions have always been preceded by social and religious revolutions."

Ambedkar's opinion regarding reasons for looking towards Sikhism instead of Islam or Christianity was that if the depressed classes embrace Islam or Christianity, they not only go out of Hinduism but go out of Hindu culture. On the other hand, if they become Sikhs they remain within Hindu culture. This is by no means a small advantage for the Hindus. Conversion to Islam or Christianity will denationalise the Depressed Classes. If they go to Islam the number of Muslims would be doubled and the danger of Muslim domination also becomes real. If they go to Christianity it will strengthen the hold of Britain on the country."

Part of the debate at the time was whether converts to Sikhism (or any other religion) would retain the rights given to them as Scheduled Castes, under the Poona Pact. Moonje had agreed that converts to Sikhism would retain these rights.

Thus, on 18 September 1936, Ambedkar sent a group of his followers to the Sikh Mission at Amritsar to study the Sikh religion. On Baisakhi day in 1939, Ambedkar participated in the All India Sikh Mission conference in Amritsar with his followers wearing turbans, and deletated his nephew to take amrit and become a Khalsa Sikh.

Way from Sikhism to Buddhism

The Sikh leadership, including Master Tara Singh, a high caste, had been advised by Gandhi and the Brahmin leaders to reject the proposed conversion as that would shift the monopoly of power from the higher caste Sikhs to the new Dalit Sikhs. Gandhi and the Brahmins also did not want the message of casteless society advocated by Sikhism to spread to the rest of India – the land of caste, to which Gandhi and Brahminical forces subscribed. If the Sikhs had accepted the proposal at that time, today Sikhs would have numbered 250 to 300 million, and would have had a lot of clout in all power structures, and what had happened to them in 1984 would probably never would have happened.

The massive numbers of untouchables would overwhelm the existing Sikhs, if conversion took place; and Tara Singh feared that Ambedkar himself would become the leader of the Panth. In one incident, money (twenty five thousand rupees) apparently promised to Ambedkar was given instead to a follower of Tara Singh, Master Sujan Singh Sarhali; it never reached Ambedkar. Apparently, the Sikh leadership was not interested in expansion of Sikhism to India as they were blinded by their selfish interest, and not the interest of Sikhism.

They feared that they would lose all control and power to the new Dalit Sikhs. If only the Sikhs leaders had followed the true agenda of Guru Gobind Singh Ji of a new casteless society in India; the Guru had hoped that his Khalsa contagion would spread rapidly throughout India especially among victims of the caste system (the lower castes i.e. the shudra varna who form nearly 80 per cent of India's population).

This was a great loss to Sikhism. The Sikhs had one chance to expand their religion out of Punjab to the rest of India, and they have lost that chance. Sikhism has become a stunted religion as a result without any missionary zeal, restricted to Punjab and largely a hereditary religion with no new conversions at national or international level. This was a great achievement for the Brahminical forces as they did not want Sikhism to spread to rest of India and threaten the hegemony of Brahmins and the Brahminical system in India. The Guru's in their infinite wisdom wanted Sikhism to be, India wide religion but the Sikh leaders at the time lacked that wisdom and had put their own agenda, above the vision of the Guru.

Thus, it can be said that during the middle period of his life, Ambedkar interacted with the Sikhs and their leaders, and showed some attraction towards conversion to Sikhism but due to some unavoidable reasons, he turned away from it. One reason was undoubtedly his awareness of the existence of untouchability within Sikhism itself. Though in principle egalitarian, in fact Dalit Sikhs retained a separate identity – as Mazbhi Sikhs, or in some cases as "Ravidasis' – and were differently treated. There was thus a kind of segregation within Sikhism. At the social level, Dalit Sikhs in the Punjab remained landless, subordinate as agricultural labourers to the landed Jat Sikhs, the dominant community.

Then, perhaps, the very factors which he early spoke of as reasons for going to Sikhism may have dissuaded him. If Sikhism was "part of Hindu culture," then what in the end was the use? The "Hindu culture" which was so infected with casteism would continue to infect the entire Sikh community; Dalits would remain as untouchables within it, only untouchables who perhaps wore turbans. Buddhism more and more was appearing to Ambedkar as something different; like Sikhism it was Indian and not "alien"; it would not irrevocably divide the nation or give domination to Muslims or greater continuity of power to British colonialists. It also offered, perhaps, a kind of rationalism that Sikhism did not – Ambedkar was undoubtedly attracted by this theme that the Buddha had so consistently put forward, that one must decide for oneself, on the basis of experience and rationality. Thus, Buddhism proved to have a stronger and more enduring appeal than Sikhism. Buddhism could not even offer the limited resources of community support that Sikhism could, but it was also a religion that Ambedkar could shape on his own, could mould to suit what he felt to be the spiritual and moral needs of Dalits. Sikhism already had its set religious hierarchy, to which Ambedkar – however strong and determined as a leader – would have been subordinate. So, it can be said that after returning in 1937 from Europe, his love for Sikhism had evaporated.

It is obvious that Ambedkar regarded Buddhism as a much more rational religion compared to Hinduism and Sikhism, rather the most rational religion. His main objection to Hinduism was that it sanctified inequality and untouchability through its doctrine of Chaturvarnya. Buddhism, on the other hand, rejected Chaturvarnya and supported equality. He commends Buddhism for rejecting God and soul and for emphasising morality. According to him, prajna (understanding as against superstition and supernaturalism), karuna (love), and samata (equality), which Buddhism alone teaches, is all that human beings need for a "good and happy life". Though he continued to talk of his proposed conversion but in the twilight of his life, on October 14, 1956, two months before his death, he left Hinduism to become a Buddhist along with half a million adherents. So, Sikhism lost out to Buddhism as the goal of conversion for Ambedkar and his lakhs of followers.

Conclusion

In a nutshell, it can be said that Ambedkar does not accept a religion in which one class alone has a right to gain knowledge, another has only a right to use arms, the third one to trade and the fourth only to serve. In his viewpoint, the religion, which has an intention to educate a few and to keep the rest in darkness, is not a religion but a conspiracy to keep the people in mental slavery. In religion, salvation is stated as the saving of the soul from sin and its consequences. Salvation is called *moksha* or *mukti* which mean liberation and release respectively. So, to liberate the people of lower castes from the chains of inequality, untouchability and discrimination, it was considered necessary at that time to get away with such religion which propagates inequality among human beings. In limelight of this opinion, Ambedkar sought to convert into such a religion which will vanish the roots of all quarrels of unjust treatment of individuals. Thus, by conversion, the affinity between the Hindus and the Untouchables can be brought about and equality of treatment can be achieved. Once, the most favourable option fulfilling all the requisites of the Dalits was Sikhism which later on changed to Buddhism due to presence of various evils in Sikhism itself and some differences with the Sikh leaders.

References

Ambedkar, B. R. (1981), *Why Go For Conversion*?, New Delhi: Dalit Sahitya Akademy.

Keer, Dhananjay. (1954), *Dr Ambedkar: Life and Mission.* Mumbai: Popular Prakashan.

Moon, Vasant. (2002), *Dr Babasaheb Ambedkar*. New Delhi: National Book Trust.

Rathore, Akash S. and Verma, Ajay. (2011), *B.R. Ambedkar: the Buddha and his Dhamma.* New Delhi: Oxford University Press.

Roy, Arundhati. (2013), *Annihilation of Caste: The Annotated Critical Edition.* New Delhi: Navayana Publication.

Singh, Bhupinder. (2006, October 14), Dr Ambedkar and Sikhism. Retrieved March 21, 2016, from http://bhupindersingh.ca/2006/10/14/dr-ambedkar-and-sikhism/

Singh, N. K. (2000), *Ambedkar on Religion*. New Delhi: Anmol Publications.

19

Dr B.R. Ambedkar – A Theoretician of Indian Brahminical Caste System and His Contribution to Understand Caste System and its Operational Mechanism

—*Tarminder Kaur*

Abstract

The paper is intended to understand Caste system from the view point of Dr B.R. Ambedkar and his vision of Caste ridden Indian society. He comprehensively analysed the factors responsible for operational success of Caste system and its continuity from centuries. This paper highlight the theoretical contribution of Dr B.R. Ambedkar to approach Indian society from a different perspective with special reference to depressed and downtrodden lowest rung of Indian Caste system i.e. Scheduled Caste and Untouchables. The role of Dr B.R. Ambedkar as a social reformer and a National Political Leader is also discussed.

[**Keywords:** *Caste system, depressed, downtrodden, untouchables*].

Introduction

"The system of Untouchability is Goldmine to the Hindus. In it 240 millions of Hindus have 60 millions untouchables to serve as their retinue to enable the Hindus to maintain pomp and ceremony and to cultivate a feeling of pride and dignity befitting a master class, which can't be fostered and sustained unless there is beneath it a servile class to look down upon."

Dr B.R. Ambedkar

Dr Ambedkar's life appears to confirm the fairy tale of a self made man. He emerged as First Dalit Leader in India. Dr Bhim Rao Ambedkar was born on April 14, 1891 in Mhow. His native village Ambavade was in the Konkan Coastal region and Ambedkar's real name Ambavadekar came from there. He was protected for many years from discrimination afflicting Untouchables because of the particular circumstances of life in the cantonment where his father was working in British Army as a soldier. He gradually exposed to the vagaries of life as an Untouchable.

It is very interesting to first read the Words of Dr B.R. Ambedkar when he says that he first proposed to handle the Law giver of India. He firmly believes that every Country has Law givers, who arise as an incarnation in times of emergency to set right a sinning humanity and to give it the law of justice and humanity. He said that "I may seem hard on Manu but I am sure my force is not strong enough to kill his ghost. He lives like a disembodied spirit. Manu didn't give the Law of Caste and that he couldn't do so. Caste existed long before Manu. He was an upholder of it and philosophised about it. He didn't ordain the present order of Hindu Society. His work ended with the codification of existing Caste rules and preaching of Caste Dharma. The spread and growth of Caste system is a gigantic task achieved by the power of cunning of an individual or of a class.

Dr B.R. Ambedkar darely said that Brahmins may have been guilty of many things. In orthodox Hinduism, there is a strong belief that the Hindu society was somehow molded into the framework of Caste system and it is an organisation consciously created by the Shastras. It is being justified on the ground that it cannot but be good because it is claimed by the Shastras and Shastras can not be wrong. Preaching didn't make the caste system neither will it unmake it. He said that my aim is to show the falsity of the attitude that has exalted religious sanction to the position of a scientific explanation.

Dr B.R. Ambedkar also discussed the viewpoint of western scholars who attempted other explanations. They stressed the nuclei, round which have formed the various castes in India. These nuclei may be occupation, survival of tribal organisations, rise of new belief, cross-breeding and migration.

Question 1: **According to Dr Ambedkar whether these nuclei do not exist in other societies and whether they are peculiar to India. If they are not peculiar to India but common to the world then why they didn't 'form' caste in other parts of this planet? Is it because other parts are holier than Vedas or that the professors are mistaken?**

The matter of particular attention is that it is essentially a class system in which individuals, when qualified could change their class and therefore classes thus change their personnel. But the unnatural thing about the so called sub-divisions (Castes) is that they lost the open door character and become self-enclosed units called Castes.

Question 2: **Whether they compelled to close their doors and become endogamous, or did they close them of their own accord?**

Dr B.R. Ambedkar submits that there is a double line of answer: some closed the door and other found it closed against them. Dr Ambedkar says close door system is a fashion in Hindu society and it has originated from the Brahmin Caste. Then it is whole heartedly imitated by all non-Brahmins who in turn become endogamous castes. It is the infection of imitation that caught all these sub-divisions into its fold.

What made Dr B.R. Ambedkar a Social Reformer and a Controversial Political Leader

Dr Ambedkar, who was a constitutional expert, philosopher and statesman emerged first as a great crusader for the oppressed and depressed. His laudable contribution in the process of nation building entitled him the exalted position of a top ranking nationalist leader, patriot and statesman of modern India. His belief that without the freedom of people, nationalism becomes a means of internal slavery, forced labour and oppression for the poor and the depressed classes informed his conception of nation building.

The political strategies which he used to secure constitutional safeguards for his community made him a controversial leader of his time. His mounting attack on Hindu religion and confrontationist and uncompromising stand which he took on Hindu Gods and Goddesses under the belief that Hindu religion was responsible for slavery and oppression of untouchables, caused a widespread resentment in

Hindu Society. His hostility to Congress and Mahatma Gandhi and his denunciation of Congress party's programmes and policies of upliftment of Harijans and abolition of untouchability was not only condemned by nationalist forces but also led to believe that he was dividing the society on the basis of caste. The demand of separate electorate for Schedule Castes which Mr Ambedkar put in the Round Table Conference was eventually recognised in the Communal Award by British Prime Minister Ramsay Mcdonald also generated lot of controversy. Dr B.R. Ambedkar himself claimed he is not against Hindu Religion but against the evils of Hinduism because he believed that they were responsible for the pathetic plight and exploitation of the downtrodden. He said that he demanded separate electorates only to avoid the total dependence on sweet will of caste Hindus. At a time when he appeared on the political scene of India there were three types of minorities demanding special protection:

1. Religious Minorities
2. Linguistic Minorities
3. Depressed Classes.

These minorities were facing basic social and economic problems. Dr Ambedkar belonged to the third minority that had suffered terrible humiliating consequences of 'Untouchability'. Consequently, it was but natural that socio-economic upliftment of this group from long age bondage had the first priority in his thought and practice.

Dr Ambedkar: A Minority Leader or a National Political Leader?

It will not be correct to say that he was a minority leader. Dr Ambedkar was a national leader who was visualising an Indian society free from all inequalities. He held the view that the problem of depressed classes in India is religio-political and not socio-economic as advocated by other leaders including Mahatma Gandhi. Unless Hindu society is restructured and the depressed classes are given due share in the political power, there problem can not be effectively solved it is for this reason he found Gandhi's approach to the problem of untouchability as cosmetic and superficial. Dr Ambedkar was a student of Sanskrit. So he had access to the core Hindu texts which untouchables were not allowed to read therefore with the help of theological facts he tried to transform emotional aversion to caste into an intellectual challenge by giving it a religio-political base. Accordingly, he wrote **"Caste is not a physical object like a wall of Bricks or a line of barbed wire which prevent Hindus from co-mingling and which has therefore to be pulled down. Caste is a notion, a state of mind; destruction of caste does not mean the destruction of physical barrier, it is a notional change"**. Dr Ambedkar argues that in Hindu society, not only Brahmins but all the three upper castes have privileges. They themselves created the caste system. It is not simply one class that benefited from the caste system: all the three classes have benefited and they are the rulers.

Dr Ambedkar's vision on Caste system: Demand High Caste status or Abolition of Untouchability or is there any other alternative?

Ambedkar never claimed high Caste status for untouchables, since such claims implied an acceptance of upper castes superiority, nor did he invoke other common claim – that untouchables were pre-Aryan. He argued that the untouchables position in Indian society was of social, not racial origin and therefore subject to change. Consisting the claim of Gandhiji that the problem of untouchability is socio-economic, he wrote that "what the mahatma seems to suggest is that Hindu Society can be made tolerable and even happy without any fundamental change in its structure if all the high caste Hindus can be persuaded to follow a high standard of morality in their dealings with the lower castes, Hindus. I can respect those of the High caste Hindus who try to realise a high social ideal in their life. Without such men India would be an uglier and less happy place to live in. But anyone who relies on an attempt to turn the members of the caste Hindus into the better men by improving their personal character is in my judgment wasting his energy... can personal character make the maker of armament a good man..... if it can not... how can you accept personal character to make a man loaded with the consciousness of caste a good man, a man who would treat his fellows as his friends and equals ?......."

Annihilation of Caste

The "Annihilation of Caste" a list of reforms for Hinduism that appears naïve and legalistic, based on abstractions rather than possibilities. The cardinal reforms listed were: there should be one standard book of Hindu religion, acceptable to all Hindus; priest should receive their office not by heredity, but by the state examination, priest should be limited in number by law and should be subject to disciplinary action by the state. His final resolution of the untouchables' religious dilemma was adopted in 1956 when he converted to Buddhism in an attempt to link the untouchables to the greatness of India's past while denying the contemporary concept of caste. Ambedkar found Gandhi's general ideology unappealing. He and some other reformers considered his philosophy outdated and rejected his programme, which was based primarily on a concern for the rural masses. Ambedkar's programmes were intended to integrate the untouchables into Indian society into modern, not traditional ways, and on as high a level as possible. Ambedkar's ideal for the depressed was to raise their educational standard so that they may know their own conditions, have aspiration to rise to the level of highest Hindu and be in a position to use political power as a means to that end. **For Ambedkar equality meant not only equal status of the varnas, but equal social, political and economic opportunity for all.**

Conclusion

Thus, he concluded that the moral consciousness of the evil of caste is meaningless if the basis of relationship between high and low caste is fundamentally wrong. Ambedkar's views as to the origin of untouchability are presented in "The Untouchables" published in 1948, late in his political career. According to this account, untouchability originated in the practices of separation and denigration imposed on those who remained Buddhists during an earlier period of renascent Hinduism. However, from 1927 to 1935 Ambedkar helped organise campaigns to force the opening of Hindu temples to untouchables. This also proved to be ineffective and in 1935 Ambedkar decided to reject all claims to Hinduism by converting to another religion. Ambedkar maintained that the untouchables were an element separate from Hinduism and went to great length to prove it. He went to the root of the matter when he said that Hindus has much to lose by the abolition of untouchability, though they had nothing to fear from political reservations leading to this abolition. The matter was economic rather than religious. Ambedkar wanted egalitarian Hinduism.

He analysed the process of Hindu Rashtra degeneration. The caste system set forth many difficulties for the downtrodden and pushed them in the asylum of the foreigners. Ambedkar pointed out that the reason of the existence of caste system was not its merit but the only thing that the foreigners didn't crush it down. He concluded that Hinduism was flexible and progressive. The predominance of handful of the aryas proved the progressiveness. They adjusted nicely with the people racially different from them. Then Ambedkar posed a question as to how such progressive a religion turned retrograde. He furnished a logical answer that till Hinduism had unity: oneness of the varna- it remained progressive and found no difficulty in its function.

References

Christopher, Jaffrelot (2004), *Dr Ambedkar and Untouchability*. Permanent Black Publication, Delhi: 2-7.

Manoranjan, Mohanty (2004), *Caste: Mechanism, Genesis and Development*. Sage Publication, New Delhi: 140, 141.

Ibid., 145-147.

Seema, Pasricha (2006), *Caste Based Reservation in India*. Deep and Deep Publications: New Delhi: 131-137.

Ibid., 139-143.

Ibid., 146-148.

Ibid., 159-160.

20

Ambedkar's Philosophy on the Emancipation of Dalit Women and its Reflection in Baby Kamble's *The Prisons We Broke*

— Parveen Kumari

Abstract

Dr Bhim Rao Ambedkar besides a scholar of genius who had significant volume of writings to his credits to lead the society on the path of Liberty, Fraternity and Equality was also a crusader for the rights of depressed and marginalised sections of the society including Dalits and women. He broke down the barriers in the way of progress of women by his sincere efforts like codification of Common Civil Code for Hindus and other sections of the Indian society. The present paper is an attempt to highlight the relevance of Dr B.R. Ambedkar's ideas on the inclusion and empowerment of women in general and Dalit women in particular who carry the double burden of gender and caste oppression in the larger framework of society. Dr B.R. Ambedkar mobilised a large number of Dalit women to join the various phases of his movements – be it the historic Mahad Satyagraha of 1927, or the Nasik Satyagraha of 1930 or his conversion to Buddhism in 1956. Dalit women have benefitted in several ways from his initiatives. Some Dalit women took up the pen to articulate their experiences of victimisation. The present paper attempts a study of Baby Kamble's narrative The Prisons We Broke to analyse why Dalit women have great reverence for their 'Babasaheb' and why he is still considered a Messiah by Dalits. It was Ambedkar's awakening regarding the rights of Dalits which ultimately moved them from periphery to centre.

[**Keywords:** *Marginalisation, Inclusion, Empowerment, Oppression, Caste, Gender*].

Introduction

Dr B.R. Ambedkar, the chief architect of Indian Constitution is regarded as one of the greatest intellectual and social reformer of modern India for his work for the cause of social justice for the downtrodden and underprivileged sections of Indian society. He not only struggled for the emancipation of the underprivileged but also worked tirelessly for the reformation of conditions of women in Indian society. His views on women's oppression, social democracy, caste and Hindu social order and philosophy are significant to modern Indian feminist thinking.

Women in India have always been the topic of concern since ancient times. The Indian women are devoted to their families and are known as perfect homemakers and 'grahlakshmi'. They are worshipped in the names of goddesses Durga, Saraswati, Parvati, Kali and so on. However, if one looks deep down at the surface visible scenario, one gets face to face with reality. On the name of goddesses, the women are trained to be silent, calm and to endure every torture and injustice.

In India, social system is highly patriarchal. Women are denied rights. They have no freedom and are not considered equivalent to men. A woman faces humiliation, taunts and at times fatal violence on giving birth to a daughter. Women are not only abstained from getting educated but also are not permitted to step out of the house.

It is said that women in Vedic period enjoyed equivalent status and rights with men in all spheres of life. Maya Majumdar testifies that women's status during the Vedic period was high. She was the presiding deity of the house:

> Over thy husband's father and thy husband's mother bear fully sway. Over the sister of thy lord, over his brothers rule supreme. 'Go to the house to be the household's mistress and speak as lady to thy gathered people. A woman has more character than impious man.' (qtd. in Majumdar 2)

K. Uma Devi in her work *Women's Equality in India: A Myth or Reality?* also testifies that position of women was better during Vedic period:

> There were no child marriages and woman had freedom to marry a man of her choice irrespective of caste. The concept of *Ardhangini*

suggests that there was equal status to woman along with man....Girls were equally educated along with boys. (17)

The deterioration of status of women started from the period of *Smritis* (800 BC – 200 AD) particularly with Manu and his *Manusmriti*. He pronounced that no woman was entitled to freedom. In *Manusmriti*, he says: "The father protects the woman during childhood, the husband during her youth, and son during her old age. Woman does not deserve freedom" (qtd. in Shukla 6).

During Medieval period, the condition of women worsened. Several evil practices like child-marriage, Sati, and female infanticide were practiced largely. Devdasi tradition was common in southern India where girls were married to deity or trees.

During the pre-Independent era, various social reformers like Ishwar Chandra Vidyasagar, Begum Kudsiyya of Bhopal (1819-44) who refused to follow purdah system, Raja Ram Mohan Roy, Jyotiba Phule with his wife Savitri Phule, Swami Dayanada Sarswati, Dr D.K. Karvae, Mahatma Gandhi and others undertook various measures to improve the condition of women in India. Dr B.R. Ambedkar was one among those nationalists and reformists.

Presently women in India have freedom of expression as well as right to education. Women are proving their worth. Various prestigious positions are held by Indian women. However, they still are not considered as equivalent to their male counterparts. Dowry system, female infanticide, poor health, domestic violence still gets in the way of women's emancipation and empowerment. The present paper is an attempt to highlight the relevance of Dr B. R. Ambedkar's ideas on the inclusion and empowerment of women in general and Dalit women in particular who carry the double burden of gender and caste oppression in the larger framework of society.

Dr B.R. Ambedkar's approach to women's empowerment is wholly different from other social reformers like Raja Ram Mohan Roy, Swami Dayanada Sarswati, Ishwar Chandra Vidyasagar and Mahatma Gandhi who tried to reform the Indian society from orthodox customs and rituals without questioning the hierarchical social order. Ambedkar saw women as the victims of the oppressive, caste-based and rigid hierarchical social system. As Simone De Beauvoir observes: "One is not born, but rather becomes, a woman" (301), Ambedkar also believed it's the socio-cultural forces which construct gender relations.

In his articles "The Riddle of the Women", "The Woman And the Counter Revolution", "The Rise and Fall of Hindu Women", "Castes in India: Their Mechanism Genesis and Development" and through his newspapers *Mooknayak* (1920) and *Bahishkrit Bharat* (1927), Ambedkar tried to show how the gender relations and differences are constructed by Hindu Brahminical patriarchy, which conditions women to assume a stereotype feminine behaviour, to be passive and submissive, suited only to a life of domestic and family responsibilities. He perceived education as an important tool for the change and stressed on the need of women's education to raise their social status.

In his article, "The Rise and Fall of Women" he makes a historical study of the women's status in ancient India and the factors which led to the decline of their status. Like other scholars, he also observes that during pre-Manu days, women occupied a high position in the intellectual and social sphere. They had access to education and he gives examples from various ancient *Shutras* like *Sharuta Shutras*, Panini's *Ashtadhyayi*, Patanjali's *Maha Bhasya* as evidence.

In "The Women and Counter Revolution" and "The Riddle of Women" Ambedkar portrays the ways by which the laws of Manu on the status of women have moulded the Hindu attitude and perspective towards women. In his paper "Caste in India: Their Mechanism, Gensis and Development" presented for the anthropology seminar of Dr A.A. Goldenweiserat Columbia University, USA in May 1916, he shows how caste as a system of distinct units within a larger system of production makes endogamy an important element which in turn affects gender. Caste system is a closed system which cannot be maintained without endogamy and therefore, endogamy acts as an important tool for the perpetuation of caste and gender subordination:

> ...*the superposition of endogamy on exogamy means the creation of caste... The problem of Caste, then, ultimately resolves itself into one of repairing the disparity between the marriageable units of the two sexes within it.* Left to nature, the much needed parity between the units can be realised only when a couple dies simultaneously. But this is a rare contingency...both the *surplus man* and the *surplus woman* constitute a menace to the Caste if

> not taken care of....Let us see what our imaginary group is likely to do with this *surplus man* and *surplus woman.* We will first take up the case of the *surplus woman.* She can be disposed of in two different ways so as to preserve the endogamy of the Caste. First: burn her on the funeral pyre of her deceased husband and get rid of her....The second remedy is to enforce widowhood on her for the rest of her life. The problem of *surplus man* (= widower) is much more important and much more difficult than that of the *surplus woman* in a group that desires to make itself into a Caste. From time immemorial man as compared with woman has had the upper hand. He is a dominant figure in every group and of the two sexes has greater prestige. With this traditional superiority of man over woman his wishes have always been consulted. Woman, on the other hand, has been an easy prey to all kinds of iniquitous injunctions, religious, social or economic. But man as a maker of injunctions is most often above them all. Such being the case, you cannot accord the same kind of treatment to a *surplus man* as you can to a *surplus woman* in a Caste. Important as he is to the group, endogamy is still more important, and the solution must assure both these ends.... It is in the interest of the Caste to keep him as a *Grahastha*....But the problem is to provide him with a wife from within the Caste. At the outset this is not possible, for the ruling ratio in a caste has to be one man to one woman and none can have two chances of marriage, for in a Caste thoroughly self-enclosed there are always just enough marriageable women to go round for the marriageable men. Under these circumstances the *surplus man* can be provided with a wife only by recruiting a bride from the ranks of those not yet marriageable in order to tie him down to the group. This is certainly the best of the possible solutions in the case of the *surplus man.* By this, he is kept within the Caste. By this means numerical depletion through constant outflow is guarded against, and by this endogamy morals are preserved. (Ambedkar)

Ambedkar voiced the cause of women within the Legislative Council as well. He strongly advocated for family planning measures for women in Mumbai Legislative Assembly. In 1942, as a Labour Minister of Executive Council of Governor General, he introduced a Maternity Benefit Bill. His work was not limited to Hindu women only. He highlighted the issues of Muslim women. His secular perspective is known through his thoughts on "Purdah" system, religious conversions and legal rights for Muslim women.

He provided several provisions in the constitution for protecting the welfare and civil rights of women. He introduced the Hindu Code Bill in the Parliament and highlighted the issues about women's property right. The bill received strong opposition from orthodox Hindus. Ambedkar resigned from the cabinet expressing his discontent over the parliament. As the architect of Indian Constitution, he tried for an adequate inclusion of women's right in the political vocabulary and constitution of India:

Article 14 – Equal rights and opportunities in political, economic and social spheres.

Article 15 – prohibits discrimination on the ground of sex.

Article 15(3) – enables affirmative discrimination in favour of women.

Article 39 – Equal means of livelihood and equal pay for equal work.

Article 42 – Human conditions of work and maternity relief.

Article 46 – The state to promote with special care, the educational and economic interests of weaker section of people and to protect them from social injustice and all forms of exploitation.

Article 47 – The state to raise the level of nutrition and standard of living of its people and the improvement of public health.

Article 51 (A) (C) – Fundamental duties to renounce practices, derogatory to the dignity of women.

Article 243D (3), 243T (3) and 243R (4) provides for allocation of seats in the Panchayati Raj System.

Dr B.R. Ambedkar in the presence of more than fifty women made a bonfire of *Manusmriti* to draw the attention of people against the orthodox system and protest against the discrimination of women and untouchables upheld by it. This event took place on 25 December 1927 at a Conference of Depressed Classes held at Mahad. He believed in the strength of women and their role in the process of social reform. Though a man, he could understand the root cause of the subordination of women due to economic void. Like Virginia Woolf who in "A Room of One's Own" demands space and stresses upon the economic independence of women "a woman must have money and a room of her own...", Ambedkar also strongly called upon women to get married after becoming financially independent. Ambedkar encouraged Dalit women participation on the social and political platform. According to him, the status of Dalit women is like waste ash who lie at the bottom of the caste pyramid:

> ...the Hindu caste system as a pyramid of earthen pots set one on top of another. Not only are Brahmans and Ksatriyas at the top and Shudras and untouchables on the bottom, but within each earthen pot, men are at the top and women of that caste are on the bottom like crushed and wasted powder. And at the very bottom are the Dalits and below them are the suppressed Dalit women. (Omvedt, 321)

He made every effort to raise Dalit women from their double marginalisation of being Dalits as well as women. The early movement of Untouchables in Maharashtra saw the active participation of Untouchable women: "A Nagpur woman, a nurse described her experiences of untouchability to the all-India women's conference of 1920" (Pawar and Moon, "We Made History, Too" 49-50). Under Ambedkar's leadership more and more Dalit women came forward to participate in the movement: "Dr Ambedkar organised several conferences of the Untouchables. He saw to it that women's conferences were held simultaneously with those for men" (50). By 1930 Untouchable women started conducting their own conferences:

> The first session of the all-India Depressed Classes Congress was held at Nagpur on 8th to 10th August 1930, presided over by Dr Babasaheb Ambedkar. In this conference a separate women's session was held on the 10th. The women gave speeches supporting the stand taken by Ambedkar in the Round Table Conference. (Pawar and Moon, *We Also Made History,* 137).

During the "the historic *satyagraha* movement" in Mahad in 1927 for the rights of Untouchables to have access to the public water tanks: "...Dalit women not only participated in the processions with Dr Ambedkar but also participated in the deliberations of the subject committee meetings in passing resolutions about the claim for equal human rights" (Pawar and Moon, "We Made History, Too", 50).

Hundreds of Untouchable women participated in sit-in agitations in front of temple and courted arrest during Nasik Satyagraha, started by Dr B.R. Ambedkar in 1930 for the right of Untouchables to enter Hindu temples. In 1956, the Untouchable women supported Dr B.R. Ambedkar's declaration of conversion to a non-Hindu religion:

> The speeches of women, reported exhaustively in *Janata Weekly*, show that women were very frank in stating that they wanted a religion that would recognise their freedom, dignity, and equal status with men. They expressed confidence that Dr Ambedkar would not drag them into a religion where women would have to wear the *burkha* or live in *purdah*. (50-51)

In his address at the Depressed Classes Women's Conference held at Nagpur on July 20, 1942 in which 25000 women were present, Dr B.R. Ambedkar said: "I am a great believer in women's organisations. I know what they can do to improve the condition of society if they are convinced. In the eradication of social evils they have rendered great services" (qtd. in Barnwal, 397).

From the encouragement and inspiration from Ambedkar, Dalit women have begun to articulate their self. They consider him their ideal, their Messiah. Many Dalit women like Baby Kamble, Urmila Pawar, Mukta Sarvagod, Shantabai Krishnaji Kamble have started writing to articulate their experiences of victimisation. In their narratives one can read reverence of the Dalit women towards their 'Babasaheb' and the documentation of his words and speeches to express their gratitude towards him. The present paper is focused on the study of Baby Kamble's narrative *The Prisons We Broke* to analyse how Dalit women still consider themselves indebted to Dr B.R. Ambedkar for the improvement of their lives as well as their community's status.

Baby Kamble comes from Phalatan, a small town in the Satara district of Maharashtra. She was a veteran of the Dalit movement in Maharashtra. Her narrative *Jina Amucha* originally written in Marathi was published in 1986. It was later translated as *The Prisons We Broke* in English by Maya Pandit which was first published in 2008.

The Prisons We Broke is a sociological and psychological exploration in which Baby Kamble describes the penury, hunger, and nakedness of the Mahar community. *The Prisons We Broke* does not glorify the lives of the Mahars but subjects them to a critical scrutiny: "...to demonstrate how Brahminical domination had turned the Mahars into slaves, forcing them to live in conditions worse than animals" (Pandit, xiii). She honestly tells about the evil practices and superstitions in the Mahar community which was responsible for their wretched conditions. *The Prisons We Broke* is also a feminist critique of the patriarchy:

> She graphically describes the physical and psychological violence women have to undergo in both the public and private spheres. If the Mahar community is the 'other' for the Brahmins, Mahar women become the 'other' for the Mahar men. (xv)

The Prisons We Broke dwells on the incidents of domestic violence prevalent in the Mahar society. Baby Kamble narrates the period of 1940 to show how a girl is treated in a Dalit family. Victimised at the hands of upper caste men, Mahars too desired power, so they made their own arrangement to find slave- their own daughters-in-law and wives:

> The other world had bound us with chains of slavery. But we too were human beings. And we too desired to dominate, to wield power. But who would let us do that? So we made our own arrangements to find slaves- our very own daughters-in-law! If nobody else, then we could at least enslave them. (*The Prisons We Broke,* 87)

Mahar girls were married young. After marriage a girl had to endure the abuses, taunts and physical violence at the hands of everybody in her house including her sisters-in-law and brothers-in-law. The husband would beat his wife to a pulp with a stick and drive her out of the house. This was the usual fate of Mahar women within the family. In such situations, the girl would try to run away but she was brought again by her in-laws and a huge square piece of wood weighing around five kilos with a hole, big enough for her foot to go through, with an iron bar through the side so as to make impossible for her to pull her foot out, was put around the wife's leg or sometimes her nose would be chopped off.

The Prisons We Broke reflects how Ambedkar created impact on the minds of Dalits which brought a significant change in their standard of living, and they began educating themselves and left their traditional jobs, gods and goddesses. They admitted their daughters in school after listening to an inspirational speech by him. Ambedkar made a special appeal to Dalit women to participate in the cause of Dalit revolution as he saw that women are the creators and put his faith in strength of Dalit women. Baby Kamble recalls how the speech of B.R. Ambedkar in Jejuri gave tremendous courage to the women:

> 'Our women have had a major role in being superstitions, but I'm sure they will now give up these superstitions and take a lead in educating their children. They will have the honour of being the first to take this step forward. I have full faith in you, my sisters. Go ahead, educate your children. Let all our women take this step. Discard all such customs that strengthen our ignorance. My poor dear brothers and sisters, do not eat carcasses any more. Don't clean it up themselves. Let us teach them this lesson. This slavery, which has been imposed upon us, will not disappear easily. For that we need to bring about a revolution. Let three-fourth of our people die in this endeavour, then, at least the remaining one-fourth will be able to live their lives with dignity. At least, their future will be better. I appeal to you, my brothers and sisters, be the first ones to step forward for reform.' (65)

Bhikai Aaji, her grand aunt (sister-in-law of Baby Kamble's maternal grandfather), climbed up onto the stage to deliver a speech. She appealed to all the women to follow Dr B.R. Ambedkar's advice and to educate their children:

> 'Let me assure you, my sisters, what Bhimrao Ambedkar says is absolutely right. We must educate our children. We must not and will not eat dead animals. We must reform our community. Let us resolve to fight along with Ambedkar. He speaks nothing but the truth. Let's follow him to the end. This is what I say.' (65)

All those who attended the Conference in Jejuri, were completely enamoured of Dr B.R. Ambedkar. Dr B.R. Ambedkar told: "Start educating all Mahar children. Stop eating dead animals. We must reform ourselves. Don't stay ignorant anymore. Don't believe in god and religion" (66).

Baby Kamble recalls that all evil practices against Dalit women continued well into the 1940s until the message of love, brotherhood and equality given by Buddha was popularised by Dr B.R. Ambedkar's principles and ethics. Baby Kamble describes the Hindu Code Bill as tearing the very net that had enslaved the women. She attributes her own awakening to Dr B.R. Ambedkar and the movement he created and led:

> It is because of him that my pen can scribble out some thoughts. It is because of him that I have understood the truth; that I can now see how morality is being trampled upon. It is because of him that I got the inspiration to join the struggle against oppression and contribute my small might to it. (102)

Baby Kamble made a resolve to lead her life according the path sketched by Dr B.R. Ambedkar: "I made a firm resolve, at a young age, to lead my life according the path sketched by Dr Babasaheb Ambedkar, the light of my life. His principles have exercised a strong influence on me" (115). Baby calls herself "a product of Ambedkar movement" (125).

Baby Kamble appeals to the community not to forget the glorious history of struggle. She appeals to them not to forget the path shown by Ambedkar. She says that Dr B.R. Ambedkar had solved issues that had troubled lakhs of generations in a period of mere fifty years is therefore, rightly the father of God. According to her, only women can make their husband and children to trot on the right path. She says:

> It is the duty of educated women to impress this upon their young children. They should portray this in poems and teach them to their children. Through all our programmes, we must portray the lives of Bhim and the Buddha. We must see to it that our children imbibe the principles of the Buddhist religion. Then alone shall we be able to call ourselves the children of Bhim. Character, truth and morality are the essence of our constitution. Character is the pillar of this constitution, truth is its roof, and morality, its the foundation. This is the home of humanity. This is our house, decorated with these three jewels. Baba wanted it to be the residence for the entire human race. If the whole of the human race treads on the path of these principles, only the sky would be the limit for Mother India. (123)

In the condolence message in parliament, on Ambedkar's death, Prime Minister Jawaharlal Nehru said "Dr Babasaheb Ambedkar was a symbol of revolt against all oppressive features of Hindu society" (qtd. in Singariya). Dr B.R. Ambedkar not only wrote extensively to answer the orthodox Hindu opinion against women but worked as an activist and social reformer at the grass roots level to organise and empower women of depressed classes. The concept of inseparability of caste and gender subordination in the construction of Hindu social hierarchical order is an important theoretical input in understanding the hurdles in the way of empowerment of women in the Indian social milieu and needs to be taken note of by the Indian feminists. His views on the financial independence of women are very crucial for women's emancipation. His thoughts are important for the social reconstruction that favours women's empowerment.

References

Ambedkar, B.R., "Caste in India: Their Mechanism, Genesis and Development." *www.ambedkar.org*. Ambedkar. org. n. date. n. page. Web. 17 March 2015.

Barnwal, Bijay K. (1973), "Dr B. R. Ambedkar's Quest for Gender Equality: It's Relevance in Beauvior, Simone de. *The Second Sex*. New York: Vintage Books.

Devi, K. Uma. (2000), *Women's Equality in India: A Myth or Reality?*. New Delhi: Discovery Publishing House.

Feminist Discourse, *Online International Interdisciplinary Research Journal* 4.2 (2014). *www.oiirj.org*. Web. 14 March 2015.

Kamble, Baby. (2009), *The Prisons We Broke*. Trans. Maya Pandit. New Delhi: Orient Blackswan Private Limited.

Majumdar, Maya (2005) ed., *Encyclopedia of Gender Equality Through Women Empowerment*. Vol. 2. New Delhi: Sarup and Sons.

Moon, Meenakshi, and Urmila Pawar. (2003), "We Made History, Too: Women In the Eraly Untouchable Liberation Movement". *Gender and Caste*. Ed. Anupama Rao. New Delhi: Kali for Women, 48-57.

Omvedt, Gail. (2003), "The Downtrodden among the Downtrodden: An Interview with a Dalit Agricultural Labourer." *Gender and Caste*. Ed. Anupama Rao. New Delhi: Kali for Women, 310-324. Print.

Pandit, Maya. (2009), *The Prisons We Broke*. By Baby Kamble. Trans. Maya Pandit, Delhi: Orient Blackswan Private Limited, xiii-xiv. Print.

Pawar, Urmila, and Meenakshi Moon. (2008)*We also Made History: Women in the Ambedkarite Movement*. Trans. Wandana Sonalkar. New Delhi. Zubaan.

Shukla, Bhasker A. (2007), "Feminism – An Overview." *Feminism and Female Writers*. Ed. Bhasker A. Shukla. Jaipur: Book Enclave, 1-19. Print.

Singariya, M.R. (2014), "Dr B. R. Ambedkar and Women Empowerment in India." *Journal of Research in Humanities and Social Science* 2.1. *www.researchgate.net*. Web.14 March 2015.

21

Did Dr B.R. Ambedkar Really Succeed in Removing the Social Barriers for Deprived in Indian Society?

— *Navneet Kaur*

Abstract

Dr B.R. Ambedkar emerged during a period when the caste-based discrimination was at its peak. Jyotiba Phule as well as Chatrapati Shahu ji Maharaj already attempted so many ways to provide the education as well as Employment to the Untouchables respectively whereas Gandhi was attempting the efforts to 'Change the Hearts' of the upper castes. During this period, Dr Ambedkar emerged as a Scholar, Philosopher, Social-Activist as well as a Reformer who sincerely raised-up the Caste-based issues in the British Councils, 3-Round Table Conferences as well as during the Constituent Assembly Debates. This paper is, therefore, an attempt to examine analytically the efforts of Dr Ambedkar for removing the Untouchability from the Hindu Society and their influence in present democratic India.

[**Key words:** *Dr Ambedkar, Untouchables, Efforts, Change in Society*].

Introduction

India's journey as a free independent State was started in 1947. On 15th August, 1947, India emerged as the first poor country in the world with full-scale democracy. The concept of democracy includes equality, liberty and justice. The democracy in simple words means the participation of all sections of society. This participation of all sections raises many doubts particularly in context of India where the caste system exists in the society. Born on April 14, 1891, Dr B.R. Ambedkar fought for the removal of this caste system throughout his life. Though he had done advanced studies and his education and caliber was recognised all over the world but he too was discriminated on basis of the caste. He was born as a Mahar and the Mahars were considered as the Untouchable community. He wanted to remove this caste-based discrimination from the Indian society. According to him, this can be done only through the radical change in the social structure of the society. In order to bring the social equality and opportunity to the deprived, he strictly opposed the *Varna Vyavstha* (hierarchy in the social structure of Indian society) and with his sincere efforts and logical reasoning he succeeded in influencing the Colonial rulers in framing the legal provisions in various Acts in favour of deprived.

Challenging the Social Hierarchy

According to Dr Ambedkar, a society is an association which appears due to joint intercourse for better realisation of the shared values. For him, the essence of human society is not present in the caste system of the Hindu society because it prevents the common activity for the downtrodden. Even he did not accept the hypothesis of an Aryan invasion from north-west India. According to Ambedkar, the Shudras were not dark skinned aboriginals who were enslaved or subordinated by the Aryans rather the Shudras were Aryans belonging to the Kshatriya solar dynasty. He emphasised that the subordinate status of Shudras was a result of bloody battle between Sudas, the Shudra king and Vasistha and due to the regular change or succession, these Shudras became degraded from their Kshatriya status.

With a passage of time, the whole society was divided into the caste-system and thus created the four *Varnas*- the Brahmins, Kshatriyas, Vaishyas and Shudras. All these Varnas had to perform their duties according to their Varnas. On the basis of purity and pollution, Untouchables (Ati-Shudras) were considered outside the Varna System and they were termed as '*Acchut*'. This category mainly consisted of butchers, hunters, removers, cremators, hangmen, sweepers, drum beaters in funerals and festivals, grave digging, making *chappals*, and manual scavengers etc. These people could not enjoy their rights and were kept away from resources. This section did not have right to live with the upper castes in their localities. Neither were they allowed to achieve education nor could they enter the temples, public places and shops. This section was denied to have water from the common tap as well as the tailors also denied to stitch their clothes and barber did not cut their hair. They could neither walk with slippers, nor could they carry umbrella or cart in the locality of upper castes. These people worked as the bonded labourers in the field of rich higher caste landlords. Without any doubt, the upper castes particularly the Brahmans and Kshatriyas were active enough to mould the society according to their benefits.

Thus, the Varnas Theory in pre-independent India was based on three important features-

(1) It includes only four classes.

(2) The inter-relations of these classes were regulated by the principle of graded in-equality.

(3) Each class had to perform the occupation already assigned to it.

Ambedkar did not agree with the principles led down under this Theory. He even opposed the Social Reform Movement launched by various Religious Social Activists like Swami Dayanand during that period. According to him, the Arya Samaj preached the social institutions of the Hindus based on Vedas which attributed the cause of present misery to past *karmas* of man. In this manner, Dr Ambedkar tried to find out the meaning of 'human harmony' in the social relations based on the actions. He wanted to abolish the aristocratic living applied to the rulers and the superior classes and considered the bureaucracy and Hindu Religion responsible for the owes of the Untouchables.

Ambedkar's Steps towards Promoting Social Changes in Society

Dr B.R. Ambedkar was a contemporary of Mahatma Gandhi. On one hand, Mr. Gandhi was preaching the philosophy of *Swadeshi, Sarvodaya and Ram Rajya* whereas, at the same time, for ending-up the sorrows and troubles of Untouchables, Dr Ambedkar started raising demands for the upliftment of deprived section by providing them the representation. Ambedkar raised the issue of representation of this section in various Round Table Conferences. He wanted the Separate Electorate for this section. The objective behind this Separate Electorate was to provide a separate representation to this particular community in the elections so that their own representative could easily resolve the troubles of their own community in better manner. Dr Ambedkar felt that the freedom by Untouchables cannot be achieved while being as a member of the Hindu society. However, Dr Ambedkar was succeeded in providing the Separate Electorate to the deprived, under the Government of India Act 1935. This Act provided the separate representation to the deprived in educational, political and economic field. With the passing of this Government of India Act, Dr Ambedkar was emerged as '*masiah*' for deprived section of society. As a consequence of this, Mahatma Gandhi went to fast against the notion of this Separate Electorate and therefore, a deal called the Poona Pact took place between Gandhi and Ambedkar in which seats were reserved for the deprived section on the basis of caste in the jobs and legislature.

During 1944-1950, Dr B.R. Ambedkar, as a member of the Constituent Assembly, put his sincere efforts in bringing the complete equality before law and equal protection of law under Article 14, to all the citizens of India. For the advancement of socially and educationally backward classes or Scheduled Castes and Scheduled Tribes, Article-15 (4) and clause (2) of Article 29 was added to the Constitution of the independent India under his supervision. He brought Article 17 in the Indian Constitution which not only abolishes the practice of Untouchability but also made its practice, in any form, an offence. Under this Article, the provision is made to give a strict punishment to that person who practices the discrimination to the deprived section of the society. He also wanted the reach of Untouchables to the public services; therefore, being as a realistic thinker, Dr Ambedkar laid down the Reservation for them under Article 16 (4) and 335. In order to protect this section from injustice and all forms of exploitation, Dr Ambedkar strictly favoured the introduction of Article-46. Dr Ambedkar knew that the casteism will not be abolished easily even with the introduction of the Constitution of India, therefore, he recommended the set–up of the Scheduled Castes and Scheduled Tribes Commission. Further many provisions for the political representation of the deprived were also laid down under Article 332, 334. As a Law Minister of independent India (1950), he introduced the Hindu Code Bill, the Hindu Succession Act, Hindu Minority and Guardianship Act,

Hindu Adoptions and Maintenance Act and Hindu Marriage Act in the Parliament.

Influence of His Efforts in Democratic India

Dr Ambedkar knew that the problems of Untouchables could not be solved by mere framing the Constitutional provisions. According to him, the social stability depends upon the best social adjustment among all the sections of the society and this adjustment must include the features of equality, liberty and dignity. As a realist thinker, Dr B.R. Ambedkar wanted to end-up the casteism from Indian society and wanted to see it as a practical democrat. He believed in the concept of Distributive Justice and wanted that the downtrodden should be brought in the mainstream with their dignity. Taking into concern his views, one cannot deny the fact that efforts of Dr Ambedkar have seemed to be succeeded to some extent. No doubt, in the present democratic India, the suppression of deprived is still existed on basis of caste but this section has uplifted to some extent. The people residing in Urban cities are interacting and dinning together with each other without any Caste discrimination. With Reservation, these downtrodden people have been brought into the offices at par with upper castes. The members of this section are being represented in the Political Parties, Committees as well as in Local Bodies. They are forming their own Associations and the Pressure Groups in order to make their demand reach to the government. This section is participating in the elections and selecting its own Representatives. In order to show their identity these people are having their own Gurudwaras, Symbols and Slogans. All this has happened because of the consciousness brought among these sections through the efforts and provisions made by Dr Ambedkar which otherwise were not possible.

Along with the bright picture of upliftment of the downtrodden, the large section of this is still living in dark. The people living in rural areas are going through caste-based discrimination in their day-to-day life. The harassment of this section by the upper castes is existing still. The Constitutional provisions related to equality, liberty and fraternity have not implemented in the backward peripheries. In public sectors like Railways, these downtrodden are engaged in in-human activities like Manual Scavenging. A large number of marriages are taking in their own communities because of fear, hatred and discrimination.

Whatsoever the present scenario is, it is clear that efforts of Dr Ambedkar have yielded the positive consciousness among the masses and the celebration of festivals and Jayanties has made the downtrodden much more stronger and unite than earlier. This is only because of his positive efforts for the upliftment of deprived that Baba Saheb Ambedkar is known as 'Massiah'.

References

1. Aloysius, G.(1997), Nationalism Without A Nation in India. Delhi: Oxford University Press.
2. Ambedkar, B.R. (1945), Pakistan or Partition of India, Thacker and Co., Mumbai.
3. Ambedkar, BR (1946), Who were the Shudras?, Thacker and Co., Ltd., Mumbai, p.155.
4. Ambedkar, Baba Saheb (2008), *Shudron Ki Khoj*, Gautam Book Centre, Delhi.
5. Iverson, Vegard and Raghavendra P.S. (2007), What the Signboard Hides: Food, Caste and Employability in Small Indian Eating Places. Sage Publication.
6. Judge, Paramjeet S. and Gurpreet Bal (2008). Understanding the Paradox of changes among Dalits in Punjab. *Economic and Political Weekly,* Vol. 43, No. 41 (Oct. 11-17), pp. 49-55.
7. Nirula (2009), Dalits- A Bruised Dignity- Recasting Casste (Vol. II). New Delhi: APH Publishing Corporation.

22

Dr Bhim Rao Ambedkar Thoughts on Conflicting Issues of Indian Foreign Policy

—*Shayama Bangar*

Abstract

India has produced many social and political thinker and philosopher in the course of her long and chequered history. Among the galaxy of thinkers and philosophers of India, Bharat Ratna Dr Babasaheb Ambedkar occupies undoubtedly the most important place. He has carved out for himself a unique position in society, whatever label he wears in future, Dr Ambedkar is not the man to allow himself to be forgotten. Dr Bhim Rao Ambedkar, popularly known as Babasaheb, Ambedkar, was one of the architects of the Indian Constitution of the Independent India. Dr Ambedkar a determined fighter and a deep scholar has made significant efforts to lead the society on the path of Liberty, Equality and Fraternity. While his views on various social, economic and political aspects have been analysed, his approaches to Indian foreign policy especially most conflicting issues of Indian foreign policy (China and Kashmir issue) have remained a rain shadow area. This paper highlights Dr Ambedkar's thought on China and Kashmir issue which are the most conflicting issues of the Indian foreign policy.

Introduction

Foreign Policy plays a prominent part in the peace and progress of every country in the world today. Every nation can aspire to be self-reliant. For this it has to depend upon others. In other words interdependence is essential factor. It leads to international relations for giving a meaning and directions to her behaviour at the international level each nation adopts a set of principles, a national guide the foreign policy. Independent India under Nehru's leadership chose the foreign policy strategy of Non-alignment not only because of considerations like enjoying independence in decision making, getting the best of aid (economic) from the power blocs, carving out for itself an independent position and leadership role in the emerging Third World, but primarily because of retaining the much needed maneuverability in the conduct of its foreign policy.The foreign policy of India largely depends upon the Panchsheela principle. Ambedkar believes that principles have little value in international relations. He said, "Principles are undoubtedly very valuable, but I take it politicians have a great dislike for principles particularly politicians who are dealing with foreign policy". He said,when I think of our foreign policy, I am reminded of what Bismarck and Bernard Shaw have said. Bismarck has said that 'politics is not a game of realising the ideal. Politics is the game of the possible.' Bernard Shaw not very long ago said that "good ideals are good but one must not forget that it is often dangerous to be too good. Our foreign policy is in complete opposition to these words of wisdom uttered by two of the world's greatest men."Ambedkar believes that principles have little value in international relations.

Ambedkar's Views on Kashmir Issue

Ambedkar's interest in more direct aspects of foreign policy had emerged in his resignation letter from the Union Cabinet on 10th October, 1951. Few major issues that he brings out on foreign policy deserve close attention. An ardent supporter of land reforms and profitable agriculture, Dr Ambedkar called for modernisation of this sector ever since the third decade of twentieth century. Side by side, analysing Indian foreign policy he said, "Thrust of our foreign policy is to solve problems of other nations rather than our own." Linking Kashmir problem with this policy, he opined, "Even if we cannot defend the entire region, at least our own people should be accorded full protection." Dr Babasaheb Ambedkar had his own vision regarding Kashmir problem. When he gave statement for his resignation he had explain various issues which was related to security matter. Dr Ambedkar did not agree with India's foreign policy and stand taken by Government of India regarding Kashmir issue. He said, "Our quarrel with Pakistan is a part of our foreign policy about which I feels deeply dissatisfied. There are two grounds which have disturbed our relations with Pakistan- one is Kashmir and the other is the condition of our people in West Bengal. He felt that we should be more deeply concerned with East Bengal where the condition of our people seems from all the newspapers intolerable than with Kashmir. Notwithstanding this have been staking out all on the Kashmir issue. Even Ambedkar felt that we have been fighting on an unreal issue. The issue on which we are fighting most of the time is who is in the right and who is in the wrong. The real issue in our mind is not who is right but what is right. 'Taking that to be the main question, my view has always been that the right solution is to partition Kashmir. Give the Hindu and Buddhist part to India and the Muslim part to Pakistan as we did in the case of India'. He said that we are really not concerned with the Muslim part of Kashmir. It is a matter between the Muslims of Kashmir and Pakistan. They may decide the issue as they like or if you like dividing it into three parts, the cease fire zone, the valley and the Jammu-Ladakh region and have a plebiscite only in the valley. Ambedkar said, "what I am afraid of is that in the proposed plebiscite, which is to be an overall plebiscite, the Hindu and Buddhist of Kashmir are likely to be dragged into Pakistan against their wishes and we may have to face the same problems as we are facing today". Ambedkar's views on Kashmir and East Bengal were significantly different from the mainstream approaches on the subject. His solutions to the question of Pakistan were based on either reaching an agreement or resorting to arbitration. While the arbitration route between India and Pakistan was not tried in his lifetime, the Indus-water treaty incorporated mediation and arbitration as dispute resolution mechanisms. Dr Ambedkar also opposed Article 370 of the Constitution of India, which granted a special status to the State of Jammu and Kashmir, and which was included against his wishes. When Sheikh Abdullah, on the suggestion of Nehru, had approached Ambedkar to get his consent for Article 370, Ambedkar had rejected the proposal right away. Ambedkar had remarked: "Mr. Abdullah, you want that India should defend Kashmir, India should develop Kashmir and Kashmiris should have equal rights as the citizens of India, but you don't want India and any citizen of India to have any rights in Kashmir. Dr Ambedkar had said that he was fortunate to be a minister of India and would not take any measures that would harm the country.

Ambedkar's Views on China

Dr Ambedkar warned the government several times about expansionist design of China. He did not agree with Indian policy-makers' belief of Panchasheela as basis of our relationship with China and said, "Mao Tse-Tung does not have faith in Panchasheela, which is an essential part of Buddhism. If it has any belief in these ideals, he would have well treated Buddhist of his own country." Panch sheel was only a "give away" with no reciprocal "take". Through Panchsheel India literally gave Tibet to China on a platter, without negotiating anything in return either for Tibet or for India. Panchsheel is actually a most eloquent example of the naivety of the Indian diplomacy and a shining example of what an international agreement should not be! There is no room for Panchsheel in politics and secondly, not in "the politics of communist country". The communist countries have to well-known principles on which they always act on is that morality is always in a flux. There is no morality. Today morality is not tomorrow's morality you can keep your word in accordance with the morality of today and you can break your word with equal justification tomorrows because tomorrows morality will be different. Prakash Yashwant Ambedkar, grandson of Dr B. R. Ambedkar, said that Dr Ambedkar insisted on creating Tibet as a buffer State between India and China and for this he wanted India to have friendly ties with international democratic forces. "This policy of Dr Ambedkar is still relevant in the context of another conflict with China looking imminent on the issue of sharing of Brahmaputra waters in Arunachal Pradesh," he said while delivering a lecture on 'Foreign Policy of Dr B. R. Ambedkar' organised by Dr B.R. Ambedkar Open University (BRAOU) at its campus.

Ambedkar's criticism of Nehru's foreign policy was highlighted by both the national and international media. In October 22, 1951, noted: "Ambedkar is the first important Indian official who has openly attacked Nehru for being too friendly to China and not friendly enough to the United State of America". Separately, speaking at a gathering of students of Lucknow University on November 8, 1951, Ambedkar said: "The government's foreign policy failed to make India stronger. Why should not India get a permanent seat in the UN Security Council?

Why has the Prime Minister not tried for it? When UNO was formed, China was ROC—Republic of China—headed by Chiang Kai-shek. In 1949, Communists took over China and founded People's Republic of China (PRC) under Mao. Chiang Kai-shek and his ROC were driven away to Formosa—now called Taiwan. ROC continued to be a member of the UN till 1971, and not PRC, as US and allies refused to recognise it. They did not wish to have another communist country as a member of the UNSC. Reportedly, both the US and the USSR were willing to accommodate India as a Permanent Member of the UNSC in 1955, perhaps in lieu of Taiwan, or as a sixth member, after amending the UN charter. This Nehru refused! Nehru wanted the seat to be given to PRC, as Nehru did not want China to be marginalised! Even though not asked by China, India, of its own accord, had been vigorously advocating PRC for the Permanent Membership of the UNSC in lieu of Taiwan.The fact remains that in 1952 it was the United State that wanted India to take the permanent seat at the UN Security Council that was then held by Taiwan. Nehru policies were based on his personal hope and aspirations they were not based on hard, factual calculations that existed in reality. "India must choose between parliamentary democracy and the Communist way of dictatorship and come to a final conclusion. If you do not want it, let us join Russia and China tomorrow". He recognised the ideological and political convulsions in the Asian continent and called on the government to align with the free nations who believe in freedom. Ambedkar envisioned a league of democracies and believed that the democracies of the world had to reach out to each other in view of the spread of communism towards which he held a deep ideological antipathy. He recognised the impact of the emergence of Asia after long years of colonialism and imperialism and wanted India to align itself with the 'free nations'. Ambedkar felt that close Indo-US relations premised on a natural affinity of democracies would lead to foreign assistance to India in various fields, thus alleviating the national burden. He challenged the government to move away from non-alignment and come to a final decision of either aligning with democratic governments such as US or making friends with communist governments and joining Russia and China. This was a dramatically opposite view on foreign policy as compared to Nehruvian non-alignment. He envisioned a strong India that took its place in the global order based on developing its economic strength and leveraging its political alliances with other democracies. Dr Ambedkar belief in the balance of power is evident when he castigates the government for not trying to obtain a permanent seat in the Security Council. After evaluation of India's foreign policy we can learn what are drawbacks in foreign policy and how government of India adopted foreign policy especially case of China and what policies were suggested by Dr Babasaheb Ambedkar but adopted by government there are followings are consequences on India's national security Consequences: India's foreign policy has been facing continuous adverse criticism, because without well-defined a geographical factor and national interest, India humiliated by China 1962. Today China claims 90.000 sq. km. of territory in India's eastern sector in Arunachal Pradesh. In addition it is in occupation of 38,000 sq. km. of territory in Ladakh including Aksai Chin 1000 sq. kms of Pok west of Karakoram pass given by Pakistan 30 Sq. km. Wong Dong in Arunachal Pradesh and 40 Sq. km. of Barahati grazing grounds in Uttar Pradesh.

Ambedkar is opposed to the policy of appeasement and co-existence. He does not see any harm in becoming the member of organisation like SEATO. The SEATO is not an organisation for committing aggression on any other country. The SEATO is an organisation for the purpose of preventing aggression on free countries. The strength of SEATO can help India in preventing the aggression from communist countries. He wants to protect his country and make her prepare for war, if any is attack. Dr Babasaheb Ambedkar the Chinese possession of Tibet he accused the government of helping the Chinese to bring their border down to the Indian border, because government allowed the Chinese to take possession of Lhasa. Due to this mistake Chinese to take occupation of Tibet in 1950 which removed the buffer state between the two giants. He argued that there is no place for 'Panchsheel' in international politics only remain national interest due to lack of vision India's defense expenditure was only two per cent of GNP from 1947 to 1962. Due to Kashmir problem we had three wars with Pakistan and arm race have been increased in South Asia. Due to Kashmir problem thousands of jawan and officers were killed at Kashmir. Due to Kashmir problem today Kashmir peoples demanding greater autonomy although Jammu and Kashmir already has sufficient autonomy. Due to Kashmir problem Pakistan consider that Kashmir is the unfinished business of partition and is the core dispute between the countries and also Kashmir problem burden on Indian economy has been increased. South Asia becomes nuclear flashpoint. Recently some section of society demanding trifurcations of Jammu and Kashmir where as Dr Babasaheb Ambedkar had given solution on Jammu and Kashmir by partition of Jammu and Kashmir. But unfortunately Government of India not adopted Dr Babasaheb Ambedkar policies related to security matter. Some of the leaders consider as he was only leader of depressed class and chief architect of Indian constitution although he was great strategic thinker, Security experts and he propounded prudent policies for external security and foreign relation but Government of India not adopted his policies from independence it is right time to think and analysed. Suggested policies of Dr Babasaheb Ambedkar and adopt his policies for overall development, unity and security of India. Ambedkar's criticism of Nehru's foreign policy was highlighted by both the national and international media.

References

Agnihotri, Kuldip Chand (2015), Babasaheb Ambedkar – The Troubleshooter Jammu-Kashmir missed! http://aseema.net.in/babasaheb-ambedkar-the-troubleshooter-jammu-kashmir-missed-part-1/*rajnikantp.blogspot.com/2016/04/ambedkar-and-nehru.html*

Appadorai, A. (1949), India's Foreign Policy, *International Affairs*, Vol. 25, No.1, pp. 37-46.

'Ambedkar was for friendly foreign policy' http://www.thehindu.com/todays-paper/tp-national/tp-andhrapradesh/ambedkar-was-for-friendly-foreign-policy/article3664663.ece

Dr Ambedkar's Resignation Speech, March, 2011.

https://ambedkarism.wordpress.com/2011/03/10/dr-ambedkar%E2%80%99s-resignation-speechhttp://www.baiae.org/resources/articles-essays/113-impact-of-dr-ambedkar%E2%80%99s-thoughts-on-indian-economy.html

Bakshi, R.S. (2009), Dr B.R. Ambedkar socio-economic and political ideology, Sarup, New Delhi.

Bharas, C.B. (2013), Ambedkar's contributions to Indian foreign policy, World Focus, Vol. xxxiv, No.12, pp. 68-72.

Bharathi, K.S (1998), Encyclopaedia of Eminent Thinkers the Political Thought of Ambedkar, Concept publications, New Delhi.

Dhanker, Sonali (2011), Ambedkar place in history http://www.boloji.com/index.cfm?md=Content&sd=Articles&ArticleID=10773#sthash.sGRziS3d.dpuf

Jayapalan, N. (2001), Foreign Policy of India, Atlantic, New Delhi.

Khare, S. Vijay (2008), Thoughts of Dr Ambedkar on India's National Security http://dalitliberation.blogspot.in/2008/03/thoughts-of-dr-ambedkar-on-indias.html

Parvathaneni, Harish (2012), Ambedkar's views on foreign policy http://www.newindianexpress.com/columns/article58431.ece

Parvathaneni, Harish (2009) What if Ambedkar had shaped India's foreign policy? http://archive.indianexpress.com/news/what-if-ambedkar-had-shaped-india-s-foreign-policy-/434288/

Rajasekhariah, M.A. and Hemalata Jayaraj (1991), Political Philosophy of Dr B. R. Ambedkar, Indian Journal of Political Science, Vol. 52, No. 3, pp. 357-375.

Index

C